Impact of Sociocultural Factors on Health Communication

Semmelweis Medical Linguistics Investigations

Edited by Katalin Fogarasi and Dániel Mány /
Semmelweis University, Institute of Languages for Specific Purposes

Volume 1

Katalin Fogarasi and Dániel Mány (eds.)

Impact of Sociocultural Factors on Health Communication

In collaboration with Sarah Bigi, Zsófia Demjén, Jan Engberg, Pascaline Faure and Rita Temmerman

Copy Editor: Judit Császár
Editorial Assistant: Tünde Vágási

PETER LANG

Berlin · Bruxelles · Chennai · Lausanne · New York · Oxford

Bibliographic Information published by the Deutsche Nationalbibliothek
The Deutsche Nationalbibliothek lists this publication in the Deutsche Nationalbibliografie;
detailed bibliographic data is available online at http://dnb.d-nb.de.

Library of Congress Control Number: 2025024910

This publication has been supported by Semmelweis University and developed within
the Institute of Languages for Specific Purposes, a research and education unit at the
intersection of language and healthcare. The copyright belongs to Semmelweis University.

ISSN 2942-7487
ISBN 978-3-631-91784-8 (Print)
ISBN 978-3-631-91785-5 (E-PDF)
ISBN 978-3-631-91786-2 (E-PUB)
DOI 10.3726/b23115

© 2025 Peter Lang Group AG, Lausanne (Switzerland)
Published by Peter Lang GmbH, Berlin (Germany)

info@peterlang.com

All rights reserved.
All parts of this publication are protected by copyright.
Any utilization outside the strict limits of the copyright law, without the permission of the
publisher, is forbidden and liable to prosecution. This applies in particular to reproductions,
translations, microfilming, and storage and processing in electronic retrieval systems.

This publication has been peer reviewed.

www.peterlang.com

Table of Contents

Preface 7

PART I
Terminology

Transition in nursing documentation:
Insights into the terminology of Hungarian nursing notes 11
Tünde Vágási – Gábor Gyenes – Zoltán Patonai – Éva Katalin Varga

Standardized medical data for optimized health communication 27
Maria-Cornelia Wermuth

PART II
ESP Instruction

Language learning strategy use and willingness to communicate
among high- and low-anxiety health science students 43
Theodora Tseligka – Ioanna Katerini

English for medical purposes: The importance of role-plays 59
Dagmar Vrběcká – Klára Čebišová – James David Clubb

Feedback criteria for simulated patients in courses of languages
for healthcare purposes 73
*Viktória Sirokmány – Tímea Takács – Enikő Földesi –
Dániel Mány – Katalin Fogarasi*

Simulated online scenarios as a form of telemedicine practice in the
English for Healthcare Purposes course for physiotherapy students 89
Tímea Takács – Or Sharabi – Vera Tick

PART III
Healthcare communication

Is there an interpreter in the house? The intercultural needs of healthcare providers in communication with immigrant patients in Spain 105
Sofía Antequera Manzano

Development and assessment of an automatically creative and flexible use of medical English as a lingua franca – terminological awareness in healthcare communication 117
Alexandra Zimonyi-Bakó

"Doctor, I have not seen for three months / Docteur, je ne vois rien depuis trois mois": A comparative lexicological analysis of words and expressions related to the body and its (dys)functions in the English and French common languages 135
Pascaline Faure

Culturally aware healthcare providers: training future physicians and midwives to work with trained interpreters 155
Tinka Reichmann – Luciana Carvalho Fonseca – Danjela Brückner – Daisy Rotzoll – Henrike Todorow – Anne Tauscher – Larissa Evers

Communication as language use in consultations: methodological considerations 169
Sarah Bigi

PART IV
Metaphors in healthcare

How mothers think about postpartum mood disorders: A metaphor analysis of Hungarian online forums 187
Petra Bialkó-Marol

Just war? Variation in COVID-19 metaphors in Hungarian public communication 203
Lilla Petronella Szabó – Réka Benczes – Utku Bozdağ

Metaphors as markers for suicidal intent: Patterns in metaphorical language used in online forum posts about suicidal thoughts 221
Gábor Simon – Tímea Borbála Bajzát – Kata Árvay – Júlia Ballagó – Kitti Hauber – Zsuzsanna Havasi – Ágnes Kuna – Emese K. Molnár – Noémi Prótár – Eszter Szlávich – Zsuzsa Kaló

Preface

Despite the profound role language plays in shaping healthcare delivery, clinical reasoning, patient experience, and professional identity, the systematic study of medical language has remained fragmented across disciplinary lines. Medical linguistics, as an emerging field at the intersection of linguistics, medicine, and communication studies, is still in its nascent stages—lacking both consolidated theoretical frameworks and an established international forum. With the launch of Semmelweis Medical Linguistics Investigations, we seek to address this lacuna. This inclusive label of medical linguistics allows us to unify diverse approaches and methodologies under a shared conceptual umbrella that highlights the essential role of language in healthcare contexts. This volume inaugurates a series dedicated to advancing scholarly dialogue, encouraging interdisciplinary collaboration, and fostering the development of medical linguistics as a distinct and evolving domain of scientific inquiry.

This first volume assembles a diverse set of research contributions that reflect the conceptual breadth and methodological richness of the field. It is organized into four thematic sections: Terminology, ESP Instruction, Healthcare Communication, and Metaphors in Healthcare. The opening section investigates the transformation and standardization of medical terminology, particularly in nursing documentation and data-driven health communication. The second section explores the pedagogical challenges and innovations in teaching English for medical purposes, highlighting role-plays, telemedicine simulations, and feedback mechanisms involving simulated patients. The third section examines multilingual and intercultural dynamics in healthcare encounters, including interpreter-mediated communication, training for cultural competence, and comparative discourse analysis. The final section turns to metaphor as a powerful lens for understanding how health, illness, and emotional experience are conceptualized and expressed in both professional and lay contexts. Together, these chapters offer critical insights into how language operates in—and often defines—the lived realities of medicine.

Our intention with this series is not only to showcase the current state of research but also to cultivate an intellectual space where medical linguistics can grow into a recognized and robust field. We hope that this volume will serve as a point of departure for further explorations and collaborations, encouraging scholars, educators, and healthcare professionals alike to engage more deeply with the language of medicine and its far-reaching implications.

PART I
Terminology

Transition in nursing documentation: Insights into the terminology of Hungarian nursing notes

Tünde Vágási[1] – Gábor Gyenes[1] – Zoltán Patonai[2] – Éva Katalin Varga[1]

ABSTRACT
The study examines the terminology and general characteristics of the nursing notes (handover) in inpatient care in Hungary, in order to determine the extent to which the move to electronic recording affects the quality of the record and thus the impact on the nursing process. The nursing notes of twenty-one anonymized patient files from a traumatology department were gradually transferred to the electronic system: at the time of the study, notes for five patients were handwritten and fourteen were electronically recorded. A manual and software-based analysis of the corpus was performed: terms, abbreviations, and acronyms, as well as stylistic features were extracted and compared. The results show that the terminological characteristics of the genre have substantially changed with the introduction of electronic recording.

Keywords: medical language, terminology, nursing notes, nursing documentation, corpus analysis, genre analysis, e-MedSolution

1. Introduction

In Hungary, the transfer of medical and nursing documents and records to electronic systems started in the early 2000s, and in some institutions this process has been fully implemented. At the moment, no standardized system exists, with each institution deciding which documents are kept electronically and which are kept in the traditional, handwritten format. As document management varies according to the local regulations of each institution, there is a need for a nationally-integrated, standardized system. The integration of the Hungarian Electronic Nursing Record (ENR) is currently in progress (Oláh et al., 2023), and the recording of bedside daily nursing activities in the system was tested in more than ten pilot institutions in the summer of 2022 (Oláh et al., 2023).

The aims of this study are firstly, to summarize the main features of the Hungarian nursing documentation system and secondly, to compare electronic and handwritten nursing documents prepared during patient care.

---

[1] Semmelweis University, Institute of Languages for Specific Purposes
[2] University of Pécs, Clinical Center, Department of Traumatology and Hand Surgery

The terminology and general characteristics of the nursing notes (handover) were examined; the notes were generated in inpatient care in 2019 and 2020 at the Department of Traumatology and Hand Surgery of the University of Pécs, Hungary, and were gradually transferred to the electronic system. The electronically recorded documents were stored in the clinic's e-MedSolution integrated healthcare IT system, which was designed to provide both inpatient and ambulatory care functionality in a single application with a Hungarian-language interface. The handwritten and electronic documents in our corpus are particularly suitable for comparing the advantages and disadvantages of each recording method.

2. Theoretical background

Studies and research worldwide have demonstrated that the introduction of electronic nursing documentation improves patient safety, care efficiency and the quality of healthcare as well as care planning and evaluation. Adereti and Olaogun (2019) argue that electronic documentation, in contrast to its analogue (paper-based) counterpart, offers a significant advantage in standardized terminology, ensuring uniform wording. Meanwhile, the data recorded in electronic systems are generally more accurate and complete, since the system provides multiple control functions. The potential for errors in nursing documentation (Oláh, 2020, pp. 24–27) can be largely eliminated by completing electronic nursing documents (Fölker, 2014).

A further advantage is that healthcare professionals have rapid access to patient data, even in multiple specialties or institutions, as they can be easily shared among authorized individuals, increasing not only information availability but also collaboration (Potter et al., 2017). Electronic documentation also enables easier analysis of data, supporting healthcare institutions to improve processes and outcomes, and to improve quality of care (Moody et al., 2004; Khuan et al., 2018; McCarthy et al., 2019).

Several studies have focused on security and privacy issues (McCarthy et al., 2019; Tajabadi et al., 2020). Electronic nursing documentation systems generally apply strict privacy measures to ensure confidentiality and protection of patient health data, and have thus been found to be more reliable than paper-based documentation.

De Groot et al. (2022) analyzed time savings with 195 Dutch community nurses. They found that electronic management of documentation enables data to be quickly recorded and retrieved from any location with access to an electronic system. Research on nurses in Florida also suggests that introducing electronic documentation would reduce the administrative burden on nurses (Moody et al., 2004). A survey of 100 nurses found that 36% of the participants agreed that electronic documentation had reduced their workload, 75% agreed that the quality of the documentation had improved and 76% of respondents felt that it had improved patient safety and therefore the quality of care (Oláh, 2020, p. 28).

In Hungary, there has been an increasing transition in the last decade to electronic nursing documentation, with e-MedSolution and Medworks used to record and store patient nursing care data and information.

Nursing care documentation is completed in accordance with the rules provided for in Act XLVII of 1997 on the processing and protection of health and related personal data. However, the nursing documentation is used solely for internal communication within the hospital department, or as evidence in possible criminal or civil legal proceedings. Nurses need to pass on correct information to their colleagues on other shifts to improve the healthcare process (Braaf et al., 2015).

Similarly to medical documentation, nursing documents are produced at the time of admission (nursing anamnesis, nursing assessment, and nursing care plan), during nursing care (patient care sheet, nursing notes or handover or course of disease, and nursing activities), and at the time of discharge (nursing discharge summary).

Table 1 details the documents, namely the parts of the nursing documentation that are generated during the admission, care and discharge of the patient, and compares them to medical documents in terms of their communication purpose and structural characteristics. Medical documents are usually kept in digital format and follow the patient throughout their hospital stay; they include medical history, examinations, tests and labs, diagnoses, and medications. However, the regulations of individual hospitals regarding documentation – which is maintained continuously throughout the care process – may include the possibility of paper records, although these should be at least partially transferred to the electronic system.

Table 1. *Document types of nursing documentation in comparison with medical records (T = type of recording: E = electronic system, H = handwritten)*

Stages of inpatient care	nursing documentation	T	medical documentation	T
Admission	Nursing anamnesis (ápolási anamnézis)	E	Patient admission form: anamnesis (kórlap / beteg-felvételi lap: anamnézis)	E
	Nursing assessment (ápolási regisztráció)	E	Patient admission form: status (kórlap / betegfelvételi lap: státusz)	E
	Nursing care plan (ápolási terv)	E		
Care / treatment/ implement	Patient care sheet (ápolási lap)	H	Course of disease (dekurzus)	E
	Nursing notes / hand-over / course of care (ápolási jelentés, átadó, dekurzus)	H		
	Nursing activities (ápolási tevékenységek)	E		
Discharge	Nursing discharge summary (ápolási záró-jelentés – eredmények)	E	Medical history summary (klinikai záró-jelentés – epikrízis)	E

From the nursing documentation, the nursing notes, also called handover or course of care, were analyzed. These contain, in diary-like form, the nursing care activities undertaken by the nurse around the patient and the observations on the patient's details (patient's condition, pain levels, current medications, etc.). The document is called the 'handover', as the day- and night shift nurses hand the information over to the next shift. The patient care sheet includes the patient's information (their name, room number, age, etc.). On the back of the form is the nursing report, which contains information about the assessment (a patient's current physical status), lab- and diagnostic tests, and should include the date of the activities and the details (name, signature) of the employee who provided the care. The nursing notes can be handwritten on the back of the patient care sheet in accordance with the quality assurance policy, or recorded electronically in the nursing care activities document.

The aim of our analysis is to describe the structural and terminological characteristics of the genre of nursing notes as a specific communication tool between healthcare assistants, providing up-to-date information about the patient. As the traditional handwritten, free-form version is gradually being replaced by nurses' short notes within the electronic documentation system, our aim is to describe the structural and terminological characteristics of the genre in both cases. In comparing the two, this study aims to observe the extent to which the efficiency-enhancing support of electronic documentation enables the genre's structure to be preserved and the linguistic and terminological guidelines for quality documentation to be fulfilled.

3. Data and methods

A comprehensive, interprofessional hospital documentation analysis was conducted, using twenty-one anonymized medical files generated in 2019 and 2020 at the Department of Traumatology and Hand Surgery of the University of Pécs. The analysis of the medical records was completed in 2021 (Varga et al., 2021), while the processing of the nursing records is ongoing. The admission and discharge documents of the nursing records are stored in the e-Medsolution medical system used in the Pécs clinic since 2007, but the 'nursing notes' (aka handover, course of disease) are still kept on paper forms.

In five of the twenty-one hospital documents examined, the nursing notes were handwritten in the traditional way, on the back of the patient report sheet, in two columns titled "Nursing notes day 6-18 h" and "Nursing notes night 18-6 h". In fourteen cases where patients stayed in a hospital more than three days, the patient report sheet was annotated 'nursing activities in eMedSol'. Two patients had a day surgery for which no patient report sheet was opened; in these cases, the nursing activities were only recorded in e-MedSol. After transcribing the handwritten nursing notes into typed text, a corpus of approximately 5400 tokens was developed and analyzed manually and using software. Terms, abbreviations and acronyms were collected manually, stylistic features typical of the genre were examined, and a frequency analysis and keyword analysis were performed using the Sketch Engine software. Individually-worded terms were also extracted from the electronically recorded nursing activities, and the resulting corpus of 2482 tokens was analyzed for terminological and stylistic aspects. For both corpora, the writing style used in the documents was retained. Hungarian language data were quoted only when the data were required for illustrative purposes; otherwise, the meaning of the quoted words and expressions was given, and the acronyms used in the documentation were given in the form common in Hungarian. The statistical analysis used a descriptive and analytical test (chi-square) to examine whether a correlation exists between the absence of custom-written sections in electronically recorded nursing activities and the use of short, handwritten notes by the nurses on the patient care form. Expressions entered during day and night shifts were also compared separately. The entries were compared in two different ways: firstly, the availability of a paper-based report for electronically recorded data was examined; secondly, it was determined whether data were entered into the electronic system from the paper-based nursing records. Data were analyzed using the IBM SPSS 22 software.

4. Results
4.1. Features of the handwritten nursing notes or handover

Two types of patient care sheets (ápolási lap) currently exist. While one features the nursing notes or handover on the back, the other has no free-form text written on the back and instead comprises several handwritten entries. In both cases, the nursing notes are composed of text, which is typologically narrative in nature and consists of freely-written complete sentences. It is also known as a handover, as day and night nurses use it to give the information to the next shift. Importantly, the patient care sheet details the patient's condition, including the date of the activities and the signature of the nurse who provided the care.

The monitoring of the patient's general condition; i.e., measuring blood pressure, pulse, respiratory rate, and body temperature several times a day, is most often recorded as 'observing the vital signs' (*vitális paraméterei ellenőrizve* 'vital signs tested') in this collocation. This being the most common entry, nurses generally use abbreviations that are not always consistent: *vitális paraméterei ell., vit. par. ell., Vit. paraméterei ell.* Unlike in medical documentation (Varga et al., 2021), with a limited number of exceptions, the negative word *nem* 'non, no', is not used to record the absence of a condition but rather to describe the patient's actions, in combination with verbs: *panaszt nem jelzett* 'no complaint', *nem eszik* 'no eating', *nem iszik* 'no drinking', *nem akar* 'not wanting', *nem fogadott el* 'not accepting', *nem kért* 'not accepted'. In addition to the anamnesis, this is the only type of nursing documentation that uses present- or past-tense verbs, and it does so typically in relation to the patient. The actions of the nursing staff are referred to the adverbial participle expressing a situation (ágynemű *cserélve* 'bed linen changed') or by the nomen actionis, which replaces the passive voice not used in Hungarian, and formed by the verb *történt* 'was made'; e.g., ágynemű *csere történt* 'bed linen has been changed'. First-person singular verbs are very rare; the actions of the healing and nursing community are indicated by the first-person plural verbs. In connection with infusion or transfusion therapies, the verbs *lefolyik* 'run down' and *lecsepeg* 'drip' are used (e.g., *infúzió / AB / vér lefolyt lecsepegett* 'infusion / AB [antibiotic] / blood has run through). Adjectives have mostly positive connotations such as *láztalan* 'feverless', *jól* 'well'.

The nursing notes use only Hungarian anatomical names both for the parts of the body (e.g., *bal kézfej* 'left hand') and for the location of the interventions (e.g., *lábán kötéscsere* 'leg bandage replacement'), usually with the laterality specified. The genre as a whole uses few Latin and Latin derived terms: *subfebrilis* 'subfebrile', *per os* 'orally', *haemokultúra* 'hemoculture', *hyperaemiás* 'hyperemic'. Among the names of the devices, *infusio* 'infusion' is common from Latin, as is *catheter* from Greek, and *drain* from English. French derived-terms include *redon* (from the name of the French surgeon Redon), *kanül* 'cannula' and *fixator/fixateur*. Meanwhile, *Branül* (from the name of the manufacturer Braun and the contamination of the word *kanül* 'cannula') is a term used exclusively in Hungary.

The terminology of the designation of diagnostic tools also includes medical acronyms such as *EKG* 'electrocardiography', *CT* 'computer tomography', and *RTG* 'radiography'. The acronyms for institutions and departments are derived from Hungarian appellatives: *OMSZ* (*Országos Mentőszolgálat*) 'National Ambulance Service', *AITI* (*Aneszteziológiai és Intenzív Terápiás Intézet*) 'Department of Anaesthesiology and Intensive Therapy'. The nature of the traumatology department explains that many of the acronyms associated with procedures are of English origin, e.g., *LMWH* 'Low-molecular-weight heparin', *VAC* 'vacuum-assisted closure', *CRP* 'C-reactive protein'.

To save space and time, the nursing notes use many abbreviations. Nursing notes are characterized by the use of Hungarian abbreviations and acronyms, generally written without spaces or periods, with acronyms generally written in capitals. The same terms can have different abbreviations and acronyms: *vit., vitál.* to *vitális* 'vital', *par., param.* to *paraméterek* 'parameters', *AB, antibiot.* to *antibiotikum* 'antibiotic', *T.L.* and *TL* to *teljes labor* 'full lab'. While there is no uniform list of abbreviations and acronyms used for each institution, and the different variants do not necessarily pose a problem for the understanding of the text, the lack of consistency may be a factor in processing speed.

4.2. Characteristics of electronically recorded care activities

Another classification of care activity, BE-06, was also used in our study. This does not include a free-form text handover but contains more handwritten entries than the other type of patient care sheet. Nurses manually complete the day and night shift records by indicating the date and the time intervals 6-18 and 18-6. Separate columns are provided to record blood pressure, pulse, and fluid intake and output. There are three columns for short, free-worded entries under the headings of ward rounds, nursing problems, observations, and nursing activities. The last column almost always contains the entry Áp. *[ápolási] lap eMedSolban* 'Nursing activities in eMedSol(ution)', indicating that the nursing activities have been recorded in the electronic system. The last column contains the signature of the nurse.

In contrast to the handwritten nursing notes, the electronically recorded nursing activities (Ápolási tevékenységek) interface allows the nurse to select from a list of activities performed on a patient; e.g., measuring oxygen saturation, heart rate, blood pressure, respiratory rate, temperature. Another new feature is that for each entry, the patient's condition is graded according to the Karnofsky scale, where 1. indicates death and 10. indicates no complaints. In the documents examined, patients were classified between grades 3 and 7. When the nurse assigns the patient to a grade on the Karnofsky scale, only the nursing care activities that belong to that grade are listed.

Examining a single nursing activity, we can see that while the electronic document only includes textual information such as 'Cleaning up the patient's environment' next to the selected codes, the handwritten handover also records, for example, whether a complete or partial bed linen change was performed, or whether the patient washed himself or herself with or without assistance. There is also much more information about the patient's urination in the handwritten documents, e.g., whether the patient needed a bedpan or was able to go to the toilet independently. Similar added detail can be observed in the measurement of body temperature and the taking of medication. In the traditional handover, not only the fact of taking the body temperature is recorded, but also the measured value and the patient's condition, e.g., *subfebrilis* 'subfebrile', *láztalan* 'afebrile'.

The electronic recording also allows for free-form entries in two menu items of the electronic interface: on the one hand, under 'Nursing observations, events', examples include *éjszaka aludt, panaszt nem jelzett* 'slept at night, no complaints'; *panaszmentes, láztalan* 'complaint-free, feverless'; and on the other hand, under the menu items of activities selected by codes, examples include *katéter vezet* 'urine flowing through catheter'; while under 'Infusion therapy', the name and amount of the administered medication can be recorded; e.g., *1500 ml Isolyte*.

In addition to the electronic nursing activities, handwritten free-form notes by nurses on the patient care sheet continue to be maintained. These are found in three columns under 'Ward round orders', 'Nursing problems, observations', and 'Nursing activities'. These entries were much shorter than even the free-worded parts of the electronically kept nursing activities; therefore, they were not examined separately and were included only in the statistical analysis.

A software analysis of the 2482 tokens of text corpus generated from 373 free-word entries of the nursing activities documents generated during the care of fourteen patients was also performed. The most common word is *panaszmentes* 'complaint-free', and the most common patterns are: *katétere vezet* 'catheter is in', *éjszaka többször ellenőrizve* 'checked several times at night', *pelenka csere* 'diaper changed', *katéterzsák ürítve* 'catheter bag emptied', *perifériás kanül van* 'peripheral cannula is inserted'. Similar to the handwritten nursing notes, these include the names of the instruments and procedures used to care for patients. The entries are stylistically similar to the handwritten records.

4.3. Statistical analysis

IBM SPSS 22 software was used for statistical analysis. First, the chi-square test was used to examine whether there was a connection between the absence of custom-written sections in electronically recorded nursing activities documents and the presence of handwritten notes in the ward round, 'Nursing problems, observations', and 'Nursing activities' columns of the patient care sheet BE-06. Then, the entries recorded during day and night shifts were compared separately. The comparison was made using two different aspects. The first determined whether there were paper records for data entered into the electronic system. The second was based on the handwritten records in the patient care sheet and determined whether there were any entries in the electronic system in addition to these. Based on these two aspects, the variables examined are shown separately in Table 2.

Table 2. *Descriptive statistics based on the variables tested, on the electronic system and on the handwritten entries on the form*

Baseline characteristics		From an electronic system perspective (n=373)		In terms of a handwritten note (n=238)	
		n	%	n	%
position	day shift	199	53.4	137	57.6
	night shift	174	46.6	101	42.4
Type of entry recorded electronically	there was no entry	89	23.9		
	nurses' note	142	38.1		
	coded entry and free-form addition	41	11.0		
	nursing entry and coded entry	96	25.7		
	other entry	5	1.3		
Handwritten note for electronic registration	yes	35	9.4		
	no	338	90.6		
Type of handwritten entry	there was no entry			56	23.5
	ward round			114	47.9
	nursing observations			19	8.0
	nursing care activities			49	20.6
Electronic entry for a handwritten note	yes			204	87.6
	no			29	12.4

Based on the electronic system, 373 entries were examined. No statistically significant association was found between the type of electronic entry and the presence of a handwritten note on the patient care sheet (p = .771). When examining the association between the type of electronic entry and the day- or night schedule of nurses, free-word additions next to coded entries were significantly more prevalent in the day schedule than in the night schedule (p = .003), while the distribution of other entry types were nearly identical between the two schedules. There was no significant association between the existence of a paper record and the nurses' rostering in addition to the electronically recorded entry (p = .074).

238 entries were examined using the patient care sheet. No statistically significant association was found between the type of handwritten entry and the existence of an entry recorded in the electronic system (p = .146). With regard to the nurses' assignment, there was a significant association between the assignment and the type of entry on the patient care sheet (p > .001). A higher proportion of entries were recorded manually on paper in the daytime than in night-time schedules. In addition, it was also found that there were significantly more individually-phrased electronic entries created during the night shift compared to the day shift (p = .043).

5. Discussion

A comparison of the two types of documents under consideration clearly shows the advantages and disadvantages of electronic recording, which may help to increase the efficiency of the new system. Although electronically recorded nursing activities are easy to read, handwritten documents contain much more information on individual nursing activities and the patient's condition. However, handwriting is often difficult to read, the documentation can be unclear, and the exact times may not be recorded. Documents in our handwritten corpus were difficult to read and disorganized in format and therefore cannot be regarded as an effective source of information for nurses and related professionals. As processing speed can be affected by the legibility of handwriting and the use of abbreviations, especially unique ones, electronic care management is accordingly more understandable for all parties. However, there is a risk that essential information contained in the more detailed handwritten notes can be lost in the more general wording of electronic systems.

All healthcare employees must use the same template when preparing their reports. A standard format ensures that the same information is included in the same way every time. Nursing documentation is intended to accurately reflect a timely flow of nursing and care events but due to the high workload, documentation is typically only completed at the end of the shift, with the result that some information may be lost. With use of the appropriate electronic tools, information can be tracked and recorded from a tablet or software-enabled mobile phone, and data can be recorded swiftly, even from the bedside, thanks to the modular system. Electronic recording can also filter out possible duplication and alert the nurse to the possibility of entering the same data in several places (e.g., patient care sheet, temperature chart, medication chart), which can occur when filling in one of the many forms by hand.

One of the main advantages of using an electronic care record is that it contains elements that can be selected from a module, so there is no information gap and it saves a significant amount of time. The nurse fills in the fields that describe the patient's condition. The nurse can also describe the events in his or her own words as a comment, so as not to compromise individual care. In 33 of the 373 electronic nursing activities documents reviewed, the entry found matched the handwritten entry on the patient care sheet. In the electronically recorded nursing activities, the free-form, individual comments under the 'Nursing observations, events' menu are usually short; e.g., *panaszmentes* 'complaint-free', or *láztalan* 'feverless'. Longer entries are similar to those observed in handwritten nursing notes.

The selection from this module shows how misunderstandings due to typing are avoided, errors due to differences in wording are eliminated, and professionally-checked, standardized definitions are used. In the case of handwritten documents recording individual events, statements that were not drafted with sufficient care were found to have been entered in the nursing documentation, while events that had already been formulated were repeated unnecessarily from shift to shift, with unnecessary jargon used in the recording. The use of standardized nursing terminology allows easy transmission of data analyzed using the nursing data system. Nurses use push-button scan schemas to formulate care schedules that occurred during a shift; e.g., infusion, medication, dressing changes. From e-Medsolution, any of the electronically recorded data can be printed, but only the completed parts, thus saving printing costs. Nevertheless, we should draw attention to the important fact that the traditional, handwritten patient care sheets are kept in some cases even if the nursing activities are recorded in the electronic system. This may be because the orders for rounds, medication, diet, and surgery appointments are recorded on the handwritten form at the bedside.

6. Conclusion

In the study, particular attention was paid to the users of the document types under investigation, and the characteristics of language use were examined in the light of this. On this basis, it was determined that only under the headings 'Nursing observations, events' and 'Other additions' in the electronically recorded document was the free-form style of the handwritten documents retained.

The integration of the Hungarian Electronic Nursing Register (ENR) has a number of problems to solve before it can fully replace paper-based documentation. In a hospital, several different specialties of medicine and nursing care exist; therefore, a module system compatible with each discipline needs to be built. After eliminating all these problems, in terms of efficiency, a digitized format may be preferable due to consistency of terminology and content; however, it would be important for nurses to retain the option for adding other information.

References

1997. évi XLVII. törvény Az egészségügyi és a hozzájuk kapcsolódó személyes adatok kezeléséről és védelméről [Act XLVII of 1997 on the processing and protection of health and related personal data]. https://net.jogtar.hu/jogszabaly?docid=99700047.tv

Adereti, C. S. & Olaogun, A. A. (2019). Use of electronic and paper-based standardized nursing care plans to improve nurses' documentation quality in a Nigerian teaching hospital. *International Journal of Nursing Knowledge, 30*(4), 219–227.

Asmirajanti, M., Hamid A. Y. S., & Hariyati, R. T. S. (2019). Nursing care activities based on documentation. *BMC Nursing, 18*(Suppl 1), Article 32. https://doi.org/10.1186/s12912-019-0352-0

Braaf, S., Riley, R., & Manias, E. (2015). Failures in communication through documents and documentation across the perioperative pathway. *Journal of Clinical Nursing, 24*(13–14), 1874–1884.

De Groot, K., De Veer, A. J. E., Munster, A. M., Francke, A. L., & Paans, W. (2022). Nursing documentation and its relationship with perceived nursing workload: a mixed-methods study among community nurses. *BMC Nursing, 21*(1), 1–12. https://doi.org/10.1186/s12912-022-00811-7

Fölker, J. (2014). *A Pécsi Tudományegyetem medikai rendszerének mobil alkalmazása.* [Mobile application of the medical system of the University of Pécs.] http://nws.niif.hu/ncd2014/docs/ehu/063.pdf

Khuan L., Hanafiah Juni, M., & Makhdzir, N. (2018). Experience of electronic nursing documentation in a hospital setting: A qualitative study. *Journal of Nursing Care, 7.* https://doi.org/10.4172/10.4172/2167-1168-C4-073

McCarthy, B., Fitzgerald, S., O'Shea, M., Condon, C., Hartnett-Collins, G., Clancy, M., Sheehy, A., Denieffe, S., Bergin, M., & Savage, E. (2019). Electronic nursing documentation interventions to promote or improve patient safety and quality care: A systematic review. *Journal of Nursing Management, 27*(3), 491–501. https://doi.org/10.1111/jonm.12727

Moody L. E., Slocumb, E., Berg, B., & Jackson, D. (2004). Electronic health records documentation in nursing: Nurses' perceptions, attitudes, and preferences. *Computers, Informatics, Nursing, 22*(6), 337–344. https://doi.org/10.1097/00024665-200411000-00009

Oláh, A., Zrínyi, M., Fullér, N., Balogh, Z., Kádár, M., Kis, T., & Szebeni-Kovács, Gy. (2023). Az ápolói munkaterhelés és ápolási intenzitás komplex mérésének lehetőségei a magyarországi Ápolástámogató Rendszer kialakításához kapcsolódó fejlesztések keretében. [The possibilities of complex measurement of nursing workload and intensity in the context of the development of the Hungarian Nursing Support System.] *Nővér, 36*(2), 1–44. https://doi.org/10.55608/nover.36.0008

Oláh, M. (2020). Az ápolási dokumentáció hatékony alkalmazásának aspektusai [Aspects of effective use of nursing documentation]. *Acta Sana, 13*(2), 22–31. https://doi.org/10.14232/actasana

Potter, P. A., Perry, A. G., Stockert, P., & Hall, A. (2017). *Fundamentals of nursing.* Elsevier.

Tajabadi, A., Ahmadi, F., Sadooghi, A., & Vaismoradi, M. (2020). Unsafe nursing documentation: A qualitative content analysis. *Nursing Ethics*, *27*, 1213–1224.

Varga, É. K., Fogarasi, K., & Patonai, Z. (2021). A kórházi ellátás dokumentumai [Hospital care documents]. InÁ. Fóris & A. Bölcskei (Eds.), *Tartalomfejlesztés és dokumentáció. Nyelvészeti kutatások* (pp. 289–326). Károli Gáspár Református Egyetem – L'Harmattan Kiadó.

Standardized medical data for optimized health communication

Maria-Cornelia Wermuth[1]

ABSTRACT

Standardized terminological resources play a key role in the collection and exchange of health-related information. This paper takes a closer look at SNOMED CT, the international reference terminology for healthcare. The system consists of a formal ontology combined with multilingual terminology. Once implemented in software applications such as the Electronic Health Record (EHR) or Hospital Information Systems (HIS), SNOMED CT enables the structured capture, documentation, and processing of a wide range of health-related data such as findings and diagnoses, procedures, social parameters, etc. in different languages, thus supporting efficient cross-lingual communication in the healthcare sector. The translation of the English-language terminology requires a collaborative and community-based approach and (inter)national translation guidelines based on ISO standards to ensure translation quality, consistency, and appropriateness, taking into account the cultural requirements of different medical contexts worldwide. The specific translation challenges are described, focusing on the importance of (inter)national teamwork and terminological principles for high-quality translation to meet the information needs of different audiences, including professionals and patients.

Keywords: health information exchange, standardization, medical translation, patient-friendly terminology, SNOMED CT

1. Health communication in the digital age

Effective health communication faces challenges from international mobility, migration, cultural diversity and patient empowerment (Ratna, 2019, pp. 1-6). Cross-border exchange of medical data, multilingual communication, and inclusive and understandable language are now essential aspects of medical communication. In addition, electronic data capture and exchange replaces paper-based communication. Electronic health and patient records (EHRs, EPRs) have become commonplace, allowing health-related data to flow seamlessly between users for different purposes, independent of time and place. The digitization of healthcare brings efficiencies but also challenges related to data security, standardization and interoperability between systems (Torab-Miandoab et al., 2023). A particular challenge is the complexity of medical

---

[1] Faculty of Arts, KU Leuven in Antwerp

terminology, which often has multiple designations for the same concept. For example, while one specialist may diagnose a condition as *kidney cancer*, other healthcare professionals may use different terms for the same concept, such as *renal cancer, malignant tumor of kidney, renal malignant tumor*, or *CA renal* (which stands for *renal cell carcinoma*). While humans may be able to correctly interpret the meaning of multiple terms, computers cannot deal with ambiguity in language. Standardization is therefore essential to ensure that information remains consistent when transferred between electronic systems. Several health informatics standards have been developed by the ISO Technical Committee 215 on Health Informatics (ISO TC 215), covering architecture, data exchange, semantic content, and security, safety and privacy standards (Payne, 2013, pp. 16-18). Recent efforts, such as the European Commission's eHealth initiative (eHealth, n.d., Web), recognize the need for structured documentation, with an emphasis on standardized data capture. In the landscape of international data exchange standards, Health Level Seven (HL7) (Health Level Seven International, n.d., Web) provides a framework for the sharing and retrieval of electronic health information. It includes several categories of standards, such as FHIR (Fast Healthcare Interoperability Resources), that specify the language, structure, and data types required to integrate systems and enable healthcare providers to effectively share clinical data across multiple healthcare software applications. This paper focuses on SNOMED CT, which stands for Systematized Nomenclature of Medicine – Clinical Terms, a globally used terminology standard published by SNOMED International and developed by the International Health Terminology Standardization Organization (IHTSDO). The aim is to highlight the importance of this reference terminology in supporting efficient cross-lingual communication in healthcare. It also describes the specific translation challenges, focusing on the role of ISO 1087:2019 *Terminology work and terminology science – Vocabulary* and ISO 704:2009 *Terminology work – Principles and methods* in this context. The following sections introduce the terminology resource, followed by an overview of the translation process and challenges.

2. SNOMED CT: the reference terminology for healthcare

SNOMED CT is a multilingual reference terminology that quantitatively and qualitatively covers all areas of medical activity. The terminology is constantly being expanded in line with the progress of scientific research. Once implemented in software applications such as EHRs and EPRs, SNOMED CT can be used to collect, document and electronically process medically relevant information (such as findings and diagnoses, procedures, drugs and agents, laboratory values, social parameters, etc.) in a structured way (e.g., in the exchange formats of the electronic patient or health record or primary systems such as practice or hospital information systems). In addition, descriptions of the same facts, which are identical in content but formulated differently in medical documentation, can be standardized by recording synonymous terms and defining a preferred term. In this way, SNOMED CT supports the standardization of medical terminology and the effective exchange of health-related information. The terminology standard, primarily published in English, is currently used in over 50 countries (through national membership of SNOMED International or use licenses). Translations are currently available in 20 languages or language variants. By removing language barriers, SNOMED CT helps to increase the usefulness of clinical documentation produced in another language. High-quality translations are, therefore, essential for reliable system use. Achieving accurate translations requires a collaborative and community-driven approach, coupled with adherence to translation guidelines based on the ISO 1087:2019 and ISO 704:2009 standards. Both standards play a crucial role in ensuring that the translation of SNOMED CT is not only linguistically accurate and consistent but also conforms to standardized principles in terminology development and presentation. The ultimate translation goal is to maintain the quality, consistency and appropriateness of the source terminology while considering the cultural nuances inherent in different medical contexts around the world. While there is extensive research on the development and application of medical ontologies (Fung & Bodenreider, 2023), the specific aspect of translating these ontologies into different languages is less frequently addressed. For example, a study of the translation of SNOMED CT concepts into Belgian French (Wermuth et al., 2022) highlighted the translation problems and the need for collaborative work, but such studies are relatively rare. More comprehensive research is needed to explore this specific area's challenges and requirements. Therefore, this paper aims to provide a first approach to filling this gap by focusing on some of the common challenges that arise when translating SNOMED CT across languages. First the structure of SNOMED CT is described, based on the Starter Guide (SNOMED CT Starter Guide, n.d., Web).

3. The architecture of SNOMED CT

3.1. SNOMED CT concept model

SNOMED CT consists of a formal ontology and a collection of standardized terms for describing objects, entities, states, processes, etc. in various medical domains. The concept model specifies how concepts are defined using a combination of formal logic and editing rules. At the top of the SNOMED CT hierarchy is the root concept or |SNOMED CT concept| (the SNOMED CT notation of concepts between two vertical pipes is adopted here). All concepts are derived from this root concept through at least one sequence of |is-a|relationships. The direct subtypes of the root concept are called top-level concepts and represent the main branches of the hierarchy (e.g., |clinical finding|, |procedure|, |body structure|, |organism|, etc.). Each of these 19 top-level concepts, together with its numerous subtypes, forms a main branch of the SNOMED CT hierarchy and contains similar concept types. The concepts become more specific as the abstraction relationships below the top-level concepts become deeper.

3.2. SNOMED CT components

The system consists of three components: (1) concepts; (2) descriptions that link concepts to human-readable medical terms (single-word and multi-word terms such as *eczema* and *open fracture of the forearm* or nominal phrases such as *cholera vaccine in an oral dosage form*); the descriptions are divided into the Fully Specified Name (FSN) and Synonyms; (3) relationships that link related concepts using abstraction relationships (|is-a| relationships) and associative relationships (so-called attribute relationships). Each concept can have several parent concepts and can be accessed in the ontology through different parent concepts. This polyhierarchical structure allows the granular representation of clinical concepts and relationships and enables complex medical data to be encoded with the necessary semantic correctness and granularity (Ingenerf, 2015, p. 42). For example, the concept |Bronchitis| may be subordinate to the concepts |Disorder of bronchus|, |Inflammation of specific body organs| and

|Inflammatory disorder of lower respiratory tract|. An attribute relationship contributes to the definition of the source concept by linking it to the value of a defining characteristic. The characteristic (attribute) is determined by the relationship type, and the value is provided by the target of the relationship. For example, the attribute relationships |Associated morphology| and |Finding site| are used to associate the source concept |Bronchitis| with the target concepts |Inflammatory morphology| and |Bronchial structure|.

3.3. Complete vs. incomplete definitions

Each concept is labelled as fully defined or primitive. A concept is fully defined when its defining characteristics are sufficient to distinguish its meaning from other related concepts. For example, the concept |Acute disease| is fully defined by two relationships, namely |is-a||Disease| and |Clinical course||Sudden onset AND/OR Short duration|. To say that this concept is fully defined means that any concept with these two relations is a subtype of this concept (or the concept itself). If the defining characteristics of a concept are not sufficient to clearly distinguish its meaning from other similar concepts, then the concept is primitive (incompletely defined). For example, the concepts |Disease| and |Drug action| have the same defining characteristics, namely an |is-a| relationship to the concept |Clinical finding|. To clarify the meaning of these concept types, natural language definitions are provided, albeit to a limited extent. For computational purposes, concepts are identified by numerical identifiers (concept IDs). Figure 1 shows the overall structure of SNOMED CT.

4. The translation of SNOMED CT

4.1. Organization of the translation

The translation of SNOMED CT is a large-scale undertaking that follows specific guidelines and organizational structures. When joining SNOMED International, member countries designate a National Release Centre (NRC) to manage national distribution and translation. In Germany, for example, the National Competence Centre for Terminologies (Nationales Kompetenzzentrum für Terminologien) at the Federal Institute for Drugs and Medical Devices (Bundesinstitut für Arzneimittel und Medizinprodukte [BfArM]) coordinates translations for the German language area. Due to the

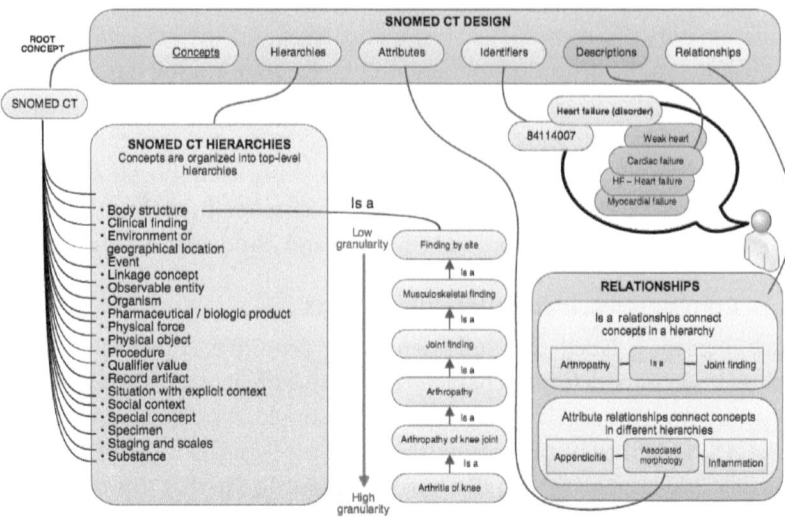

Figure 1. *Design of SNOMED CT (SNOMED CT Starter Guide, Web)*

huge volume of the terminology (the system contains more than 350,000 concepts), the translation process focuses on the priorities set by the NRCs, often emphasizing legal tasks to support electronic health and patient records. Interdisciplinary teams of experts in medical informatics, (bio)medicine, linguistics and terminology work together on translation. The international Translation User Group facilitates the exchange of experience to improve the consistency of SNOMED CT translation and ensure system interoperability. International and national translation guidelines, based on ISO standards, provide rules for achieving standardized translations in all target languages. The Guidelines for Translation of SNOMED CT 3.0 (SNOMED International, n.d., Web) are based on ISO 1087:2019, which systematically describes notions and principles related to terminology work and terminology science. Internal guidelines (International Health Terminology Standardization Organization [IHTSDO], 2010) are based on ISO 704:2009 and define the organizational framework for translation projects, such as planning, the composition of the translation team, distribution of roles, work steps in the translation process, quality control, translation tools and similar (the original version is currently being revised based on the latest version of ISO 704:2022). While each NRC decides on its specific implementation, the document provides recommendations for cost-effective, high-quality translation projects. In terms of content, the standard emphasizes the importance of maintaining terminological uniformity, which in the context of SNOMED CT means that clinical concepts are presented consistently across different language versions. This is essential for healthcare professionals, researchers, and systems that rely on SNOMED CT for standardized communication.

4.2. Translation challenges

The translation of SNOMED CT presents a number of hurdles to translators, covering a wide range of aspects. Some of the most important of these are summarized below.

A key challenge is the need for semantic equivalence between SNOMED CT concepts and their translations to support meaningful communication and successful data exchange. Therefore, translation should be concept-based, starting from the formal representation of concepts in the SNOMED CT ontology. Translators should decipher the meaning of the terms to be translated based on the hierarchical classification and relationships of the underlying concepts to ensure accurate translations into the target language. The Fully Specified Name (FSN) and (a limited number of) free-text definitions complement the formal descriptions to provide unambiguous, understandable meanings. The Guidelines for Translation of SNOMED CT 3.0 introduce the basic notions and principles related to terminology work and terminology science and explain the steps to be followed in the prescribed onomasiological approach. The benefits of the recommended approach are obvious, but it is not easy for translators without prior ontological, medical and theoretical knowledge of terminology to apply the recommended approach consistently. For example, the difference between a concept (i.e., abstract mental notions representing ideas, phenomena, or categories of objects in a general and abstract way) and a term (i.e., words or phrases used to describe a specific concept in language) is difficult for a translator who is a domain expert with no prior knowledge of terminological principles. Conversely, assessing the completeness and accuracy of the formal definitions requires a sufficient level of medical expertise. Logical errors in the SNOMED CT ontology, which lead to incorrect descriptions of the meaning of a concept and thus to misinterpretations, are another difficulty. For this reason, translators need specific training in the principles of terminology and its working methods, the basics of medical terminology and the architecture of the SNOMED CT ontology to understand and translate accurately. The SNOMED CT Browser[2] provides a tool to explore the ontology and search for concepts and terms in different SNOMED CT editions from SNOMED International and its member countries. There is also the opportunity to gain competence in the practical use of SNOMED CT through e-learning courses offered by SNOMED International. The evolving nature of healthcare practices and terminology also mandates translators to keep abreast of healthcare developments to maintain accurate translations in the context of new medical knowledge and technologies. Ongoing training is therefore essential to ensure that translators are familiar with updates and changes to the SNOMED CT system. Another important consideration is the complexity and cultural specificity of the concepts. An example is the concept of |neck|, which has a broader meaning in English than in some other languages. In Dutch and Norwegian, for example, the term *neck* refers to the back of the neck (*nek/nakke*), whereas *hals* refers to the front of the neck. SNOMED CT is also used in a wide variety of medical contexts around the world, including different healthcare practices, norms and beliefs, which necessitate cultural sensitivity to ensure appropriate translations. Examples include culture-bound concepts such as |susto|, a disease characterized by chronic somatic suffering due to emotional trauma in Latin American cultures. For this concept, several local synonyms are listed in SNOMED CT in addition to the preferred term *susto*, such as *chibib, espanto, pasmo, pérdida del alma, tripa ida* (cf. SNOMED CT Browser International Edition). Translators are also confronted with ensuring interoperability between different language versions of SNOMED CT to enable the global adoption of the terminology. A multidisciplinary approach, involving collaboration between translators, terminologists, healthcare professionals and technology experts, is therefore essential for accurate and consistent translations. Another impediment is the availability of reliable resources, including comprehensive dictionaries and glossaries specific to SNOMED CT. A lack of standardized resources can hinder the translation process. Managing the significant number of concepts within SNOMED CT is an additional challenge that requires prioritization during translation. Balancing completeness with practicality is an ongoing task for translation

---

[2] https://browser.ihtsdotools.org/?

teams, who must meet the specific priorities set by the National Release Centers (NRCs). The diversity of SNOMED CT users is another difficulty for translators. The system is used by different audiences, including different types of healthcare professionals and patients. Translators must tailor their translations to meet the information needs of these user groups, adapting terminology for both technical accuracy and accessibility. Finally, translation quality is a major issue. Ensuring the quality and consistency of translations, including accuracy, completeness and compliance, requires robust quality control processes described in the translation management guidelines. This includes checking for errors and inconsistencies and validating translations against the source. Overcoming the various translation obstacles mandates a combination of advanced translation methodologies, collaborative efforts and ongoing communication between translation teams, healthcare professionals and linguistic experts.

5. Relevance and challenges of patient-friendly terminology

SNOMED CT is not only used by healthcare professionals but is increasingly accessible to medical laypersons. Sharing medical information with patients is recognized as a particularly important aspect of effective care. Well-informed patients understand their condition better, feel confident to ask questions and can participate in decision-making. Data accessibility is therefore important and requires not only standardized data entry but also the provision of terms that patients can understand. The Consumer Health Vocabulary (UMLS, n.d., Web) defines patient-friendly terms as "[...] informal, common words and phrases about health. It includes jargon, slang, ambiguous, and misspelled words as used by consumers and health care professionals." For some time, efforts have been made to create consumer health terminologies, such as the Wellmed Consumer Health Terminology and the Consumer Health Vocabulary Initiative and others (Zielstorff, 2003, pp. 331-332). These resources are based on the Unified Medical Language System (UMLS), whose component terminologies use standard terminologies such as SNOMED CT as the "source of truth" for the meaning of medical terms.

Patient-friendly terms (PFTs) (also known as consumer-friendly terms) are important for several reasons. Patient-friendly terminology helps patients understand the technical jargon typically found in patient records and test results. The Electronic Patient Record (EPR) is gaining increasing attention due to its many benefits, including improved patient care and care coordination, increased patient engagement, unrestricted data availability, and accessibility. From one perspective, the use of SNOMED CT as a common vocabulary for the documentation of clinical information guarantees the uniformity and precision of such data. This enables the transfer of clinical information between systems. For example, clinical information in a discharge summary can be entered directly into a patient record, obviating the need for a healthcare professional to re-enter the data by hand. This saves time and reduces the risk of human error. Conversely, the comprehension of data within the EPR requires the availability of terminology that is accessible and comprehensible to patients. By associating patient-friendly synonyms with clinical terminology, healthcare professionals can document health information in their medical jargon, while patients can access this information in readily comprehensible language. For example, if a healthcare professional documents the conditions of *anosmia* and *dyspnea due to SARS-CoV-2* in the medical record, the patient will see the terms *inability to smell* and *difficulty breathing due to COVID-19 (corona)* in the EPR. The use of patient-friendly terminology also facilitates the retrieval of information, as it enables the automated mapping of consumer-entered queries to clinical terms, thereby improving the quality of search results. For example, a search for the clinical equivalents of *IBS* (frequently used abbreviation for *Irritable Bowel Syndrome* by patients) via the SNOMED CT Browser yields the clinical terms *Irritable bowel syndrome, Irritable colon syndrome* or *Functional bowel disease*. The use of any of these synonyms will result in a link being established back to the same concept in SNOMED CT. Ultimately, the implementation of patient-friendly terminology serves to eliminate obstacles to data collection in instances where a familiar term is not accessible to users (e.g., the clinical term *epistaxis* is automatically mapped to the corresponding familiar term *nosebleed*).

However, systematically introducing patient-friendly terminology into electronic terminology resources is challenging. Firstly, the potential number of PFTs for a given medical concept is unlimited, as patient-friendly terminology is often idiosyncratic and colloquial, requiring clear criteria for acceptability. Consider, for example, the many synonyms for *common cold* in English: *head cold, cold, flu, runny nose, chest cold, rhinitis, nasal catarrh*, etc.

Furthermore, the actual meaning of the PFT is not always obvious. This is because of the semantic ambiguity that arises when lay terms are used as interchangeable synonyms to express clinical concepts (as in the case of *headache* and *migraine*), leading to misinterpretation. Finally, the same PFT may have different meanings in different cultural contexts. For example, the Spanish patient-friendly term *intoxicación* means 'poisoning by food', while the English term *intoxication* refers to the (negative) effects of alcohol and other substances on the body (i.e., *envenenamiento* in Spanish). It must also be noted that when mapping PFTs to standardized terminologies such as SNOMED CT, there is often a 1:N relationship where a single PFT can be mapped to several medical terms in the reference terminology. In SNOMED CT, for example, the following correspondences are possible: exact match of the PFT with a preferred medical term in the standard resource, both having the same meaning; synonymy, the PFT is missing in the standard resource, but corresponds to a clinical term that denotes the same concept; hyponymy or hypernymy, the PFT is narrower or broader than the equivalent clinical term (SNOMED CT Editorial Advisory Group, n.d., Web). The specific challenge for translators is to determine the semantic equivalence of PFTs with the corresponding standardized clinical term, which adds an extra layer of complexity.

6. Summary

The evolution of medical communication in the digital age presents many opportunities but also challenges. Increasing globalization, cultural diversity, and patient empowerment underscore the need for effective cross-border exchange of medical data and multilingual communication. The transition from paper-based to electronic communication, exemplified by electronic health and patient records, has improved the accessibility and exchange of health-related data. However, the digitization of healthcare also poses challenges in terms of data security, standardization, and interoperability between systems. This paper focuses on SNOMED CT, a globally used multilingual terminology standard, and highlights its important role in facilitating cross-lingual communication in healthcare. Designed primarily for clinicians, SNOMED CT contains an enormous amount of specialized knowledge, making translation a major challenge. In this context, the importance of translation guidelines based on ISO 1087:2019 and ISO 704:2009 and multidisciplinary teamwork is discussed. The recommended concept-based translation approach establishes the conditions for producing consistent and internationally standardized translations. This ensures that SNOMED CT fulfills its claim to be a terminology standard in the medical domain. In this context, it is also important to emphasize the value of SNOMED CT in domains beyond the medical, as it represents an invaluable resource for those engaged in the fields of medical translation and copywriting. Because the creation and translation of terminology into different languages is based on ISO guidelines, and because the quality and accuracy of all terms (including synonyms) are checked by both subject matter experts and terminologists, the use of SNOMED CT as a terminology resource guarantees high-quality translations. Of course, as in every field, machine translation software (such as DeepL, Google Translate, ChatGPT) is now systematically used in medical translation (this also applies to the translation of SNOMED CT), but the collaborative review of these automatically generated translations by experts and terminologists remains essential, which makes SNOMED CT a criterion standard for medical translation and copywriting in the healthcare sector.

The importance of patient-friendly terminology is increasing as SNOMED CT becomes more accessible to lay people. Sharing medical information with patients is recognized as a critical element of effective care, promoting understanding, trust and active participation in decision-making. Despite the benefits, there are challenges to implementing patient-friendly terminology in electronic resources. Ambiguity, the potential for an unlimited number of idiosyncratic terms, and cultural differences make systematic integration difficult. For translators, the particular challenge is to determine the semantic equivalence of patient-friendly terms to their standardized clinical counterparts, adding an additional layer of complexity to the translation process. Careful consideration of these challenges is essential to ensure accurate and meaningful communication in healthcare contexts. Among the key players in the complex landscape of health communication, medical translators stand out as indispensable contributors who play a pivotal role in ensuring that health information is accessible, understandable, and culturally sensitive to diverse populations.

References

eHealth. (n.d.). *European Commission*. Retrieved January 24, 2025, from https://digital-strategy.ec.europa.eu/en/policies/ehealth

Fung, K. W., & Bodenreider, O. (2023). Knowledge representation and ontologies. In R. L. Richesson, J. E. Andrews, & K. F. Hollis (Eds.), *Clinical research informatics* (pp. 387–388). Springer. https://doi.org/10.1007/978-3-031-27173-1_18

Guidelines for Translation of SNOMED CT 3.0. (n.d.). SNOMED International. https://confluence.ihtsdotools.org/display/DOCTRANSLATE

Health Level Seven International (HL7). (n.d.). *HL7 Standards*. https://www.hl7.org/implement/standards/index.cfm?ref=nav

Ingenerf, J. (2015). Classifications and terminologies – an overview. In O. Rienhoff, & S. C. Semler (Eds.), Terminologies and classification systems in medicine. *Assessment and need for action in the German-speaking countries* (pp. 35–50). Medizinisch Wissenschaftliche Verlagsgesellschaft. https://library.oapen.org/bitstream/handle/20.500.12657/39874/1/terminologien-und-ordnungssysteme-in-der-medizin.pdf

International Organization for Standardization. (2019). *Terminology work and terminology science — Vocabulary* (ISO 1087:2019). https://www.iso.org/standard/62330.html

International Organization for Standardization. (2009). *Terminology work — Principles and methods* (ISO 704:2009). https://www.iso.org/standard/38109.html

Payne, J. D. (2013). The state of standards and interoperability for mHealth among low- and middle-income countries. *mHealth Alliance*. https://lib.digitalsquare.io/server/api/core/bitstreams/3dda1cb3-fc2f-4746-8a95-e0cf5ba78090/content

Ratna, H. (2019). The importance of effective communication in healthcare practice. *Harvard Public Health Review*, 23, 1–6. https://www.jstor.org/stable/48546767

SNOMED CT Editorial Advisory Group. (n. d). *SNOMED International*. https://confluence.ihtsdotools.org/pages/viewpage.action?pageId=38262933

SNOMED CT Starter Guide. (n. d). SNOMED International. https://confluence.ihtsdotools.org/display/DOCSTART

Torab-Miandoab, A., Samad-Soltani, T., Jodati, A., & Rezaei-Hachesu, P. (2023). Interoperability of heterogeneous health information systems: a systematic literature review. *BMC Medical Informatics and Decision Making*, 23(1), 18. https://doi.org/10.1186/s12911-023-02115-5

Unified Medical Language System (UMLS). (n.d.). CVH (Consumer Health Vocabulary) – Synopsis. https://www.nlm.nih.gov/research/umls/sourcereleasedocs/current/CHV/index.html

Wermuth, M-C., Walravens, M., & Lambot, M-A. (2022). Collaboration and communities of practice in the field of medical ontology translation. *The Journal of Specialised Translation*, 37, 75–98. https://jostrans.soap2.ch/issue37/art_wermuth.php

Zielstorff, R. D. (2003). Controlled vocabularies for consumer health. *Journal of Biomedical Informatics*, 36(4–5), 326–333. https://doi.org/10.1016/j.jbi.2003.09.015

PART II

ESP Instruction

Language learning strategy use and willingness to communicate among high- and low-anxiety health science students

Theodora Tseligka[1] – Ioanna Katerini[2]

ABSTRACT
The use of language learning strategies (LLS) has been widely researched, foregrounding their facilitatory role in foreign language (FL) learning and communicative competence. This is directly pertinent to health science students who are expected to engage in FL interaction in sensitive healthcare settings, where advanced oral proficiency is linked with effective doctor-patient relationship and improved interpersonal care. Against this backdrop, the current study examined the frequency of use of self-reported LLS and its correlation with willingness to communicate (WTC) among a group of Greek health science students (N=172). Using a convenience sampling approach, data were collected employing a four-part survey instrument administered via Google Forms. The research tools included: the Strategy Inventory for Language Learning (SILL), the Short-form Foreign Language Classroom Anxiety Scale (S-FLCAS) and the Willingness to Communicate in a Foreign Language Scale (WTC-FLS). The impact of anxiety was also computed regarding WTC. Overall, our findings compare favorably to the results of previous studies pointing to a more frequent employment of cognitive and metacognitive strategies than that of memory and affective strategies. Indirect strategies appear to create a more conducive environment for students' WTC, compared to direct strategies, both among high- and low-anxiety students. The present findings could shed light on future directions of LLS instruction to health science students.

Keywords: language learning strategies, willingness to communicate, foreign language anxiety, health science students

1. Introduction

Foreign language (FL) communicative competence in today's medical setting is widely perceived as an invaluable skill for all healthcare practitioners as it essentially fosters clinical interaction and patient care. Challenging communicative situations that require coping with sensitive personal issues, delivering bad news, interacting with patients with low health literacy, addressing health inequities or arranging end-of-life care, especially among speakers who do not share a common native language, are among the most demanding contexts

---

[1] University of Ioannina, Faculty of Medicine
[2] University of Ioannina, Department of Primary Education

of FL health-related interaction. Language concordance between doctors and patients has been shown to ascertain patient safety, reduce medical errors, establish rapport and trust to the medical care, increase patient satisfaction and adherence, ultimately leading to a better understanding of the social determinants of health and an overall improved healthcare ecosystem (Molina & Kasper, 2019). To this end, extensive research has been conducted in FL learning settings investigating the ways that best facilitate health science students' oral competence, with a primary focus on medical English (being the lingua franca). In particular, the use of language learning strategies (LLS) has been often associated with learners' advanced FL progress (O'Malley et al., 1985; Oxford, & Ehrman, 1995; Cohen et al., 1998).

2. Language learning strategies, Willingness to Communicate and FL anxiety

Language learning strategies (LLS) broadly refer to the conscious initiatives, behaviors and skills learners undertake to enhance their FL learning process and become more autonomous, facilitating the comprehension, retention, retrieval and use of the new FL material across different settings and contexts (Oxford, 1999; Gavriilidou & Psaltou-Joycey, 2009). LLS have been classified in different ways, including goal, function, skill (Cohen, 2017). One of the most popular taxonomies is the Strategy Inventory for Language Learning (SILL) by Oxford (1990), in which strategies are grouped into direct and indirect ones. The former demand mental engagement with the target language and include memory (e.g., reviewing, semantic mapping), cognitive (e.g., note-taking, summarizing) and compensatory strategies (e.g., using synonyms, guessing), while the latter contribute indirectly to FL learning, subdivided into metacognitive (e.g., paying attention, self-monitoring), affective (e.g., discussing feelings with others), and social strategies (e.g., cooperation with peers, developing cultural understanding) (ibid.).

Research has shown that LLS are not similarly utilized across different ages, genders, individual learning styles, motivation, study disciplines, cultural backgrounds, academic settings or proficiency levels (Oxford, & Ehrman, 1995; Gavriilidou & Psaltou-Joycey, 2009; Cohen, 2017; Sukying, 2021). Nevertheless, frequent and constructive employment of LLS has been generally found to be conducive to a betterment of FL language performance, both productively and receptively. Oxford, & Ehrman (1995) note that the active employment of cognitive strategies is correlated with improved outcomes in speaking, while Nakatani (2005) found that a group of Japanese EFL learners, having received strategy training in oral communication strategies, increased their metacognitive FL learning skills and significantly improved their oral performance, both quantitatively and qualitatively. In Sukying's study (2021), which included health science students, a frequent LLS application was positively correlated with a moderate English proficiency improvement, while have demonstrated that explicit strategy training can help learners to better monitor their speech, employ self-reflection, increase oral grammatical accuracy, and, thus, advance their speaking proficiency. Similarly, training in metacognitive, cognitive, and socioaffective LLSs in O'Malley et al.'s study (1985) provided evidence for a significant improvement in participants' speaking skills owing, primarily, to the application of functional planning and peer evaluation of recorded speeches.

Relevant to the achievement of speaking proficiency is the notion of willingness to communicate (WTC), which refers to the learner's psychological readiness and intention to engage in conversation using a FL, whether inside or outside the FL classroom (MacIntyre, 2007). In particular, WTC appears to be underpinned by two fundamental concepts, namely anxiety and motivation, both of which are involved in "what might be the critical decision for language learning success: Does a learner choose to communicate when the opportunity arises?" (MacIntyre, 2007, p. 567). With specific reference to foreign language classroom anxiety (FLCA), Horwitz et al. (1986) have defined it as a distinct concept associated with the feelings, beliefs, and reactions occurring during the language learning process, which can impede oral language performance due to communication apprehension, test anxiety and fear of negative evaluation. Numerous studies provide evidence that anxiety associated with communication apprehension and peer negative evaluation in a FL classroom could have a debilitating impact on students' performance in speaking tasks (Horwitz et al., 1986). Communication apprehension has also been recorded in a study with Greek English for Specific Purposes (ESP) students, in which case a significantly negative correlation was noted between FL classroom anxiety and language performance (Tzoannopoulou, 2016).

Notably, the application of LLS has been shown to increase WTC and lower FL anxiety. In an experimental study, Farzam (2018) found that both cognitive and metacognitive strategy training significantly enhanced Iranian learners' WTC, connecting the positive effect with increased confidence and reduced anxiety. Demir Ayaz (2017) equally affirmed the strong correlation between a higher frequency of LLS and WTC, although in her case affective and memory strategies emerged as the best predictors for FL readiness to communicate. Metacognitive and affective strategies appear to be the most preferred ones, particularly among learners with high levels of WTC (Najafi & Dehghani, 2022). Equally, for Mandarin learners, the use of LLS proved to be beneficial for their communicative readiness; however, "[i]t was discovered that indirect LLS were the best predictors for students with low-level anxiety, whereas direct and indirect LLS were both good predictors for students with high-level anxiety" (Munchen et al., 2021, p. 58).

3. Research method

3.1. Purpose of the study

In light of the above, the present study was designed to address the following research questions:

1. What is the frequency of LLS use among Greek health science students?
2. 1) Is there a correlation between FL learning strategy use and willingness to communicate (WTC)? How is this impacted by FL classroom anxiety?

3.2. Methodology

The study was a cross-sectional survey conducted from April 4 to May 25, 2023. It was distributed electronically to the students at the School of Health Sciences of the University of Ioannina (Greece), comprising four Departments: Medicine, Biological Applications & Technologies (B.A.T.), Nursing, and Speech & Language Therapy (S.La.Th.), where the study's authors serve as the main English and German language instructors. Hence, the data was obtained using a convenience sampling approach. At a following stage, the survey will expand to all six Health Sciences Schools in Greek Higher education for a more representative sample. Collected data were analyzed using the SPSS 28.0 and the significance level was set at 5%, $p < .05$.

Participants suitable for this research were considered students who had attended at least one university FL course for general or specific academic purposes. In total, 172 students (N = 172) responded, who were Greek undergraduates, almost equally divided between first year of studies (1st – 2nd year = 37.8%) and senior years (3rd – 4th year = 41.8%), with 1/5 (20.4%) of our respondents attending their ≥5th year of studies. There were 133 female (77.3%) and 39 male (22.7%). Almost half of the participants studied Medicine (48.8%), followed by 34.3% who studied Nursing, while only 10.5% and 6.4% responses originated from the Departments of B.A.T. and S.La.Th. respectively. The unequal sample sizes could be attributed to the fact that only the former Departments (i.e., Medicine and Nursing) include compulsory FL courses in their program of studies and, therefore, a higher student enrollment, while the latter have only elective FL courses. Almost all respondents (95.9%) had attended at least one English for (Specific) Academic Purposes course, with English remaining the most popular language among Greek HE students, as documented earlier (Tseligka, 2016). Correspondingly, participants displayed a high level of previous English language competence with ¾ (= 76.6%) of the group being holders of a C1-C2 certificate and 18.1% holding a B1-B2 certificate. In the case of German, the respective percentages were 5.9% for C1-C2 holders and 23.4% for B1-B2, while French certificate holders were 3.5% and 11.7% respectively.

3.3. Instruments

The research tools employed for the main data collection technique included the following:

a. An introductory online questionnaire (7 items) structured by the authors with the use of Google Forms to collect basic demographic data (gender, age), students' field and year of study, information about their FL course attendance and previous language certification. The questionnaire was anonymous, and assured recipients of the confidentiality of their responses.

b. The Strategy Inventory for Language Learning (SILL) by Oxford (1990), adapted for Greek by Psaltou-Joycey and Kantaridou (2009). The SILL 7.0 is a self-reported questionnaire and consists of 50 Likert scale items, representing the taxonomy by Oxford (1990) in a 5-point Likert frequency ranging from 1 = strongly disagree to 5 = strongly agree.

c. The Short-form Foreign Language Classroom Anxiety Scale (S-FLCAS) (8 items) (Dewaele & MacIntyre, 2014), adapted for Greek by the authors, following a pilot with a small group of students. This is a shorter version of the original, more extensive 33-item Foreign Language Classroom Anxiety Scale (FLCAS) developed by Horwitz et al. (1986), which has been recently validated and found to be a reliable measure (Botes et al., 2022). Since the current study utilized 3 different instruments, the shortened S-FLCAS proved beneficial in minimizing the response time for the participants. It uses a 5-point Likert agreement format ranging from 1 = strongly disagree to 5 = strongly agree, with two items reverse scored. The higher the score, the greater anxiety respondents appear to experience when speaking English.

d. The Willingness to Communicate in a Foreign Language Scale (WTC-FLS) (20 items) (Baghaei, 2011; Baghaei et al., 2012), adapted for Greek by the authors, after being piloted on a small group of students. The WTC-FLS requires respondents to report their agreeability with the items on a two-point scale: agree/disagree. Higher scores indicate higher WTC levels.

4. Results and Discussion

4.1. R.Q.1. *What is the frequency of LLS use among Greek health science FL students?*

In line with former studies (Cretu, 2018; Shehadeh & Dwaik, 2022), our participants displayed a medium[3] strategy use, with an average mean score ranging from 2.79 (affective strategies) to 3.38 (cognitive strategies). However, contrary to Psaltou-Joycey & Kantaridou's research (2009), our results were invariable for proficiency level and department of studies for all LLS categories, probably owing to the overall homogeneity of our sample (i.e., high proficiency health science students) which did not allow for much variance. No significant differences were noted in the case of gender either, except for memory strategies, where female students used significantly more memory strategies ($M = 3.14$, $SD = 0.57$, $n = 133$) than male learners ($M = 2.83$, $SD = 0.59$,

---

[3] According to Oxford (1990), frequency of strategy use is measured as follows: low = ≤ 2.40; medium = 2.50-3.40; high = ≥ 3.50.

n = 39, *p* = .001), a finding frequently recorded in the literature (ibid., Demir Ayaz, 2017). In descending order of preference, LLS use among our students was recorded as follows:

Table 1. *Language learning strategy use (in order of preference)*

Strategies	Mean	SD
Cognitive	3.39	.587
Compensation	3.32	.569
Metacognitive	3.24	.769
Social	3.22	.822
Memory	3.04	.543
Affective	2.69	.679

Table 2. *Medical students' language learning strategy use (in order of preference)*

Strategies	Mean	SD
Cognitive	3.38	.595
Metacognitive	3.36	.767
Compensation	3.32	.609
Social	3.26	.797
Memory	3.07	.587
Affective	2.79	.639

Overall, our participants appear to use cognitive strategies the most, followed by metacognitive strategies, in alignment with prior findings with high proficiency learners (Oxford, 1990; Gavriilidou & Psaltou-Joycey, 2009). Memory and affective strategies were the least resorted to, as has been frequently reported (Sukying, 2021; Shehadeh & Dwaik, 2022; Demir Ayaz, 2017). With regards to medical students, the order of preference remains almost the same, except for compensation and metacognitive strategies found in the 2nd and 3rd position respectively (see Table 2 above). Similar results were documented in a study with Romanian medical students, who displayed the same order of preference in terms of the most and least LLS used (Cretu, 2018). Specifically, in both studies, the practicing cognitive strategy *"I watch English language TV shows or go to movies spoken in English"* appeared to be among the most popular ones, ranked fifth in preference in our sample (M = 3.90). We speculate that if this questionnaire item was adapted to include the access of English websites and social media, it would have been prioritized even more by our Gen Z respondents, whose learning preferences appear to be significantly impacted by the English-dominated internet (Poláková & Klímová, 2019).

On the contrary, in Psaltou-Joycey & Kantaridou's study (2009), cognitive strategies appeared 4th in order of preference among Greek medical students. This difference could be attributed to the fact that their respondents were primarily first- and second-year students, while almost half of our participants (41.8%) were in their senior year of studies. It might be the case that employment of cognitive strategies, which requires a conscious manipulation of the language learning process, becomes more frequent as students become more experienced in their studies. Additionally, the higher FL level proficiency of our learners (76.6% are C1-C2 certificate holders in our study, compared to 54.9% in Psaltou-Joycey & Kantaridou's study) might have impacted the LLS selection, since cognitive and metacognitive strategies are more popular among advanced learners.

Furthermore, we should note that the two most preferred strategies among our respondents belong to the compensation strategies, namely (SILL no. 29) *If I can' t think of an English word, I use a word or phrase that means the same thing* (M = 4.23) and (SILL no. 24) *To understand unfamiliar English words, I make guesses* (M = 4.02). These results corroborate with previous findings (Psaltou-Joycey & Kantaridou, 2009; Cretu, 2018; Shehadeh & Dwaik, 2022), confirming that paraphrase (SILL no.29) and guessing from context (SILL no.24) are widely favored by medical and health science students. This is not surprising since such skills are often explicitly taught to (Greek) undergraduates, who are instructed how to rephrase complex academic texts using their own vocabulary, thus, avoiding plagiarism (Rizouli & Kantaridou, 2019). We also concur with Shehadeh and Dwaik (2022) that medical students' increased confidence in the use of such strategies might relate with their overall learning profile, i.e., being high achievers, good learners throughout their lives and with an increased English language proficiency.

Conversely, our study underscored a low preference for affective and memory strategies, consistent with past research (Psaltou-Joycey & Kantaridou, 2009; Nemati et al., 2010; Cretu, 2018; Shehadeh & Dwaik, 2022). On the one hand, the most infrequent strategies in our data, i.e., SILL no.43 (affective strategy, M = 1.22), SILL no.7 (memory strategy, M = 1.95) and SILL no.6 (memory strategy, M = 1.98) that require learners to write down their feelings in a diary, physically act out or use flashcards to learn a new English word respectively, might not be appropriate for adult learners (Oxford, 1990). Furthermore, Psaltou-Joycey & Kantaridou (2009, p. 119) suggest that medical students' low scores in affective strategies might indicate that they "do not indulge in language learning at all, they merely view it as a tool for more 'valued' learning goals".

Finally, it is worth noting that SILL no.14, *I start conversations in English* (cognitive strategy, M = 2.64) and SILL no.47, *I practice English with other students* (social strategy, M = 2.53) were among the ten least preferred strategies. Apparently, the predominantly monolingual environment in which most students practice their English in Greek universities does not promote the initiation of authentic dialogic interactions among classroom participants, thus, undermining their communicative competence.

4.2. R.Q.2. Correlation between LLS use and willingness to communicate. How does this differ among high- and low-anxiety students?

When assessing the relationship between participants' LLS use and their WTC (using a Pearson correlation coefficient), a positive correlation was indicated, in agreement with previous research (Munchen et al., 2021; Farzam, 2018; Demir Ayaz, 2017; Yunus & Singh, 2014).

Table 3. *Correlation between LLS and WTC* (*$p \leq .005$ **$p \leq .000$) Correlation coefficient: (very) weak = r, 0–.39; moderate = r, .40–.59; (very) strong = r, .6–1 (Bland & Altman 1986)

LLS use	Willingness to Communicate
Metacognitive	.494**
Cognitive	.464**
Social	.453**
Affective	.415**
Memory	.228*
Compensation	.218*

While the use of metacognitive, cognitive, social and affective strategies appears to have a moderate correlation with WTC, strategies for storing and retrieving information (i.e., memory), as well as making guesses and using gestures (i.e., compensation) seem to be less conducive to oral interaction. This was overall corroborated when WTC was correlated separately with direct (.430*) and indirect LLS (.538*) (*$p \leq .000$). Hence, we could posit that indirect LLS, which assist learners to plan and evaluate their learning, control their anxiety and cooperate with their peers, are more strongly linked with learners' volition to initiate communication in a FL compared with direct strategies.

When exploring the impact of FL classroom anxiety on WTC (with a Pearson correlation analysis), a statistically significant and negative correlation was found between the Short-form Foreign Language Classroom Anxiety Scale score (S-FLCAS) and WTC (r = -.428) unveiling that the more stressed learners feel in the FL classroom, the less eager they are to initiate conversations.

Table 4. *Correlation between FL classroom Anxiety and WTC* ** Correlation is significant at the .01 level (2-tailed).

Correlations			
		Anxiety	WTC
Anxiety	Pearson correlation	1	−.428**
	Sig. (2-tailed)		.000
	N	172	172
WTC	Pearson correlation	−.428**	1
	Sig. (2-tailed)	.000	
	N	172	172

Additional evidence in our study supported these results. Following the Ward Method anxiety cluster (Ward, 1963; Losiak, 2005) respondents were clustered into two distinct groups based on S-FLCAS: Low-anxiety students N = 95 (55.2%) and High-anxiety students N = 77 (44.8%). Students with lower anxiety levels appeared to be more willing to communicate compared to students with high anxiety levels t(170) = 4.454; p < .001 (See Table 6 below). Furthermore, even though both direct and indirect language strategies were positively correlated with WTC, there was a larger effect size in the case of high-anxiety students. Thus, students with high levels of anxiety were more likely to seize opportunities to communicate when they mostly used indirect strategies.

Table 5. *Correlation between high- and low-anxiety*

LLS	Low Anxiety	High Anxiety
	WTC	
Direct	.332***	.501***
Indirect	.449***	.595***

Table 6. *Language learning strategy use, students, and WTC* ***p ≤ .000

	Ward Method anxiety cluster	N	Mean	St.Dev.
WTC	Low anxiety	95	72.96	14.778
	High anxiety	77	62.73	15.224

Finally, to investigate the predicting effects of LLS use on WTC between low- and high-anxiety students, linear regression models for the effect of the LLS were performed, showing that the indirect LLS had a statistically significant positive impact on WTC, overwhelming any formerly significant effect observed by the direct LLS since the R square was notably higher in students with high anxiety levels (.371) vs low anxiety students (.205). Thus, it can be concluded that employing indirect strategies appears to have a significant impact on predicting WTC for students of both high- and low-anxiety.

refAll the above underscore the importance of integrating LLS in foreign language learning since their contribution to increasing WTC appears to be confirmed. In view of the greater predictive ability of indirect strategies on WTC, it would be advisable to explicitly guide students in their effective and frequent use. Even though metacognitive strategies seem to be widely applied by FL learners, social and affective strategies are usually ranked low among learners' preferences. Hence, it is imperative to train students in anxiety-reducing and social interaction strategies to help them overcome their frustration, insecurity and reticence about cooperative learning, which can impede their oral language performance. Previous studies with Greek learners attest to the 'teachability' of LLS use through explicit and integrated strategy training (Sarafianou & Gavriilidou, 2015).

5. Conclusion

In concert with earlier research, our study unveiled a moderate application of LLS among health science students. Based on our findings, cognitive strategies proved to be the most frequently used ones, followed by metacognitive and compensation strategy types. On the contrary, affective and memory strategies were ranked low in our students' preferences. With regard to WTC, our findings suggest that it is strongly correlated with LLS employment, and more instigated by the use of indirect strategies both for high- and low-anxiety students. All the above point to the need of integrating LLS instruction in FL courses in Higher Education. For students of health sciences specifically, such training is deemed even more significant, as they could leverage the potential benefits from LLS use in the classroom, increase their confidence, overcome their speaking anxiety and, hopefully, engage in future effective healthcare-related conversations, by transferring these strategies in authentic medical settings. Arguably, further research is required to test these results with a larger sample of health sciences students and to supplement it with qualitative data in order to gain a more comprehensive understanding of the complexity of factors involved in LLS use.

References

Baghaei, P. (2011, September 21-23). *Validation of a multidimensional scale of willingness to communicate.* Paper presented at the Meeting of the Methodology and Evaluation Section of the German Association of Psychology. Bamberg, Germany.

Baghaei, P., Dourakhshan, A., & Salavati, O. (2012). The relationship between willingness to communicate and success in learning English as a foreign language. *Modern Journal of Applied Linguistics, 4*(2), 53–67.

Bland, JM., & Altman, DG. (1986). Statistical methods for assessing agreement between two methods of clinical measurement. *Lancet, 1*(8476), 307–310.

Botes, E., van der Westhuizen, L., Dewaele, JM., MacIntyre, P., & Greiff, S. (2022). Validating the short-form foreign language classroom anxiety scale. *Applied Linguistics, 43*(5), 1006–1033.

Cohen, A. (2017). Language learner strategies: From theory to practice. In Z. Gavriilidou, K. Petrogiannis, M. Platsidou, & A. Psaltou-Joycey (Eds.), *Language Learning Strategies: theoretical issues and applied perspectives* (pp. 20–38). Saita Publications.

Cohen, A., Weaver, S., & Li, T-Y. (1998). The impact of strategies-based instruction on speaking a foreign language. In A. Cohen (Ed.), *Strategies in learning and using a second language* (pp. 107–156). Longman.

Cohen, J. (1988). *Statistical power analysis for the behavioral sciences* (2nd ed.). Routledge.

Cretu, I. (2018). Personal epistemology: A "dark matter" that matters in how we teach and learn languages at university. In. L. Grosu-Rădulescu (Ed.), *Foreign Language Teaching in Romanian Higher Education: Teaching Methods, Learning Outcomes. Multilingual Education* (Vol. 28, pp 149–169). Springer.

Demir, A. A. (2017). The relationship between EFL learners' language learning strategy use, willingness to communicate, and L2 achievement. *International Journal of Language Academy, 5*(5), 78–92. DOI 10.18033/ijla.3620

Dewaele, J-M., & MacIntyre, P. (2014). The two faces of Janus? Anxiety and enjoyment in the foreign language classroom. *Studies in Second Language Learning and Teaching,* IV (2), 237–274.

Farzam, M. (2018). The effect of cognitive and metacognitive strategy training on intermediate Iranian EFL learners' willingness to communicate. *International Journal of Applied Linguistics and English Literature, 7*(1), 193–202. DOI 10.7575/aiac.ijalel

Gavriilidou, Z., & Psaltou-Joycey, A. (2009). Language learning strategies: an overview. *Journal of Applied Linguistics,* 25, 11–25.

Horwitz, E., Horwitz, M., & Cope, J. (1986). Foreign language classroom anxiety. *Modern Language Journal,* 72, 125–132.

Losiak, W. (2005). Shapes of anxiety: Analysis of anxiety profiles measured with S-R inventory of anxiousness. *Ansiedad y Estrés, 11*(2–3), 159–173.

MacIntyre, P. (2007). Willingness to communicate in the second language: Understanding the decision to speak as a volitional process. *The Modern Language Journal*, 91(4), 564–576. DOI 10.1111/j.1540-4781.2007.00623.x

Molina, R., & Kasper, J. (2019). The power of language-concordant care: a call to action for medical schools. *BMC Medical Education*, 19(1), 378. DOI 10.1186/s12909-019-1807-4

Munchen, L., Razali, F., & Mohamad A. N. (2021). Influence of language learning strategies on willingness to communicate in Chinese among students with high and low anxiety. *Asian Journal of University Education*, 17(4), 158–169. DOI 10.24191/ajue.v17i4.16183

Najafi, S., & Dehghani, A. P. (2022). Language learning strategy preferences and levels of willingness to communicate by Iranian EFL learners. *Journal of Translation and Language Studies*, 3(1), 50–61. DOI 10.48185/jtls.v3i1.368

Nakatani, Y. (2005). The effects of awareness-raising training on oral communication strategy use. *The Modern Language Journal*, 89(1), 76–91.

Nemati, M., Nodoushan, M., & Ashrafzadeh, A. (2010). Learning strategies in proficient and less proficient readers in medicine. *Journal on Educational Psychology*, 4(2), 19–32.

O'Malley, J. M., Chamot, A. U., Stewner-Manzanares, G. A., Kupper, L., & Russo, R. (1985). Learning strategy applications with students of English as a second language. *TESOL Quarterly*, 19, 557–584.

Oxford, R. (1999). Learning strategies. In B. Spolsky (Ed.), *Concise encyclopedia of education* (pp. 518–522). Elsevier.

Oxford, R. (1990). *Language learning strategies: What every teacher should know.* Heinle & Heinle.

Oxford, R., & Ehrman, M. (1995). Adults' language learning strategies in an intensive foreign language program in the United States. *System*, 23, 359–386.

Poláková, P. & Klímová, B. (2019). Mobile technology and Generation Z in the English language classroom—A preliminary study. *Education Sciences*, 9(3), 203. DOI 10.3390/educsci9030203

Psaltou-Joycey, A., & Kantaridou, Z. (2009) Foreign language learning strategy profiles of university students in Greece. *Journal of Applied Linguistics*, 25, 107–127.

Rizouli, T., & Kantaridou, Z. (2019). Investigating students' strategies and processes in a reading-to-write integrated task in the Greek academic context. In Z. Gavriilidou, L. Mitits, & C. Dourou (Eds.), *Situating Strategy Use in the Greek setting*, (pp. 133–155). Saita Publications.

Sarafianou, A., & Gavriilidou, Z. (2015). The effect of strategy-based instruction on strategy use by upper-secondary Greek students of EFL. *Electronic Journal of Foreign Language Teaching, 12*(1), 21–34.

Shehadeh, A., & Dwaik, R. (2022). Palestinian language learners' learning strategies: A case study of medical students. *International Journal of Instruction, 15*(2), 659–674. DOI 10.29333/iji.2022.15236a

Sukying, A. (2021). Choices of language learning strategies and English proficiency of EFL university learners. *LEARN Journal: Language Education and Acquisition Research Network, 14*(2), 59–87.

Tseligka, T. (2016). Developing a foreign language policy in Greek HE: striving between Scylla & Charybdis. *International Journal of Language, Translation and Intercultural Communication, 4*(1), 54–67. DOI 10.12681/ijltic.10352

Tzoannopoulou, M. (2016). Foreign language anxiety and fear of negative evaluation in the Greek university classroom. In M. Matthaioudakis, & K. Nikolaidis (Eds.), *Selected Papers of the 21st International Symposium on Theoretical and Applied Linguistics (ISTAL 21)* 21, 823–838. DOI 10.26262/istal.v21i0.5272

Ward, J. H., Jr. (1963). Hierarchical grouping to optimize an objective function. *Journal of the American Statistical Association, 58*, 236–244.

Yunus, N. M., & Singh, K. K. (2014). The use of indirect strategies in speaking: Scanning the MDAB students. *Procedia - Social and Behavioral Sciences, 123*, 204–214. DOI 10.1016/j.sbspro.2014.01.1416

English for medical purposes: The importance of role-plays

Dagmar Vrběcká[1] *– Klára Čebišová*[2] *– James David Clubb*[3]

ABSTRACT
The focus of this study is on teaching methods promoting active learning, role-plays, in particular. In the field of teaching English for Medical Purposes (EMP), role-plays represent one of the main tools, where students can practice doctor-patient communication. Role-plays provide numerous opportunities to counter and re-encounter and use the target vocabulary. They are essential for developing medical students' communicative competence on linguistic, sociolinguistic, and pragmatic levels. Both the positive and negative aspects of role-plays are discussed in this paper. Key aspects of successful role-plays, such as preparation, implementation, and feedback are included. Samples of role-plays are provided. Additionally, this paper includes research on EMP: The Importance of Role-Plays and Other Activating Teaching Methods on Vocabulary Acquisition.

Keywords: role-plays, doctor-patient communication, medical history taking, English for Medical Purposes (EMP)

1. Introduction

The objective of the EMP course at Charles University, Faculty of Medicine in Hradec Kralove is to equip students with professional vocabulary related to body systems, diseases, and their symptoms, and to develop doctor-patient communication skills. Medical students must be able to take a patient's history, explain diagnostic methods, disclose diagnoses, inform patients about potential treatment options, and carry out other similar professional tasks in their future careers. However, third-year students of general medicine are novices in this field and must be exposed to simulated situations in which they have opportunities to practice such communication in a safe and consequence-free environment. This paper focuses on role-plays, which represent one of the main tools through which students can practice such communication.

This study comprises three parts. At the start, teaching of medical terminology is provided as students must acquire a large corpus of technical or

---

[1] Charles University of Prague
[2] Faculty of Medicine of University of Hradec Kralove
[3] Department of Languages of University of Hradec Kralove

specialized terms, as well as lay terms, needed for effective communication with patients. Next, role-plays are described, and both the positive and negative aspects of role-plays are presented. Key elements of successful role-plays, such as preparation, implementation, and feedback are included. The final part contains the research focused on the use of activating teaching methods and their influence on the acquisition of medical terminology.

2. Teaching medical terminology

English is known for its impressively large lexicon. Regarding EMP, medicine is well known for its large number of technical or specialized terms, mostly borrowed from Greek and Latin (Ferguson, 2015, p. 253). Medical students must acquire medical terminology as well as lay terms necessary for communication with patients. It must be also clarified if the term is needed for receptive or productive use (Nation, 2007, pp. 24–33). When teaching vocabulary, there are three important general processes leading to word acquisition. Firstly, students must be given enough opportunities to notice the word. Secondly, they must retrieve it. Finally, they must acquire the ability to generate the word (Nation, 2007, pp. 63–72).

Noticing means to give attention to an item, and certain factors might influence this process: the salience of the item, previous contact, and the learner's acknowledgment that the item fills a certain gap in language knowledge (Nation, 2007, p. 63). Noticing is realized by looking up a word in a dictionary, deliberately studying it, guessing it from context, hearing it explained, etc.

Once a word is noticed and understood, it can be retained and retrieved later (Laufer, 2003, p. 569). The **retrieval** can be receptive (perceiving the form, retrieving its meaning when the word is met in listening or reading) and/or productive (communicating the meaning of the word and retrieving its spoken or written form). Repetition is crucial for retention, with studies suggesting multiple exposures are needed for effective vocabulary acquisition. Ur (2012, p. 69) states that students need to re-encounter a new item several times in order to remember it. Regarding the typical number of repetitions needed for vocabulary acquisition, Nation (2007, p. 81) references Kachroo and Crothers-Suppes, who suggest that words should be repeated 6 or 7 times. Additionally, Tinkham found that learners vary significantly in how they acquire words, with most needing 5 to 7 repetitions, although some may require up to 20 or more. Laufer (2003, p. 569) cites Horst, Cobb, and Meara, who recommend 8 exposures, while Saragi, Nation, and Meister suggest 12 exposures. Another important factor to consider when discussing vocabulary repetition is the timing of when the learner re-encounters the word. If too much time is allowed to pass, the word will be forgotten, and the re-encounter will be processed as a first encounter. Clearly, repetition is an extremely important factor in vocabulary acquisition and instructors need to provide systematic and cumulative vocabulary review activities in the classroom.

Creative or generative use involves encountering and using a word in different contexts and forms, which helps reinforce and expand the learner's understanding. Generation can be both receptive (new contexts in listening and reading) and productive (new contexts in speaking and writing).

3. Role-plays

Role-plays are a perfect tool to ensure both retrieval and generative use as they provide numerous opportunities to re-encounter and use the target vocabulary. As for linguistic competence, role-plays offer a number of opportunities to counter and re-counter word stock, which help with the language acquisition. They enable receptive and productive use encouraging students to make the shift from passive recipients into active ones. As far as sociolinguistic and pragmatic competences are concerned, students can develop and improve their understanding of human relationships, acquire appropriate ways to respond in specific situations, and develop a broad range of communication skills (Jankovcová et al., 1988, p. 127; Kotrba & Lacina, 2011, p. 147).

Considering this characterization, role-plays might seem favorable activities for both the instructors and the students. However, they place high demands on time, both the instructors' time spent in detailed preparation (including level, interest, aim, classroom interaction, and additional aids) and organization and the classroom time spent on the activity itself. This perhaps could explain why students and instructors sometimes consider role-plays ineffective. If a role-play is not well-prepared, well-organized, appropriately implemented, and supported by feedback, it can easily turn into a chaotic

> **Role-play - offer a 'scaffolding'**
> **Taking a patient's history**
> 1) Say hello and make eye contact to build rapport.
> 2) Ask about the presenting complaints (*How can I help you? What has brought you here today...*)
> 3) History of presenting complaint (*When, How long, How, Why, aggravation/alleviation, associated symptoms*)
> 4) Social history (diet, stress, exercise, hobbies, occupation...)
> 5) Explain the diagnosis to the patient (use lay terms) and suggest potential treatment.

Figure 1. *Variety scaffolding (Burke, Dvořáčková & Klapilová, 2021)*

waste of precious time. In order to eliminate these negative attitudes, it is necessary to explain certain key organizational aspects: detailed preparation (variety), proper organization including clear instructions, and the giving of feedback.

To avoid monotony and student reluctance in role-plays, it is important to introduce **variety**. This can be achieved by providing different scenarios, modifications, and new elements to maintain student interest and motivation. One way to introduce variety is by offering scaffolding for the entire role-play (see Figure 1).

Since students often lack real-world experience in doctor-patient interactions, scaffolding helps guide them in structuring professional communication. It allows students to focus on language use without worrying about the sequence of the role-play. This approach is particularly useful for introducing doctor-patient role-plays in instruction.

In addition to the scaffolding, students can benefit from the content provided. This can be achieved in a wide variety of different ways. Symptoms of certain diagnoses in English or in L1 (see Figure 2), medical reports (see Figure 3), or a detailed description of the roles (see Figure 4) can be provided, for example.

Offering **variety** by providing scaffolding and/or content might eliminate the monotony of role-plays preventing students' reluctance to participate. Providing that the role-play is carefully planned, adequate performance is the new issue to be addressed.

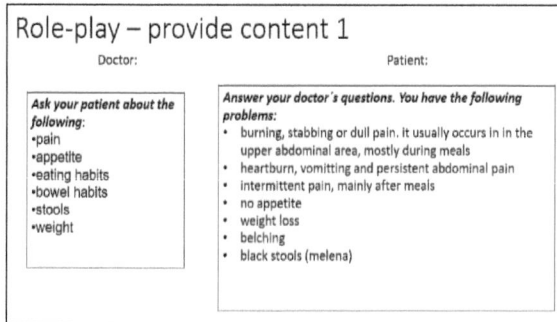

Figure 2. *Variety provide content 1*

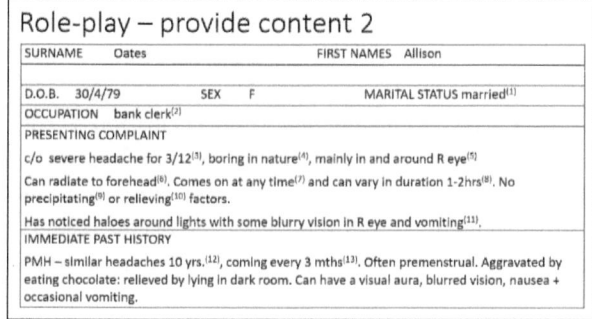

Figure 3. *Variety provide content 2*

Role-play – provide content 3

You're a patient. B is your family doctor. You know your doctor very well and you think that he/she likes you. That's why you call him/her by his/her first name (Paul/Paula) and not Dr Woods.

- Today you've made an appointment with the doctor because you have some very strange symptoms (what are they?), and you are convinced that you have a problem with your heart. You want the doctor to take you seriously and confirm your suspicions!
- Explain all your symptoms to the doctor.
- Ask the doctor to take your blood pressure and temperature.
- Tell him/her that you would like to see a specialist. Be prepared to argue with him/her if necessary.

You're a family doctor. A is your patient. You've been working for seven hours and you're very tired. Your last patient is a man/woman who comes to see you very often, always with a different problem. You think he/she might be a hypochondriac. For some reason, this patient always calls you by your first name. You hate that!

- Ask him/her not to call you by your first name. Ask him/her to call you Dr Woods.
- Ask what his/her symptoms are (this week) and how long he/she has had them.
- Give your diagnosis (a virus) and refuse to send him/her to a specialist.
- Prescribe some painkillers.

Figure 4. *Variety provide content 3 (Oxenden & Latham-Koenig, 2012)*

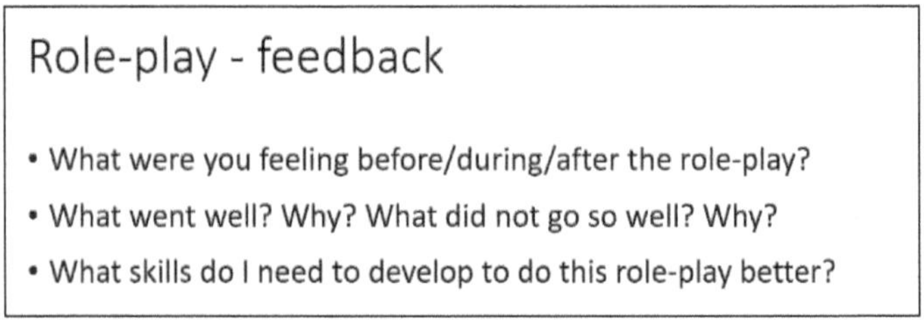

> **Role-play - feedback**
>
> - What were you feeling before/during/after the role-play?
> - What went well? Why? What did not go so well? Why?
> - What skills do I need to develop to do this role-play better?

Figure 5. *Feedback (Burke, Dvořáčková & Klapilová, 2021)*

Clear and brief instructions are crucial for successful role-plays (Harmer, 2013, p. 172; Scrivener, 1994, p. 97; Ur, 2012, p. 49). Instructions should be given before dividing students into groups and distributing handouts. Repetition can involve paraphrasing and using the L1 if needed. Redundant information should be omitted, and examples are preferred over verbal explanations.

Lack of **feedback** can cause reluctance in participation. Feedback should include assessment (how well the activity went) and correction (specific performance aspects). Corrections should be selective and tailored, highlighting positive elements. Feedback should be encouraging and tactful. Self-assessment and peer assessment are also beneficial, promoting a reflective learning environment. (see Figure 5).

Peer assessment encourages attention to peers' performances, creating a constructive and formative learning experience.

4. Research on activating teaching methods

In today's technology-driven environment, activating teaching methods (role-plays particularly) have not obtained much attention in the field of research in the Czech Republic. However, those methods provide numerous opportunities to practice and automatize medical terminology. They also provide an endless resource of variable pair/group work activities. Those aspects (acquiring medical terminology in the theoretical, pre-clinical, and clinical fields, as well as improvement of communicative competence through pair-work activities) were the most frequently listed requests in student needs analysis questionnaires conducted prior to the research on activating teaching methods. Those factors initiated the research of the activating teaching methods conducted at the Department of Languages, Charles University, Faculty of Medicine in Hradec Kralove in the academic years 2015–2019. The objective of this research was to identify the extent to which the implementation of activating teaching methods helped influence target vocabulary acquisition. A secondary objective was to find out if the activating teaching methods positively influence student motivation.

4.1. Methodology

The experimental research was conducted under standard school conditions. It contained implementation of activating methods in the form of 15 activities – eight in the winter term (Noughts and Crosses focusing on parts of the body, Describe and Guess practicing functions of the body, Snakes and Ladders revising locomotive system, Ping-Pong focusing on GIT, Words and Definitions reviewing CVS, Jigsaw focusing on GUS, Ask the right question I for medical history taking) and seven activities in the summer term (Risk it revising the winter term medical terminology, Describe and Swap focusing on NS, What is the Diagnosis revising psychiatric disorders, Crosswords practicing skin lesions and injuries, Ask the right question II and Describe and Guess for investigation methods, Find Someone Who practicing explaining diagnosis). All of those activities focused on the acquisition of professional vocabulary. The degree of acquisition of professional vocabulary was measured with 4 progress tests (tests taken at fixed points during the semester on a limited number of units covered up to that point for both formative and summative purposes) and 2 credit tests (tests taken at the end of the course, testing all units taught during the semester for final summative purposes). Evaluation questionnaires were used as a supplementary tool for gathering student opinion on activating teaching methods.

Through the administration and collation of these tests, we obtained a research sample with a total number of 152 participants, out of whom CEFR level B1 was represented by 41 participants in the experimental group and 35 in the control, while level B2 was represented by 32 participants in the experimental group and 44 in the control.

By analyzing the results, we were able to ascertain the statistically significant differences, if any, between the experimental and the control groups.

The set of four progress tests was designed to objectively measure vocabulary acquisition in experimental and control groups. The tests were aligned with the content of activating teaching methods used throughout the semesters. The tests focused on form, meaning (synonyms, antonyms, meronyms, hyponyms, and hypernyms), and use (definitions, making questions), using both receptive and productive knowledge. Each progress test included a listening comprehension exercise (receptive knowledge) and a lexical component (both receptive and productive knowledge). Difficulty index (p) was calculated to ensure appropriate testing items. Items answered correctly by more than 80% or less than 20% of respondents were considered extremely easy or difficult, respectively. Sensitivity (ULI coefficient) was measured to ensure the tests differentiated between students with better and worse language knowledge.

Measuring the effects of student exposure to activating teaching methods was further realized by the final credit tests. The Manual for Language Test and Development and Examining (Council of Europe, 2011) was used as the main source when constructing the test. The credit tests consisted of three parts, part one focusing on listening comprehension, part two on lexical acquisition, and part three on reading comprehension. Difficulty Index (p) was calculated to ensure appropriate difficulty levels and sensitivity (ULI coefficient) was measured. The credit tests were carefully adapted to include research items, ensuring they could measure the impact of activating teaching methods on vocabulary acquisition while maintaining standardized testing procedures.

The supplementary objective of the research was to find out student opinion on the implemented activities employing activating teaching methods. A short-form evaluation questionnaire for 15 activities employing activating teaching methods was created involving questions concerning the overall evaluation of the activity and the main benefits. The short-form evaluation was chosen to avoid issues like random completion due to length and students predicting expected answers. The questionnaire included questions on the activity's overall evaluation, likes and dislikes, and benefits such as making lessons interesting, improving vocabulary, speaking, and grammar. An open question allowed students to freely express advantages and disadvantages. The questionnaires were distributed in paper form at the end of each class to ensure high return rates and accurate recall of the activity.

The final evaluation questionnaire was a crucial step in our research, designed to further explore students' attitudes towards activating teaching methods. This tool provided valuable insights into the effectiveness of these methods and helped us understand student preferences and areas for improvement. The final evaluation questionnaire focused on the instructors' choice of methods and emphasis on language skills and professional vocabulary. Students could indicate favorable and unfavorable activities and suggest course improvements. It was distributed in paper form during the penultimate week of classes to ensure high return rates and minimize test result influence. The questionnaire was prepared for the students in Czech to avoid any possible confusion and/or influence on the results.

5. Results

Concerning the progress tests and credit tests, results between the control group and the experimental group were compared and analyzed in order to determine whether the implementation of activating teaching methods could positively influence the acquisition of the professional vocabulary. Student results remained anonymous due to the ethical considerations of the experiment. For the elementary description of results, mean and standard deviations were used. The mean showed the sum of all scores of all subjects in a group divided by the number of subjects. It provided information on the average performance of the group on the particular task, and demonstrated how the group performed as a whole. Standard deviation measured data dispersion around the mean (Hendl, 2006, p. 97). To test the statistical hypotheses, the results were processed and assessed by means of statistical methods of a two-sample t-test as well as nonparametric Mann-Whitney and Kolmogorov-Smirnov tests. It was important to keep the results of the measurements separate for the B1 and B2 levels in order to exclude any bias potentially caused by the heterogeneity (in terms of language knowledge) between groups.

The probability level shows how likely it is that results within the group are similar. The level of significance is $\alpha = .05$. If the value is above .05, it can be inferred that the results of the two samples are similar. If the value is below .05, it signifies a statistical difference in the two samples.

At the B1 level, the progress and credit tests failed to reveal a significantly statistical difference between the experimental and control groups. From this, it could be inferred that activating teaching methods used for target vocabulary acquisition did not facilitate such acquisition.

At the B2 level, the experimental group achieved statistically significant results in the medical vocabulary acquisition compared to the controls. Such

Table 1. Overview of B1 progress tests and credit tests results

	No of B1 participants experimental group	No of B1 participants control group	B1 experimental group Mean ± standard deviation	B1 control group Mean ± standard deviation	Probability level
OAJ I Progress test 01	30	29	67.42 ± 21.3	65.46 ± 20.81	0.722
OAJ I Progress test 02	24	19	47.491 ± 19.297	53.368 ± 18.604	0.32
OAJ II Progress test 01	23	14	54.913 ± 19.195	54.771 ± 24.613	0.985
OAJ II Progress test 02	23	16	44.05 ± 30.233	49.732 ± 22.451	0.53
OAJ I Credit test	39	35	57.267 ± 15.82	59.874 ± 17.822	0.625
OAJ II Credit test	26	19	70.769 ± 16.474	69.474 ± 21.0206	0.832

Table 2. Overview of B2 progress tests and credit tests results

	No of B2 participants experimental group	No of B2 participants control group	B2 experimental group Mean ± standard deviation	B2 control group Mean ± standard deviation	Probability level
OAJ I Progress test 01	17	20	89.7 ±11.547	65.81 ±22.085	0.00542
OAJ I Progress test 02	12	22	77.333 ±13.0878	50.436 ±17.316	0.00005
OAJ II Progress test 01	14	15	63.121 ±14.0222	51.613 ±17.954	0.06629
OAJ II Progress test 02	7	14	52.057 ±23.22	37.236 ±21.555	0.164
OAJ I Credit test	31	43	84.565 ±11.635	75.654 ±14.731	0.00664
OAJ II Credit test	17	30	75 ±12.99	64.833 ±14.473	0.02068

a difference clearly indicates that activating teaching methods facilitated an increase in the acquisition of medical terminology.

In the short-form evaluation questionnaires and final evaluation questionnaires, the vast majority of the B1 groups, in both the experimental and control groups, perceived the methods very positively. Both groups believed the activities to be beneficial in terms of medical vocabulary acquisition, the promotion of speaking (increased student talking time), and increased student motivation. The B2 groups were of the opinion that the implemented activities helped facilitate acquisition of medical vocabulary while also promoting speaking. Students also indicated a slight rise in interest levels. However, the number of activities marked as beneficial in terms of increasing student interest was lower compared to the B1 level. The vast majority of students appreciated activating teaching methods for their potential to facilitate medical terminology acquisition, to promote speaking, and to increase student motivation (in terms of interesting activities and creating a positive classroom environment).

Though the research did not manage to show a significant influence of activating teaching methods on professional vocabulary acquisition at the B1 level, the study revealed that activating teaching methods had the potential to enhance professional vocabulary acquisition and positively influenced motivation. We also found that activating teaching methods had the potential to promote speaking skills, but the extent to which this takes place was not obvious. As it would be helpful to quantify the increase in terms of a percentage figure, our department is now turning our attention to role-plays and measurements to what extent the implemented role-plays increase the student talking time (STT).

6. Conclusion

Regarding professional vocabulary, the acquisition of professional word stock is integral to every EMP course. In EMP courses, it is essential to provide students with an adequate amount of professional vocabulary items; however, merely providing such vocabulary is not enough. Students must be given the opportunities to practice and automatize the given lexical items. Such automatization can be done through activating teaching methods, role-plays respectively. Role-plays, when properly prepared, introduced, and integrated, can be recommended as an endless resource of variable pair/group work activities in which students can use the target vocabulary through speaking (taking patients' history, explain diagnostic methods, explain diagnoses and potential treatment, etc.). However, the potential for role-plays to become monotonous and counter-productive through overuse, misuse, and lack of variety must be borne in mind to ensure they support learning goals.

References

Beran, J. (1999). *Doctor-patient communication*. Karolinum.

Burke, M., Dvořáčková, V., & Klapilová, J. (2021, September 9-10). Health behaviour change – Use of authentic tools in teaching the language of clinical communication [Lecture]. MUNI.

Čáp, J., & Mareš, J. (2001). *Rozvíjení osobnosti a způsob výchovy*. Portál.

Červenková, I. (2024). *Výukové metody a organizace vyučování*. http://projekty.osu.cz/svp/opory/pdf-cervenkova-vyukove-metody-a-organizace-vyucovani.pdf

Csikszentmihályi, M. (2017). *Flow a práce*. Portál.

Council of Europe. (2011). *Manual for language test development and examining*. Council of Europe.

Ferguson, G. (2015). English for medical purposes. In B. Paltridge, & S. Starfield (Eds.), *The handbook of English for specific purposes* (pp. 243–261). Blackwell Publishing.

Harmer, J. (2013). *The practice of English language teaching*. Pearson Education Limited.

Jankovcová, M., Průcha, J., & Koudela, J. (1988). *Aktivizující metody v pedagogické praxi středních škol*. SNP.

Hendl, J. (2006). *Přehled statistických metod zpracovní dat: Analýza a metaanalýza dat*. Portál.

Kotrba, T., & Lacina, L. (2011). *Aktivizační metody ve výuce*. Barrieser & Principal.

Laufer, B. (2024). *Vocabulary acquisition in a second language: Do learners really acquire most vocabulary by reading? Some empirical evidence*. https://www.researchgate.net/

publication/250196400_Vocabulary_Acquisition_in_a_Second_ Language_Do_Learners_Really_Acquire_Most_Vocabulary_by_ Reading_Some_Empirical_Evidence

Morgan, J., & Rinvolucri, M. (2004). *Vocabulary*. Oxford University Press.

Nation, I. S. P. (2007). *Learning vocabulary in another language*. Cambridge University Press.

Oxenden, C., & Latham-Koenig, C. (2012). *New English file upper-intermediate teacher's book*. Oxford University Press.

Pecina, P., & Zormanová, L. (2009). *Metody a formy aktivní práce žáků v teorii a praxi*. MUNI.

Pelikán, J. (2011). *Základy empirického výzkumu pedagogických jevů*. Karolinum.

Petty, G. (2008). *Moderní vyučování*. Portál.

Scrivener, J. (1994). *Learning teaching*. Oxford University Press.

Ur, P. (2012). *A course in language teaching*. Cambridge University Press.

Vrběcká, D. (2019). *English for medical purposes: Activating teaching methods and their influence on vocabulary acquisition* (Doctoral thesis). Univerzita Karlova.

Feedback criteria for simulated patients in courses of languages for healthcare purposes

Viktória Sirokmány[1] – Tímea Takács[1] – Enikő Földesi[2] – Dániel Mány[1] – Katalin Fogarasi[1]

ABSTRACT
Effective communication is essential in healthcare, yet language barriers and inadequate professional-patient interactions remain challenges in medical education. The integration of Simulated Patients (SPs) into Language for Healthcare Purposes (LHP) offers a structured approach to developing both linguistic and professional skills. This study examines how SP-provided feedback influences students' verbal and non-verbal communication, as well as their professionalism, in LHP courses. A qualitative survey was conducted among 55 third-year students from four LHP courses at Semmelweis University, covering medicine, dietetics, public health, and health visitor programs. Using thematic content analysis, we categorized feedback into three key areas: verbal communication, non-verbal communication, and professionalism. The findings highlight that structured feedback from SPs dominantly enhances students' communication skills, particularly in real-world patient interactions. These results provide a foundation for refining SP-based feedback mechanisms and optimizing the role of SPs in healthcare language education.

Keywords: simulated patient (SP), languages for healthcare purposes (LHP), feedback, patient-professional interaction, healthcare communication

1. Introduction

Adequate communication is a key in successful healthcare when it comes to make the right diagnosis, build trust with patients, and make sure treatments are actually followed. Yet, for many healthcare students, language barriers and limited experience with real patient conversations make these interactions a challenge. Simulated Patients (SPs) have been widely used in clinical training to improve communication skills, yet their role in Language for Healthcare Purposes (LHP) education remains underexplored. While existing studies primarily focus on SPs in clinical skill development (Barrows, 1993; Nestel, 2015), few address their contribution to refining language competence and professional-patient communication in healthcare settings. To address this gap, our study explores how SP-provided feedback improves verbal communication, non-verbal communication, and professionalism in healthcare

---

[1] Semmelweis University, Institute of Languages for Specific Purposes
[2] Semmelweis University, Faculty of Medicine, Institute of Behavioral Sciences

language courses. By identifying key aspects of effective feedback, we aim to offer a structured approach to optimizing SP-student interactions and improving the integration of SPs in healthcare language education. The findings contribute to a deeper understanding of how SPs can support healthcare students in developing patient-centered communication skills, ultimately benefiting real-world professional interactions.

2. Simulated Patients in the instruction of Languages for Healthcare Purposes (LHP)

Simulated Patients (SPs) have become essential in helping healthcare students enhance communication skills. The SP method was first introduced by Howard S. Barrows, who defined SPs as individuals trained to accurately portray patients in clinical scenarios (Barrows, 1993).

SPs help students develop both verbal and non-verbal communication skills, including the psychosocial and cultural dimensions of patient care, as noted by Epstein and Street (2007). This focus on patient-centered communication aligns with broader healthcare models that emphasize the integration of patient preferences and experiences into care. As Lantos et al. (2018) note, person-centered health services play a critical role in generating value for patients by actively involving them in their own care processes.

Studies have also shown that SP integration leads to improved communication proficiency, particularly in medical terminology and patient interaction strategies (Halász et al., 2021; Eklics & Fekete, 2020). Structured SP-student interactions are designed to provide constructive feedback focused on practical, real-world application, thus preparing students for the complex linguistic and interpersonal demands of healthcare communication (George et al., 2022).

Semmelweis University in Hungary is a medical university offering training programs in three languages (English, German, and Hungarian). At the Institute of Languages for Specific Purposes (ILSP), Semmelweis University, SPs are integrated into language courses for students in medical, dental, health sciences, and pharmaceutical fields, with the aim of cultivating patient-centered communication skills essential for professional-patient interactions (Fogarasi et al., 2021). ILSP offers courses from A1 to C1 proficiency, focusing on medical terminology, documentation and professional-patient communication. SPs, drawn from teaching assistants and native speakers, undergo training organized by actors and language instructors at the University of Pécs to simulate healthcare scenarios using detailed patient profiles, thus allowing students to practice real-world interactions under realistic conditions (Jámbor et al., 2021).

At ILSP, SPs are provided with detailed patient profiles covering healthcare scenarios such as emergency care and general practice. These profiles developed in cooperation by healthcare professionals and LHP instructors are designed to simulate real-life medical interactions, allowing students to practice their professional communication skills. After each scenario, SPs give feedback focusing on both linguistic (terminology, syntax, pragmatics) and communication aspects (Nestel et al., 2015; Schlegel et al., 2012).

The feedback process is supported by the Kalamazoo Consensus Statement (Schirmer et al., 2005), which provides a framework for assessing essential communication skills. These include the ability to gather information effectively, show empathy, build rapport, and explain medical conditions using layman's terms. This form has proven useful in evaluating communication skills in simulated patient interactions (Peterson et al., 2014). However, during the semester, we identified areas for improvement, particularly in the feedback provided for non-verbal communication and empathy. To address these limitations, we initiated a needs analysis, aiming to refine the feedback forms to better assess the specific communication challenges encountered in our LHP courses. The ultimate goal is to make feedback more actionable and tailored to the professional needs of our healthcare students.

3. Material and methods

The purpose of this study was to analyze and improve the feedback provided by Simulated Patients (SPs) during professional-patient communication interactions in LHP courses. The study also aimed to assess the appropriateness of the feedback form used during these interactions by gathering student reflections on verbal communication, non-verbal communication, and professionalism.

3.1. Participants

The study involved 55 third-year Hungarian students from four different LHP courses at Semmelweis University: English for Medicine I, Professional-Patient English Communication for Dietitians, Professional-Patient English

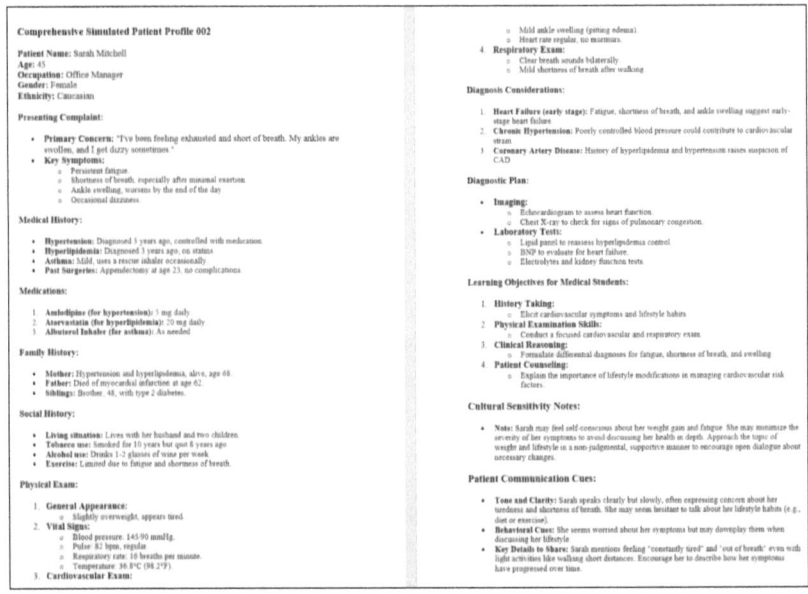

Figure 1. *Example of patient profile simulating real-life scenarios*

Communication for Public Health Inspectors, and Health Visitors. These students were enrolled in an LHP course designed to improve their professional-patient communication skills. Throughout the spring semester of the academic year 2021/22, SPs engaged in various healthcare scenarios based on detailed patient profiles. As an example, see Figure 1.

The SPs provided each student with individual feedback using an oral feedback form based on the Kalamazoo Consensus Statement (Schirmer et al., 2005) and adapted for the course by Takács & Czar (2021), as shown in Table 1. At the end of the semester, students completed a questionnaire (Table 2) reflecting on their interactions with the SPs and the feedback they received.

3.2. Scenario Description and Patient Profile

The SPs used patient profiles (Figure 1) to simulate authentic, real-life healthcare situations. Figure 2 presents an example of a scenario provided to students who acted as medical professionals. This scenario required the students to assess the patient's condition and develop a communication strategy based on the information provided.

Table 1. *Oral feedback form for simulated patient-student interactions at ILSP*

Criteria For Feedback	Rating Scale (1 = Strongly Disagree, 5 = Strongly Agree)
Opens the discussion (Introduces self to the patient properly in English)	1 2 3 4 5
Gathers information (Applies interview techniques, listens effectively, engages the patient in dialogue)	1 2 3 4 5
Understands the patient's perspective (Shows verbal and non-verbal gestures of empathy)	1 2 3 4 5
Builds rapport (Assesses emotional state, reacts appropriately, makes the patient feel comfortable)	1 2 3 4 5
Shares information (Uses lay terms instead of medical terms, answers patient's questions clearly)	1 2 3 4 5
Provides closure (Reaches an agreement on the next steps, makes plans with the patient)	1 2 3 4 5

Preparation Course for the University Medical Language Exam:

Topic 6

Participants:

General Practitioner (examinee)

(Young woman) patient (examiner)

Task:

- Greet the patient, introduce yourself [**say hello, introduce yourself**]
- Get information about the symptoms and how the patient feels [**weight loss, palpitations, increased sweating, rapid heartbeat, sleep problems present for a few months but not considered to be important**]
- Ask the patient about diarrhoea and blood in stool [**sometimes, no**]
- Get information about family history, particularly about thyroid disease [**yes, Mum**]
- Tell the patient about the physical examination examining the thyroid glands. You will stand behind the patient and will palpate the neck
- Suspected diagnosis is hyperthyroidism. Send the patient for a lab test and refer them to an endocrinologist. Give directions on how they can make an appointment

Figure 2. *Scenario for simulated patient-student interactions*

3.3. Data collection

A questionnaire, adapted from the study of George et al. (2022), was used to gather anonymous information on four key areas: positive feedback on SP interactions, areas requiring improvement, organizational suggestions, and communication feedback (verbal and non-verbal skills). The questionnaire, as can be seen in Table 2, provided students with four open-ended questions to express their views on the feedback process, allowing for a more in-depth exploration of their experiences.

To analyze the qualitative data collected from student responses, a thematic content analysis was employed. Responses were manually coded into three predetermined thematic categories (verbal communication, non-verbal communication, and professionalism) which were identified based on previous research in SP-based training (Jámbor et al., 2021). A double coding process was conducted, ensuring reliability and thematic consistency while allowing for emerging themes to be incorporated into the analysis.

This structured approach provided a comprehensive understanding of the strengths and areas for improvement in SP-based feedback, forming the basis for refining the feedback process in future LHP courses.

Table 2. *Survey on student experiences with simulated patient feedback*

Question	Focus Area
What are the existing positive features of SP interactions?	Positive feedback on SP interactions
What areas of SP interactions do you feel need improvement?	Areas that require improvement
What suggestions do you have for improving the organization of SP sessions?	Organizational suggestions
How would you assess verbal and non-verbal communication skills during SP interactions?	Feedback on communication skills (verbal and non-verbal)

3.4. Data Analysis

Qualitative data collected from the questionnaire responses were analyzed using a thematic content analysis approach. We followed a clear, step-by-step process to keep the analysis consistent and reliable.

First, open-ended survey responses were gathered from students at the end of the semester. The data were then preliminarily categorized into three predetermined thematic areas (verbal communication, non-verbal communication, and professionalism) based on the study's focus and previous research on SP-student interactions (Takács & Czar, 2021). Following this, two independent researchers conducted a manual double coding process, ensuring inter-rater reliability and allowing for the refinement of emerging subthemes. The identified themes were then compared with findings from existing literature on SP-based training to validate their relevance. Finally, a frequency analysis was performed to quantify commonly mentioned aspects of SP feedback, highlighting key strengths and areas requiring improvement. Responses were grouped according to their thematic categories, and the results were systematically summarized. This step-by-step approach provided a comprehensive overview of students' experiences, ensuring that the analysis accurately captured their perspectives on SP feedback and its role in improving healthcare communication skills.

4. Results

The findings of this study are based on a comprehensive analysis of the students' needs and reflections. The results reveal both the positive aspects of the current feedback process and areas for improvement, particularly concerning verbal and non-verbal communication, and professionalism. A total of 55 students from four different ESP groups completed the questionnaire. The open-ended questions focused on four areas: positive aspects of SP interactions, areas needing improvement, suggestions for organizational changes, and communication feedback (both verbal and non-verbal).

4.1. Verbal Communication

Verbal communication features, highlighting both strengths and areas for improvement are presented in Table 3.

Grammatical and lexical correction was noted as a primary strength, with 15 responses, followed by positive emotional feedback (6 responses), pronunciation improvement (15 responses), and conversation fluidity (4 responses). Areas for improvement included asking specialists more questions (6 responses) and making situations more interactive (4 responses). Conversation fluidity was also noted as an area needing improvement (1 response). These results show a balance between positive feedback on correction and emotional support, as well as areas where further refinement in questioning and interactivity is desired.

Table 3. *Key features of verbal communication in SP-student interactions*

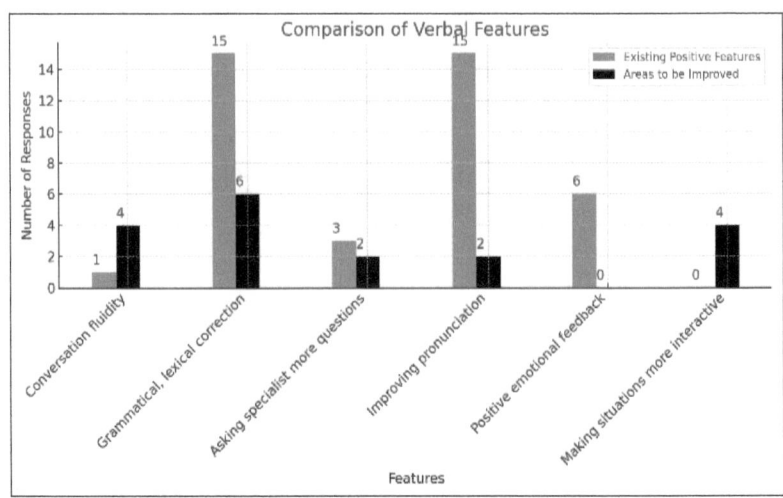

4.2. Non-verbal Communication

Non-verbal communication, while recognized as critical for patient-centered care, presented both strengths and challenges in the feedback provided by SPs. Table 4 presents a comparison of positive features – such as effective use of body language, eye contact, and empathy – versus areas that students struggled with, including maintaining consistent non-verbal cues in the scenarios. The number of mentions in the Table 4 reflects how many students identified each specific feature.

Helpfulness and empathy were recognized as the primary strengths (10 responses), followed by posture and body language (4 responses). Areas for improvement included better psychosocial preparation of SPs (3 responses) and the expression of emotions through tone (1 response). Additionally, there was one suggestion for more emphasis on being polite.

4.3. Professionalism

Feedback on professionalism in SP-student interactions was generally positive, with many students acknowledging the importance of maintaining professional attitude during patient interactions. Table 5 shows a comparison of features regarding professionalism, highlighting existing positive features, areas for improvement, and suggestions.

Table 4. Key features of non-verbal communication in SP-student interactions

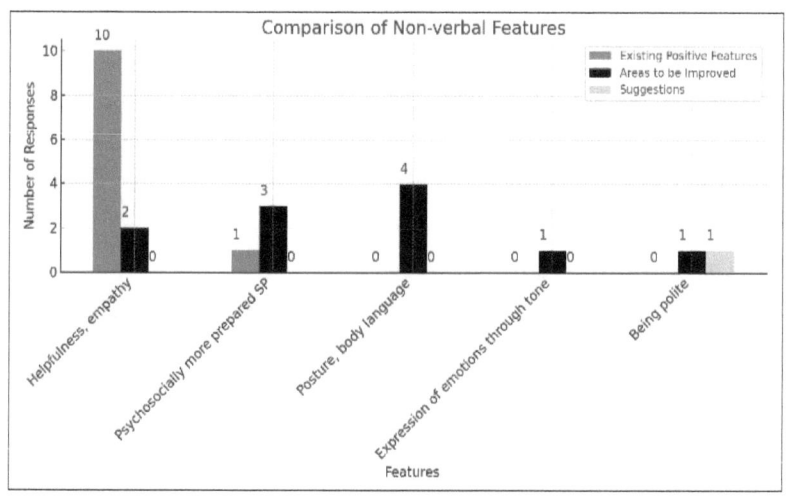

Suggesting the adequate use of terminology was the most commonly identified area for improvement (8 responses), followed by the need for SP suggestions regarding instruction and advice (4 responses). Creating an

Table 5. Key features of professionalism in SP-student interactions

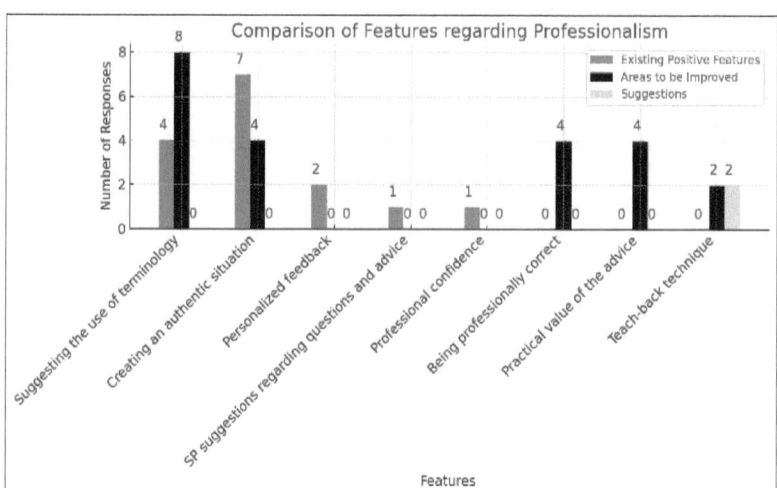

authentic situation (7 responses) and personalized feedback (2 responses) were highlighted as positive features of the feedback. Additionally, the teach-back technique [i.e., asking patients to explain in their own words what a health provider has just told them (Talevski et al., 2020)] (2 responses) was also noted positively. There were suggestions to enhance the practical value of the advice (the feedback) (4 responses) and ensure professionalism is consistently correct (2 responses).

4.4. Organizational suggestions

Students offered several suggestions to improve the structure of SP-based courses. Table 6 summarizes these recommendations, including requests for terminological glossaries, group-based preparation, and written feedback.

Table 6. *Student suggestions for enhancing organizational aspects of simulated patient-based courses*

Suggestion	No. of responses
Preparation of terminological vocabulary glossaries	8
Provision of written feedback	4
Group-based instead of individual preparation	4
Clearer communication of expectations	3
Preparation of specific grammar exercises in advance	3
Support for stress management	3
Feedback provided at the end of the lesson instead of after each conversation	1
More detailed patient profile activities for SPs	1
Incorporation of shadowing exercises	1
Video introduction to the Professional-SP interaction	1

The number of responses reflects how many students supported each suggestion. As highlighted in Table 6, key suggestions included the preparation of terminological glossaries (8 responses) and written feedback (4 responses). Students also recommended group-based preparation instead of individual (4 responses), clearer communication of expectations (3 responses), and grammar exercises in advance (3 responses). Other suggestions included offering support for stress relief (3 responses), more detailed Patient Profile activities for SPs, and the use of shadowing [i.e., a paced, auditory tracking task which involves the immediate vocalization of auditorily presented stimuli (Lambert, 1992, p. 266)] during sessions to enhance the learning experience.

5. Discussion

This study underlines the essential role of SPs in enhancing communication and professionalism in healthcare education. The integration of SPs into LHP courses has proven to effectively simulate real-world healthcare interactions, a concept originally advocated by Barrows (1993), who highlighted the educational value of scenario-based simulations in medical training. These simulations align with current evidence suggesting that patient-centered communication is central to successful healthcare outcomes (Fogarasi et al., 2021).

Regarding verbal communication, students valued real-time feedback from SPs, particularly in refining medical terminology, supporting Eklics & Fekete's (2020) emphasis on simulation practices to enhance terminology use in healthcare communication. However, students encountered challenges when attempting to articulate complex information during simulated professional scenarios, a difficulty similarly observed by George et al. (2022), who explored the delicate balance between providing relevant feedback and maintaining student confidence. The need for more structured, scenario-based feedback to address such communication gaps, as advocated by Barrows (1993), remains crucial in medical education. Tailoring this feedback to help students manage complex dialogues can further enhance their readiness for professional interactions.

Beyond verbal feedback, non-verbal communication also emerged as a crucial component of SP-student interactions, especially in building patient rapport. Students recognized the importance of body language and empathy, with Epstein & Street (2007) reinforcing how non-verbal cues help build rapport in patient interactions. This focus on the patient experience aligns with Lantos et al. (2018), who emphasized the value of person-centered health models in improving healthcare outcomes by integrating patient preferences and communication needs into everyday practice. However, maintaining consistent non-verbal communication, particularly in high-pressure scenarios, was reported as a significant challenge. This gap echoes Nestel et al. (2015), who observed that non-verbal communication is frequently neglected in training but remains essential for patient-centered care. Enhanced focus on training that addresses maintaining non-verbal cues and professional demeanor under stress could significantly improve outcomes in both educational and clinical settings.

Professionalism was another key area highlighted by students, many of whom valued the opportunity to observe and model the professional behaviors demonstrated by SPs. This finding supports the work of Takács & Czar (2021), who emphasized the importance of professionalism training in healthcare education. Nonetheless, students indicated a need for more detailed guidance on managing complex patient scenarios, especially concerning maintaining professional boundaries. This observation reflects recommendations by Halász et al. (2021), who argued that a stronger focus on feedback related to professionalism, particularly in challenging interactions, is critical for developing competent healthcare professionals.

In terms of course structure, students offered several suggestions for improving SP-based courses. Among these were calls for more comprehensive preparatory materials, such as terminological glossaries and grammar exercises, to better equip them for SP interactions. This recommendation aligns with findings by Richards & Rodgers (2001), who emphasized the importance of structured preparation in language education. Additionally, students advocated for more written feedback, a method shown to enhance reflection and retention in communication training (Qureshi & Zehra, 2020). The desire for clearer communication of expectations and more group-based preparation reflects the broader need for improved organization in SP-based courses, a theme echoed in research on healthcare-specific language education (Fogarasi et al., 2021).

6. Conclusion

This study highlights the vital role of Simulated Patients (SPs) in boosting communication and professionalism within healthcare education. By combining language-specific training with SP interactions, this study demonstrates how patient-centered communication can be improved even further. The value of real-time feedback, especially in sharpening medical terminology and communication strategies, was clear in preparing students for professional interactions. Non-verbal communication also stood out as an essential factor, particularly in helping students build rapport and provide better patient-centered care.

While the positive impact of SPs in these training settings is clear, this study also identified several areas for improvement, particularly around managing complex verbal exchanges and providing detailed feedback on students' profession-specific skills. Tailoring these aspects could better prepare students for the challenges of real-world patient interactions. However, the study's findings are somewhat limited by the small sample size and specific regional focus, which may affect broader generalizability. Future research should address these limitations by exploring SP-based training across more diverse healthcare settings, providing a deeper understanding of how these methods can be optimized.

In conclusion, the integration of SPs into healthcare language education offers valuable opportunities to enhance communication skills, but there is still room for refinement. By focusing on both verbal and non-verbal communication, and providing detailed, scenario-based feedback, SP-based courses can more effectively prepare students for the particular demands of real-world patient care.

References

Barrows, H. S. (1993). An overview of the uses of standardized patients for teaching and evaluating clinical skills. *Academic Medicine: Journal of the Association of American Medical Colleges, 68*(6), 443–453. https://doi.org/10.1097/00001888-199306000-00002

Eklics, K., & Fekete, J. (2020). The role of simulation practices in acquisition or activation of medical terminology. *Porta Lingua*, 103–110.

Epstein, R. M., & Street, R. L., Jr. (2007). *Patient-centered communication in cancer care: Promoting healing and reducing suffering.* National Cancer Institute.

Fogarasi, K., Kránicz, R., Halász, R., Barta, A., & Hambuch, A. (2021). A betegközpontú diagnózisközlés gyakorlati oktatása [Practical training for delivering patient-centered diagnoses]. *Porta Lingua, (1)*, 161–174.

George, R. E., Wells, H., & Cushing, A. (2022). Experiences of simulated patients in providing feedback in communication skills teaching for undergraduate medical students. *BMC Medical Education, 22,* Article 339. https://doi.org/10.1186/s12909-022-03415-6

Halász, R., Kránicz, R., & Hambuch, A. (2021). Die Besonderheiten der Diskurshandlungen zwischen MedizinstudentIn und PatientIn. In T. Schnedermann, Y. Ilg, & M. Iakushevich (Eds.), *Linguistik und Medizin* (pp. 51–70). De Gruyter.

Jámbor, M., Sirokmány, V., Czar, D., & Fogarasi, K. (2021). Native speaker playing simulated roles in ESP courses. *FORLANG, 8,* 177–183.

Lambert, S. (1992). Shadowing. *Meta, 37*(2), 263–273.

Lantos, Z., & Simon, J. (2018). The Community Health Experience Model - Value generation from person-centered health transaction networks. *Public Health Reviews, 39,* Article 5. https://doi.org/10.1186/s40985-018-0105-8

Nestel, D. F., Bearman, M. L., & Fleishman, C. (2015). Simulated patients as teachers: The role of feedback. In. D. Nestel, & M. Bearman (Eds.), *Simulated Patient Methodology* (pp. 71–78). John Wiley and Sons Ltd.

Peterson, E. B., Calhoun, A. W., & Rider, E. A. (2014). The reliability of a modified Kalamazoo Consensus Statement Checklist for assessing the communication skills of multidisciplinary clinicians in the simulated environment. *Patient Education and Counseling, 96*(3), 411–418. https://doi.org/10.1016/j.pec.2014.07.013

Qureshi, A. A., & Zehra, T. (2020). Simulated patient's feedback to improve communication skills of clerkship students. *BMC Medical Education, 20*(1), 15.

Richards, J. C., & Rodgers, T. S. (2001). *Approaches and Methods in Language Teaching.* Cambridge University Press. https://doi.org/10.1017/CBO9780511667305.021

Schlegel, C., Woermann, U., Rethans, J.-J., & van der Vleuten, C. (2012). Validity evidence and reliability of a simulated patient feedback instrument. *BMC Medical Education, 12,* Article 6.

Schirmer, J. M., Mauksch, L., Lang, F., Marvel, K. & Stiles, W. B. (1978). Verbal response modes and dimensions of interpersonal roles: A method of discourse analysis. *Journal of Personality and Social Psychology, 36*(7), 693–703. https://doi.org/10.1037/0022-3514.36.7.693

Takács, T., & Czar, D. (2021). Enhancing professional communication skills in teaching English for specific purposes. *International Journal of Second and Foreign Language Education, 1*(2), 48–59.

Talevski, J., Wong Shee, A., Rasmussen, B., Kemp, G., & Beauchamp, A. (2020). Teach-back: A systematic review of implementation and impacts. *PLOS One, 15*(4), e0231350. https://doi.org/10.1371/journal.pone.0231350

Simulated online scenarios as a form of telemedicine practice in the English for Healthcare Purposes course for physiotherapy students

Tímea Takács[1] – Or Sharabi[2] – Vera Tick[1]

ABSTRACT
At the Institute of Languages for Specific Purposes (ILSP) at Semmelweis University, language courses in professional-professional and professional-patient communication provide students with the opportunity to develop not only their foreign language skills but also their ability to navigate specific professional genres and communication contexts essential for their future roles as healthcare providers (Jámbor et al., 2021; Halász et al., 2021). In response to emerging global challenges and the increasing demand for IT-based solutions in healthcare, our courses also focus on developing essential telehealth communication skills, particularly in patient-centred remote consultations (Bouamra et al., 2021). Additionally, expanding students' English healthcare vocabulary and enhancing their ability to communicate effectively in foreign languages make learning more engaging and practical (Voynatovskaya et al., 2018). To achieve these goals, we integrate various online tools, apps, and webpages into our courses. Furthermore, our research explores the use of simulated patients and online scenarios as effective techniques for improving healthcare communication skills. This pilot qualitative case study examines the transcriptions of simulated online conversations between simulated patients (SPs) and physiotherapy students in the English for Healthcare Purposes (EHP) professional-patient communication course, using conversation analysis (Seuren, 2024; Drew et al., 2000). With their consent, we recorded online sessions between the SP and physiotherapy students on Zoom. The recordings were transcribed into written text using the Alrite software, and we applied conversation analysis transcription symbols based on Drew et al. (2000). Our findings confirm the relevance of integrating telehealth into English for Specific Purposes (ESP) classes. Online scenarios effectively simulate real-life consultations, allowing students to practice essential skills such as preparing for online consultations, adapting communication techniques, conducting remote examinations and guided exercises, and explaining telehealth applications to patients in the rehabilitation phase.

Keywords: ESP, physiotherapy students, simulated patient, online conversation, telehealth

---

[1] Semmelweis University, Institute of Languages for Specific Purposes
[2] St.-Elisabeth Krankenhaus Geilenkirchen, Assistenzarzt der Orthopädie und Unfallchirurgie

1. Introduction

Numerous studies and research have highlighted the crucial importance and impact of communication in the delivery of healthcare, as well as in the outcome and the success of the medical treatment (Gayef, 2019; Drew et al, 2000). Language and communication strategies, therefore, must be an integral part of healthcare practice. The pragmatic functions of language give power to words that have a psychological effect on others. With language as an intermediary, we make decisions and respond to people. It also means that the utilization of words in discourses is rather a matter of choice than a matter of time or circumstance. How we react to others and what communication strategies we choose can and should be a conscious decision. Consequently, communication techniques, at least to a certain extent, can be acquired.

It is necessary then to incorporate communication into the education of future healthcare practitioners, and Language for Specific Purposes (LSP) classes are proving to be one of the possible fields that have a role in supporting and strengthening healthcare communication skills (Eklics & Fekete, 2020). The rapid spread of telehealth and telemedicine services, eHealth, and AI-assisted applications raises the question of whether healthcare communication skills should enframe the skills needed to use these platforms (Davis et al., 2021; Kumar et al., 2022) and if this content should appear in the LSP curriculum. To explore this question, our research analyzed online scenarios in which a non-native English-speaking, non-Hungarian simulated patient (SP) interacted with Hungarian undergraduate physiotherapy students in an ESP professional-patient course. The goal was to assess the applicability of telemedicine simulations and the conclusions that can be drawn from them.

2. Research questions and theoretical background

In this paper, we explore whether online scenarios in English for Healthcare Purposes (EHP) classes simply function as a virtual adaptation of face-to-face educational materials (Bandalaria, 2023) or whether they hold distinct relevance and added value when interpreted as teleconsultation sessions. Specifically, we examine whether these scenarios can serve as real-life simulations in English for Specific Purposes (ESP) courses, and if so, in what ways. Additionally, we investigate what knowledge, practice, and skills are essential for students to effectively engage in these scenarios. To address these questions, we consider two interrelated aspects that shape our research:

1. The role of simulations in Language for Specific Purposes (LSP) courses
2. The relevance of telehealth and teleconsultations in professional communication training

2.1. The role of simulations in LSP courses

As Angelini (2023, p. 383) points out, "Simulation is one of the tools that has proved to be effective in engaging ESP students in real-life situations". Undoubtedly, simulations serve as necessary tasks for the activation of the specific vocabulary and knowledge students acquire during the course. Based on Vygotsky's theory, Angelini draws attention to another important aspect of simulations, the "social interaction and collaboration with educators and peers" (Angelini, 2023, pp. 48). Regarding the applicability of peer simulation in LSP classes, there is a consensus in research on its contribution to "improved empathy, […] realism, and improved clinical reasoning and confidence" that have a positive effect on the learning process (Granger, 2024, pp. 40). The research Dennis et al. conducted (2021) also proved that undergraduate physiotherapist students can efficiently perform the role in peer-simulated patient activities. Furthermore, peer simulation addresses lay-language awareness and the usage of English as the lingua franca, which are both linked to intercultural communication. The complexity of linguistic and psychological aspects of simulations, therefore, should be taken into consideration during the preparation and implementation phases of this method. It does not necessarily mean that peer simulation could completely substitute simulations with a trained simulated patient (SP). We believe that if possibilities are given, SP and peer simulations should be combined to approach the goal that Javaherian et al. (2020, pp. 69-71) explained in the following way: simulation can enhance students' engagement and motivation and can also help make "the transition from initial theoretical courses to the clinical environment".

2.2. Telehealth, telemedicine, teleconsultations

In LSP, digital tools have also become important due to the development of the increasing availability of virtual healthcare services (Bouamra et al., 2021).

The concept of telemedicine and telehealth, by the definition of the WHO: "Telemedicine is a component of telehealth, which is a broader application of technologies to distance education and other applications wherein electronic communications and information technologies are used to support health-care services" (WHO, 2022, pp. 2). It includes several genres, different applications, webpages, video-conferencing, telephone calls, e-mails, blogs, electronic bulletin boards, and online health forums (Harvey & Svenja, 2012).

During the COVID-19 pandemic, it was inevitable to move the majority of services, healthcare services included, online. Due to the circumstances, this shift was abrupt and must have been prompt, which meant that most professionals had to do so and continue their work in the online space without any guided assistance or guidelines and had to acquire the skills by doing it. In the post-COVID era, most services returned to face-to-face contact. In physiotherapy, for instance, palpating the affected area and observing its color and shade are of utmost importance. However, the experience and knowledge derived from the online shift did not disappear without a trace; on the contrary, some elements were built into the working process.

In comparison with the COVID pandemic, teleconsultations are still in use in some healthcare settings, especially in cases where a patient is at a long distance or is at home in the rehabilitation process and only needs some follow-up. Based on a systematic review, in most cases, telemedicine in physiotherapy rehabilitation was reported effective (Kumar et al., 2022). Due to the fact that Davis et al. (2021, pp. 17) stated, "[w]earables, smart sensors, and natural language processing platforms have also gained prominence in patient rehabilitation and will continue to evolve." That leads to the conclusion that "we must then seek avenues to educate in areas where physiotherapists can also gain the essential skills necessary to be at the forefront of this wave of innovation for better patient outcomes." (Davis et al. 2021, p. 17). LSP classes are related to these skills from the aspect of language usage. The following statement by Kumar et al. (2022, pp. 418) is essential to our perspective: "use of effective results by telemedicine, depends upon the efficiency of a physiotherapist for the effective explanation of the method for assessment as well as therapeutic intervention." This emphasizes a key skill that can be practiced during LSP classes. Proper language application in LSP classes is always closely intertwined with technical knowledge and background; in this case, it is important to involve the usage of the techniques and how to assist patients in their application throughout the online discourse and what kind of problems and emotions may arise from the patients' side. Roberts & Osborn-Jenkins (2021) also highlighted the role of giving help to patients in preparation for the online consultation:

> "Information sent to the patient in advance should provide details of the agreed time of the call [...], an estimate of the likely duration, and guidance about taking the call in an appropriate physical location. [...] the clinician needs to be aware of their own personal appearance, including attire (if they do not wear uniform), as well as any background behind them that will be visible to the patient on screen, to help create a professional image and favorable first impression. [...] With online consultations, it is important to remember the patient may be anxious, not only about their health issue, but also about using technology" [...] "the opening sequence of a video consultation was very different from that of a face-to-face interaction, due to the 'technical phase', which inevitably preceded the clinical talk." (Roberts & Osborn-Jenkins, 2021, p. 3).

Another aspect to discuss with students regarding teleconsultation/telemedicine is rapport-building in the online space. As Roberts & Osborn-Jenkins (2021, p. 3) also stated, "In remote consultations [...] it can be more difficult to build rapport with reduced non-verbal cues".

Previous research has shown that simulation can be successfully applied in various ways in language courses. In LSP (Language for Specific Purposes) courses at ILSP, medical students have participated as teaching assistants (TAs). Fifth- and sixth-year students with clinical experience and proficient English language skills were selected to further enhance their professional communication in multiple foreign language courses (Jámbor et al., 2021). In 2020, alongside the use of TAs, the Institute introduced the method of incorporating native lecturers in the role of simulated patients for English courses (Jámbor et al., 2021).

Building on the previous research, the present case study aims to describe simulated telehealth online consultations, focusing on the technical and linguistic challenges that may impact the success of building rapport and conducting an effective medical consultation, especially in physiotherapy, which is largely based on direct perceptive experiences from the expert for accurate diagnosis and from the patient for effective treatment. The feedback provided by the non-native English-speaking medical expert, who acted as the simulated patient (SP), addressed both the linguistic and professional skills of the students. This allowed for an examination of whether these scenarios can function as real-life simulations in English for Specific Purposes (ESP) courses, and if so, how they can be applied.

3. Data and methods

This study was conducted with physiotherapy students at Semmelweis University. In 2022, we partnered with a medical doctor, a non-native English speaker, who played the role of the simulated patient (SP), adding a unique element to the experience. This created a complex situation, as the SP had to continuously engage in code-switching, balancing the patient's and the expert's perspectives simultaneously. During the debriefing phase, the SP provided feedback to the students from both viewpoints. He evaluated the examination and advisory parts of the sessions from a professional standpoint, while also reflecting on the patient's understanding. Additionally, students had the opportunity to experience working in English as a lingua franca. Given the distance, these SP sessions were conducted online via Zoom.

We involved two professional-patient communication course groups of physiotherapy undergraduate students, in their 3rd year in the research, with a total of thirty students. Five physiotherapy students gave their consent to record their dialogues with the SP. Through this method, we gained insight into some SP online sessions for analysis.

The scenarios were adapted to the topics in the course material. This way, students activated their vocabulary and the related dialogues. Students received situation cards, handouts, or hints about the possible conditions that may have arisen in the scenarios. The duration of the online sessions, between the students pairs and the SP, lasted approximately ten minutes. Students could connect to the SP online outside of the class. Following the scenarios, they returned to their classroom activities.

To assess students' professional communication skills, we used a 13-item, 4-scale (2 = Good, 1 = Adequate, 0 = Not done / poor, N/a = Not applicable) feedback form that we previously created, adapting the Calgary Cambridge-Global Consultation Scale (Mány et al., 2022).

During these sessions, students received personalized feedback from the SP. At the end of the course, students filled out a survey on the Google Forms platform regarding the course and the SP encounters. This process was invaluable for us to identify the positive practices and reveal those that needed improvement. With their consent, we recorded three online sessions between the SP and five physiotherapy students on Zoom. The forty-minute-long voice recordings were transcribed in Alrite speech-to-text software and examined by discourse analysis. For the transcription, we applied Drew's (2000) transcription symbols. We gained eleven pages of transcription to analyze. In the analysis, we used the structure that medical consultations generally follow by Have (2001), 1. opening; 2. complaint; 3. elaboration, examination, and/or test; 4. diagnosis; 5. treatment and/or advice; 6. closing. Based on the conclusions of the research Seuren et al. (2024, pp. 33) conducted: "physiotherapists need to be extra attentive to subtle communication cues such as extended silences, uncomfortable laughter or non-responses", we also examined the changes in the tone, the characteristics of turn-taking, and lay-language awareness.

4. Results and discussion

The analysis of the transcribed conversations and the end-of-the-term survey also revealed some challenges that emerged during the discourse.

4.1. Technical challenges

Some of the technical challenges are related to the logistics of finding a suitable place in the building with a stable internet connection, and altering or finding certain functions in the Zoom app. It takes time from task-solving, and the possibility of disconnected speech, overlaps, interruptions, or delayed sound can sometimes evoke a bit of embarrassment and anxiety that were signified by the giggles or the change of tone. Similarly to Roberts & Osborn-Jenkins' (2021) research, in the case of our recordings, utterances about adjusting the techniques unavoidably emerged, as displayed in examples 1–5.

1. Where's the chat?
2. Sorry, we have lost the connection.
3. I hear it.
4. Can you hear me?
5. We get wi-fi over here as I'm guessing.

We also consider it essential to encourage students to always reflect on when teleconsultations are applicable and when they are not recommended (Le et al., 2023). Key questions to consider include: Is the patient, along with their concerns, mental state, and technical conditions, suitable for teleconsultation/telemedicine? To effectively assess these factors, eye contact is one of the most critical elements.

Regarding the reduced non-verbal cues in teleconsultations (Roberts & Osborn-Jenkins, 2021), the simulated patient we worked with noted a lack of eye contact in several cases. The technical aspects of teleconsultations, such as screen positioning, can be shared and applied to improve this issue, with recommendations for adjusting the screen angle to create the feeling of eye-to-eye contact.

Since perceptive experience is essential in physiotherapy for both diagnostic and therapeutic purposes, the recorded scenarios also highlighted challenges arising from the absence of manual assistance, as demonstrated in examples 6–9.

6. It's really hard to do it in an online way because I can't really see your leg and I can't really give you handouts and things like that.
7. And are there any signs of inflammation or redness there?
8. And if you palpate it in the area, so you try to push it with your fingers.
9. Is it hurting even more or not really?

4.2. Linguistic challenges

Physiotherapists can gather and communicate a great deal of information through palpation, such as the temperature and texture of the affected area. Through touch, they can not only provide corrections but also convey the importance of physical and psychological support. Our findings confirmed that the online environment significantly influences how physiotherapists give instructions to patients, whether guiding them in performing the correct movement or asking the appropriate questions. Questions need to be precise in order to receive the proper amount of information about the pain and/or the condition of the patient. In his feedback, the SP suggested that more explanation and instructions would have been needed in this sense from the physiotherapy students in the role of the professional. Also, regarding question formation, he advised students to inquire from patients in a more tentative way. They mainly used factual questions, focusing on gathering information that is appropriate for history-taking; however, building rapport and tentativeness became relatively marginalized, as in the following examples:

10. When did the pain start? Exactly.
11. What's your question?
12. Sorry?
13. Okay, what do you do?
14. You're doing what? I can't hear it.

If we look at the structure that medical consultations by Have (2001), as for the recorded situations, we concluded that the 3rd (elaboration, examination, and/or test) and the 5th (treatment and/or advice) phases were the ones that, in some cases, students might have omitted if the SP had not reminded them with guided questions. Two situations were excellently accomplished where students involved the patient in the establishment of the diagnosis. In these cases, students could successfully instruct the SP in the role of the patient on how to do some parts of the examination without professional physical presence and assistance.

Lay-language awareness was another important aspect that emerged in the SP feedback. In these situations, some illustrative examples can be mentioned by the patients where the SP indicated that he needs more information about certain terms, as displayed in examples 10–16.

15. Where is the patella or what is the patella tendon?
16. I have no idea.
17. What does it mean?
18. Kinesio tape?
19. Extensor muscle?
20. What is that?
21. Because you said tennis elbow and I don't play tennis, I said I'm playing badminton.

Further important points emphasized in the SP's feedback were that, in some cases, students did not address the patient's emotional state, which could be more challenging online. Also, he suggested that we raise students' attention, along with the non-verbal cues, to the utilization and relevance of hand gestures in physiotherapy. During anamnesis, it is significant to let patients relate their own situation so the suitable question-formation can be more accessed. Also, how do you give the right amount of information and easily understandable explanations to patients? To reach these goals, giving more emphasis on pre-teaching the connected phrases and expressions and the preparation of more detailed patient profiles and scenarios can be effective.

Based on the results of the students' self-evaluation forms, we found that they found the simulated patient (SP) sessions and feedback relevant, providing a more real-life and real-time experience. Students highlighted that the course focused on communication, and during the process, they acquired useful expressions. They also suggested they would prefer more preparation time before the SP sessions. In relation to the scenarios, they proposed the inclusion of communication with patients' relatives.

Followed by the examination of the transcripts, we could conclude that the online environment affected the professional-patient dialogues due to the challenges derived from technical issues and the lack of personal presence. The online space also influenced turn-taking, by increasing the number of overlaps and brief pauses. Changes in the tone reflected when the speaker faced challenges due to the above-mentioned reasons, and when encountered delay or difficulties in conveying the message directly. The practice of question formation also proved to be essential not only because questions and instructions must be very precise to compensate the lack of physical presence, but also because it may affect rapport building and the expression of tentativeness.

Based on our research, we confirmed that incorporating the theme of telehealth in the ESP (English for Specific Purposes) classes is relevant, and the online scenarios can be used as real-life situations. These scenarios offer students the opportunity to confront real-life challenges and practice essential skills, such as preparing for an online consultation, conducting certain examinations and exercises, and explaining telehealth applications for patients in the rehabilitation phase. To do so, students need to be aware of different forms and possibilities of telehealth in physiotherapy and get acquainted with relevant guidelines available on the webpage of the WHO or the Telerehab toolkit guidelines (Buckingham et al., 2023). Being open to and assessing patients' needs, applying conscious, tentative question formation, and tailoring the exercises to certain situations are proven to be essential techniques and skills.

5. Conclusion

The genre of the online SP session, as our case study revealed, can be clearly accepted as a form of teleconsultation. As Tonbuloğlu & Gürol (2016) also claimed in connection with ICT integration, it is not simply "transferring face-to-face education materials in the virtual setting" (Tonbuloğlu & Gürol, 2016, p. 19); there are more learner skills that can be activated by the online space. Adapting a different method to interact with the patient in the online space poses a challenge, at least on the first occasions. We claim that these obstacles have value and can be adapted more consciously as real-life situations that students can solve, as task-related elements.

Based on our case study, it would be beneficial to incorporate elements from the Telerehab toolkit guidelines (Buckingham et al., 2023) and some available applications (Davids et al., 2021) into the class materials and teleconsultation scenarios.

Our research has helped us identify challenges in online healthcare communication and how these simulated experiences can serve as real-life examples in the classroom. The study clearly revealed elements that could enhance and improve our SP scenarios, such as longer simulations, more sessions with the same patients, communication examples with relatives, using a written plan with the patient, and the need to develop more detailed SP profiles.

References

Ayuob, N. N. (2017). Evaluation of a communication skills training course for medical students using peer role-play. *Journal of the Pakistan Medical Association, 67*(5), 745–751. https://pubmed.ncbi.nlm.nih.gov/28507364/

Angelini, L. M. (2023). Simulation in teacher preparation. In L. M. Angelini & R. Muñiz (Eds.), *Simulation for participatory education: Virtual exchange and worldwide collaboration* (pp. 43–51). Springer.

Bandalaria, M. D. P. (2023). Program and course evaluation in open, distance, and digital education. In O. Zawacki-Richer, & Jung, I. (Eds.), *Handbook of open, distance and digital education* (pp. 764–768). Springer.

Bouamra, B., et al. (2021). Simulation-based teaching of telemedicine for future users of teleconsultation and tele-expertise. *JMIR Medical Education, 7*(4) e30440 https://doi.org/10.2196/30440

Buckingham, S., et al. (2023). Telerehabilitation for people with physical disabilities and movement impairment: Development and evaluation of an online toolkit for practitioners and patients. *Disability and Rehabilitation, 45*(11), 1885–1892. https://doi.org/10.1080/09638288.2022.2074549

Dennis, D., et al. (2021). Can physiotherapy students develop and portray simulated patients authentically to their peers during an activity aimed at improving communication skills? A mixed-methods study. *Collegian, 28*, 572–579. https://doi.org/10.1016/j.colegn.2021.02.002

Davids, J., Lidströmer, N., & Ashrafian, H. (2021). Artificial intelligence for physiotherapy and rehabilitation. In N. Lidströmer & H. Ashrafian (Eds.), *Artificial intelligence in medicine*. Springer Nature Switzerland. https://doi.org/10.1007/978-3-030-58080-3_339-1

Drew, P., Chatwin, J., & Collins, S. (2001). Conversation analysis: A method for research into interactions between patients and health-care professionals. *Health Expectations: An International Journal of Public Participation in Health Care and Health Policy, 4*(1), 58–70. https://doi.org/10.1046/j.1369-6513.2001.00125.x

Gayef, A. (2019). Using simulated patients in medical and health professions education. *SHS Web of Conferences, 66*. https://doi.org/10.1051/shsconf/20196601016

Granger, C. L., et al. (2024). Students experienced near peer-led simulation in physiotherapy education as valuable and engaging: A mixed-methods study. *Journal of Physiotherapy, 70*, 40–50.

Halász, R., Kránicz, R., & Hambuch, A. (2021). Die Besonderheiten der Diskurshandlungen zwischen MedizinstudentIn und PatientIn [The peculiarities of discourse between medical students and patients]. In T. Schnedermann, Y. Ilg, & M. Iakushevich (Eds.), *Linguistik und Medizin* (pp. 51–70). De Gruyter.

Harvey, K., & Adolph, S. (2012). Discourse and healthcare. In. J. Gee & M. Handford (Eds.), *The Routledge handbook of discourse analysis* (pp. 470–481). Routledge.

Javaherian, M., et al. (2020). Review paper: The role of simulated patients in physiotherapy education: A review article. *Journal of Modern Rehabilitation, 14*(2), 69–80. https://doi.org/10.18502/jmr.v14i2.7704

Jámbor, M., Sirokmány, V., Czar, D., & Fogarasi, K. (2021). Native speaker playing simulated roles in ESP courses. In E. Kaščáková (Ed.), *FORLANG* (pp. 177–183). https://www.researchgate.net/publication/358886262_Jambor_Mark_Sirokmany_Viktoria_Czar_Daniel_Fogarasi_Katalin_Native_Speaker_Playing_Simulated_Roles_in_ESP_Courses

Kumar, S., Rishi, P., & Sharma, A. (2022). Importance and uses of telemedicine in physiotherapeutic healthcare system: A scoping systemic review. In P. Nanda, et al. (Eds.), *Data engineering for smart systems* (Lecture Notes in Networks and Systems, Vol. 238). Springer Nature Singapore. https://doi.org/10.1007/978-981-16-2641-8_39

Mány, D., Sirokmány, V., Takács, T., Földesi, E., Fekete, J., Hambuch, A., & Fogarasi, K. (2022, September 17). Feedback criteria for simulated patients in language courses for healthcare. *CercleS, The Future of Language Education in an Increasingly Digital World: Embracing Change.* Porto, Portugal.

Roberts, L. C., & Osborn-Jenkins, L. (2021). Delivering remote consultations: Talking the talk. *Musculoskeletal Science and Practice, 52*(4), 102275. https://doi.org/10.1016/j.msksp.2020.102275

Seuren, L. M., et al. (2024). Video analysis of communication by physiotherapists and patients in video consultations: A qualitative study using conversation analysis. *Physiotherapy, 123*, 30–37. https://doi.org/10.1016/j.physio.2023.10.002

Le, T. V., Galperin, H., & Traube, D. (2023). The impact of digital competence on telehealth utilization. *Health Policy and Technology 12*(1), 100724. https://doi.org/10.1016/j.hlpt.2023.100724

Tonbuloğlu, B., & Gürol, A. (2016). Evaluation of distant education programs with regards to various shareholder opinions. *Journal of Education and Practice, 28*(7), 9–22.

Voynatovskaya, S. K., Antonova, S. V., & Sevinç, S. (2018). Innovative learning platforms in LSP teaching at the university level. *Herald of Chelyabinsk State Pedagogical University*, *6*, 68–77. https://doi.org/10.25588/CSPU.2018.88..6..005

World Health Organization. (2022). *Consolidated telemedicine implementation guide.* https://www.who.int/publications/i/item/9789240059184

PART III

Healthcare communication

Is there an interpreter in the house? The intercultural needs of healthcare providers in communication with immigrant patients in Spain

Sofía Antequera Manzano[1]

ABSTRACT

Despite efforts to improve language service provision in the healthcare context, immigrants living in Spain currently face significant difficulties when accessing medical care. Since the concepts of health and illness are contextualized differently depending on the culture, communication issues between healthcare providers and immigrants extend well beyond the linguistic barriers. Additionally, since interpreting services are not guaranteed in the healthcare context, intercultural competence is a fundamental skill for healthcare providers to ensure successful communication with immigrant patients. To assess the intercultural competence of providers, a qualitative study was carried out in a Spanish public hospital, in which ten doctors were interviewed about their experiences caring for immigrant patients. Interviews aimed to analyze their familiarity and perception of cultural differences, the main issues they experience when communicating with immigrant patients, and their previous training on intercultural competence. Results showed that, although providers often experience cultural difficulties when caring for immigrant patients, intercultural competence training in healthcare is very limited in Spain. Therefore, providers typically only improve their intercultural skills through experience, often only when prompted by a situation in which a patient's health has been compromised. In light of these results, a series of training measures is proposed, with the aim of improving providers' intercultural skills and, ultimately, guaranteeing equal healthcare access for all patients, regardless of origin.

Keywords: public service translation and interpreting, healthcare interpreting, intercultural competence, cultural training, language rights, migratory rights

1. Introduction

Increasing immigration to Spain in the 21st century has in turn increased the need to learn about multiculturalism and its influence in the public service sector. According to the Spanish National Statistics Institute (INE 2023), there are over six million immigrants living in Spain. This immigrant group, comprising nearly 15% of the population, needs access to public services in equal conditions to Spanish service-users.

Research shows that, despite governmental efforts to ensure equality in healthcare, immigrants face many different issues when they try to access

---

[1] University of Alcalá, Department of Modern Philology

healthcare services. The lack of linguistic proficiency in a new language, the high level of specialization in medical communication, the administrative difficulties surrounding a different healthcare system, and the power differences between healthcare providers and users are variously described as some of the main issues that enforce unequal access to care between local patients and immigrants (Corsellis, 2010). As a result, when they do manage to access health services, immigrant patients tend to ask fewer questions even if they have a reduced understanding of their condition; they do not adhere to treatment in the same way as local patients do; and they are more prone to being misdiagnosed (Schouten et al., 2023). These care discrepancies are compounded by gender, since women tend to experience more difficulties when accessing healthcare because of their added vulnerability whilst in a migratory setting (Chauvin et al., 2015). Moreover, in Spain, immigrant women seek medical specialties like Obstetrics at higher rates than Spanish women do, and yet they receive less effective care and treatment (Ostrach, 2012). This situation, and the resulting poor health conditions overall, has been documented both nationally and internationally (Bains et al., 2020).

2. Theoretical background

In the current migratory climate, translators and interpreters become key agents in ensuring proper communication and guaranteeing the basic rights of immigrants. However, the interpreting profession is not regulated in Spanish healthcare; i.e., there is no legislation that ensures language interpreting services (Del-Pozo, 2013) and no official professionalization standards for interpreters (Pena-Díaz, 2018). This leads to the widespread use of *ad hoc* interpreters, such as patients' relatives or friends (Aguilar-Solano, 2015). This practice not only compromises ethical principles of impartiality and confidentiality but may also prevent successful communication in both linguistic and cultural terms. Cultural elements also play a fundamental role in communication, since they influence the way speakers interact with each other, understand information, and comply with advice or not. Concepts like health, illness, death, and treatment are conceptualized differently in every culture (Valero-Garcés & Wahl-Kleiser, 2014), which may lead to patients refusing procedures or treatments out of cultural preconceptions.

This is where the concept of intercultural competence is usefully applied. Since it is not typical for Spanish hospitals to have in-house interpreters, healthcare providers often find themselves with the responsibility of responding appropriately in the context of the cultural differences encountered with immigrant patients. In this situation, intercultural competence, which has been defined as the "knowledge, motivation, and skills to interact effectively and appropriately with members of different cultures" (Wiseman, 2002, p. 208), and is characterized by "the ability to be empathetic, the experience of living in different cultures" (Gibson & Zhong, 2005, p. 623), becomes a necessary skill for healthcare workers as it is key to securing health outcomes for patients.

In this context, the following research attempts to determine the intercultural competence of healthcare workers in a public hospital in Spain. Our hypothesis is that the lack of intercultural competence of healthcare workers directly affect the health outcomes of immigrant patients. Some of the main research questions concern healthcare workers' difficulties when communicating with immigrant patients, the differences they perceive in comparison to communication with local Spanish patients, and any previous intercultural competence training that may have been provided. The initial aim of gathering this information is to identify particular gaps in intercultural knowledge, with the further aim of informing training proposals that could ultimately improve healthcare provision for all.

3. Data and methodology

To assess intercultural competence, a series of interviews were carried out with healthcare providers working in La Paz University Hospital, one of the largest public hospitals in the city of Madrid (Spain). A total of ten healthcare providers were interviewed: six women and four men, variously employed in the Obstetrics, Genetics, and Psychology departments. It is worth noting that the geneticists all focused on prenatal diagnosis, so all interviewees bar one typically interact with patients in the pregnancy setting. Providers were at least 30 years of age and had been practicing doctors or midwives for at least five years. All spoke at least one language other than Spanish and had used it at some point in their practice when communicating with immigrants. All were of Spanish origin except geneticist 3, who was born in a Latin America. Throughout the Discussion section, respondents will be referred to by their department role in the order they are presented in the following table (e.g., geneticist 1, midwife 1, obstetrician 3, psychologist 1, etc.).

Table 1. *Characteristics of the respondents*

	Department	Respondents	Gender	Profession	Origin	Languages other than Spanish
1	Genetics	3	Woman	Physician	Spanish	1, intermediate
2					Spanish	1, advanced
3					Latin-American	3, advanced
4	Obstetrics	6	Woman	Midwife	Spanish	1, intermediate
5					Spanish	1, intermediate
6				Physician	Spanish	4, advanced
7			Man		Spanish	1, intermediate
8					Spanish	1, intermediate
9					Spanish	1, intermediate
10	Psychology	1	Man	Physician	Spanish	1, advanced

The structured interviews were carried out on-site in the hospital, throughout the course of one morning in the spring of 2023. They were recorded and subsequently transcribed and analyzed manually to gather qualitative results of their content. Since interviews took place in between appointments, efficiency and conciseness were prerequisites. Interviews consisted of the the following questions:

1. What are the most common immigrant cultures you have encountered in the hospital?
2. Are immigrants fully integrated in the Spanish healthcare system or do providers have to accommodate their specific cultural needs?
3. What is the greater obstacle, language or culture?
4. Have you ever encountered patients that used traditional medicine?

5. Are cultural differences still relevant with immigrants who are Spanish native speakers?
6. What are the main issues that arise in communication with immigrants?
7. Is creating trust relationships with immigrant patients difficult?
8. Have you ever received training on intercultural communication?
9. Have you tried to improve your own intercultural competence?
10. What tools do you consider necessary to improve communication with immigrant patients?

4. Results and discussion

The results section of this paper presents insights gained from the ten interviews, together with analysis of healthcare providers' reported experiences of caring for immigrants, their perception of cultural differences, and their training in intercultural skills.

It must be noted that the providers interviewed have been exposed to immigrants of a limited selection of cultures, thus shaping their views and experiences of communicating in a multicultural setting. According to providers' responses, the most typical immigrant cultures presenting at La Paz are Latin American, Chinese, Arab, and Philippine, while migration from Slavic countries had been increasing since February 2022 as a result of the intensification of the Russo-Ukrainian war.

4.1. Cultural integration

When asked about the level of integration of immigrants and the hospital politics to ensure appropriate care for them, interviewees reported that La Paz Hospital offers translated information leaflets and guides, as well as informed consent forms, to some of the immigrant communities, depending on the language. However, the interviewees confirmed that interpreters are only present when arranged by the immigrants themselves, since the hospital provides no interpreting service. Such a service would be very helpful for appointments, according to all interviewees. Geneticist 1 stated that "the system doesn't make things easy for immigrants, who are constantly facing obstacles" and yet the immigrants "often do everything in their power to make matters easier, both for their own treatment and providers". Most interviewees stated that they felt "no pressure to adapt to the patient's cultural needs" (midwife 1), although all reported that cultural differences could sometimes make patients hesitant to follow certain treatments or disclose important information. Only one respondent (geneticist 2) shared that some cultures "definitely lack integration", so "the hospital often has to work towards opening up to the patient".

4.2. Language or culture?

Providers were then asked if their interactions with immigrants were most affected by language or culture. In this regard, six respondents answered that culture was the main obstacle, even when they communicated in a language that immigrants were not fluent in. Providers with higher proficiency in other languages were also more aware of cultural issues, possibly because they can see past the linguistic barrier. For instance, psychologist 1 stated they require "not just interpreters, but cultural agents, people whom I can ask 'is this appropriate?' before making decisions, someone that explains there may be underlying reasons for things that go beyond the individual".

The four respondents that struggled the most linguistically also mentioned several instances where cultural unawareness on their part had negatively affected patients. For instance, obstetrician 2 talked about how "Chinese patients always agree with our decisions but fail to do what they are advised without informing us". Midwives mentioned that Arab patients tend to either have difficulties measuring their glucose levels during pregnancy or communicating irregular results, although the providers were unable to specify the cause. As a result, these patients risk lacking a gestational diabetes diagnosis when they need one. Midwives also reported the need "to be very insistent if we need patients to abstain from making efforts and to rest during pregnancy – if you tell a Spanish woman to look after herself, she'll know what you mean, but maybe some other cultures have a different conception of rest."

Similar problems were encountered in the use of traditional medicine. Although providers did not report issues on a regular basis, there were instances of practices that compromised the health state of patients. Obstetrician 1 mentioned treating infections in Arab patients caused by the use of medicinal herbs to stop hemorrhages after childbirth. Similarly, obstetrician 3 reported that consuming moringa tea is a common practice among Latin American pregnant women, despite it being an abortifacient. These instances are particularly important because they were only discovered once the health of the patient had become compromised, since providers had no way to enquire about them before they occurred. This highlights how crucial it is for healthcare professionals to receive information on the potential cultural practices their patients perform.

Finally, when asked about cultural differences found in Spanish-speaking patients of Latin American origin, obstetricians and geneticist 1 mentioned a key factor in communicating with them: socio-educational background. Providers reported that Latin American speakers usually experience more comprehension issues than Spanish speakers from Spain and find it harder to adhere to a specific treatment, since their socio-educational level hinders communication in comparison with speakers from Spain. In this regard, we might conclude that issues in interaction with immigrants do not fully depend on cultural or linguistic differences, but on the overall communication skills of healthcare providers. Whether communication issues with Latin American patients result from their socio-educational background or from their different varieties of Spanish, it is still paramount for providers to adapt their discourse to their patients.

4.3. Building trust

In the next part of the interview, providers were asked about the difficulties they had encountered when establishing trust relationships with immigrant patients. All interviewees stated that building trust with immigrants took longer than with local patients, even when linguistic differences did not pose a problem. Some patients failed to understand medical decisions within their cultural context, not just in terms of treatment – they also experienced issues understanding the Hospital's approach to matters such as pregnancy, which they perceived as heavily medicalized in comparison to their home countries. However, the psychologist and the midwives also mentioned how, once they had gained immigrants' trust as professionals, offering treatment options to immigrant patients was sometimes even easier than with Spanish patients. As mentioned in the introduction, immigrant patients experience many obstacles when trying to access healthcare; therefore, once they have experienced cultural empathy and understanding, they may develop a special trust in providers. Geneticist 3 supported this idea of cultural empathy, reporting how Latin American patients followed her advice and decisions more willingly than those of her Spanish colleagues.

4.4. Intercultural competence training

In the last part of the interview, providers were asked about the intercultural competence training they had received during their studies. The general answer was "little to none". Out of the ten interviewees, seven stated that they had received no training during their Medicine Degree, nor was it included in their postgraduate specialization period. However, geneticist 2 mentioned acquiring some general information on multicultural issues at master's level. The psychologist had received in-depth training in multicultural issues and communication skills in subjects such as Social or Community Interpreting that are available in some Psychology Degrees in Spain. In addition, geneticist 3, who received her bachelor's degree in Latin America, had taken courses such as Anthropology that did touch on intercultural training. However, she mentioned that intercultural issues were completely neglected during her postgraduate specialization in Spain.

In these circumstances, the question arises as to whether providers have felt the need to improve their intercultural skills on a personal level. Answers on this matter differ, but division seems to be a result of the different understanding providers have of what intercultural competence training entails. Midwives mentioned they had taken side-courses on patient communication that had provided them with some knowledge on multicultural issues. Only geneticists 1 and 2 admitted to doing specific research prior to an appointment if they knew they would be communicating with immigrant patients. They reported researching potentially controversial topics (e.g., abortion) and gathering some general knowledge about the ways immigrants relate to their culture, religion and their peers, especially for heavily hierarchical cultures. The rest of providers did not make specific efforts to prepare their appointments with immigrants, despite acknowledging potential cultural issues. Obstetricians stated that, although they had not actively improved their skills, they had been passively exposed to many situations and implemented those experiences into their practice. The psychologist and geneticist 3 had not conducted any cultural research either, but along with the midwives, they had received intercultural competence training at some point. Therefore, they felt well-equipped to deal with general intercultural issues and displayed levels of empathy and cultural sensibility that stood out when compared to the rest of interviewees.

Finally, providers were asked to list the tools they would appreciate the most to communicate efficiently with immigrant patients. Unanimously, all providers answered that they would need an interpreter or cultural broker to bridge the cultural gap between themselves and their patients.

5. Conclusion

This research aimed to shed light on the current issues faced by health providers when communicating with immigrant patients in Spain. A total of ten providers were interviewed regarding their experience dealing with immigrants and their previous training on intercultural training. Interviewees were all workers from La Paz University Hospital, Madrid, and belonged to the departments of Genetics, Obstetrics, and Psychology. Their answers confirmed that culture plays a crucially important role in healthcare communication and the success of treatment. Since the current Spanish regulations on medical interpreting do not guarantee the presence of an interpreter during a medical appointment, the responsibility for bridging the cultural gap often relies on providers themselves, who need intercultural competence training to provide the best care possible. In this regard, interviews confirmed our hypothesis that providers trained in intercultural competence have higher awareness of intercultural issues and are more likely to enquire about them when communicating with patients from other cultures.

Some of the most problematic consequences of cultural differences that providers had witnessed included 1) cultural practices that are unknown to healthcare providers and that compromise patients' health; 2) difficulties in establishing trust relationships with immigrant patients, affecting their compliance to treatment and overall health outcomes; 3) different ways of communicating due to social and hierarchical relationships, and 4) different conceptions of health, illness, rest, effort, etc. Although most healthcare providers had not received intercultural competence training during their studies, all of them had noticed the cultural issues that arise during appointments throughout their years of practice. However, providers admitted that they only found out about certain cultural practices once the health of their patient had been compromised, which shows how experience cannot be the only source of knowledge for multicultural issues. Bearing this in mind, all interviewees requested the presence of a cultural broker tasked with facilitating communication with their patients.

Meanwhile, and especially due to the lack of interpreting regulation in the Spanish healthcare setting, the results of this study support the improvement of intercultural training resources for healthcare providers. Introducing intercultural training in the workplace would be problematic due to the limited time availability of health providers; a more logical proposal would be to incorporate intercultural training into university education, with a view to continuing its development during professional practice. Accordingly, intercultural competence training should be introduced on an undergraduate level in Medicine degrees, as is already the case in other disciplines like Psychology. In terms of content, the measures proposed include both general and specific intercultural training. General training should focus on values such as openness to other cultures, empathy, and sensibility towards social differences, to raise awareness among healthcare workers about the intricacies of intercultural communication. Specific cultural training is essential, since different cultures require different needs to ensure successful communication. In the case of hospitals in the community of Madrid, general overviews of Chinese, Arab, Slavic, Latin American and Philippine cultures are necessary to help providers anticipate the issues they may encounter during their practices. Importantly, the training must be conducted in a professional way that avoids harmful stereotypes.

Finally, our last training proposal focuses on communication skills in general. Healthcare providers need to acquire abilities to simplify and adapt their highly specialized medical discourse, in order to be understandable and ensure health services are accessible for people of all educational backgrounds. To this end, interprofessional practice and teamwork between healthcare providers and language and culture specialists are key. Health and communication are necessarily interlinked; therefore, is essential for both professional groups to learn from each other and work together towards a more equal society for all cultures.

References

Aguilar-Solano, M. (2015). Non-professional volunteer interpreting as an institutionalized practice in healthcare: A study on interpreters' personal narrative. *The International Journal for Translation and Interpreting*, 7(3), 132–148.

Bains, S., et al. (2020).Communication barriers in maternity care - a questionnaire study among migrants to Norway. *European Journal of Public Health*, 30(Suppl. 5).

Chauvin, P., et al. (2015). *Access to healthcare for people facing multiple vulnerabilities in health in 26 cities across 11 countries. Report on the social and medical data gathered in 2014 in nine European countries, Turkey and Canada*. Doctors of the World – Médecins du monde international network.

Corsellis, A. (2010). *Traducción e interpretación en los servicios públicos, primeros pasos*. Comares.

Del Pozo Treviño, M. (2013). El camino hacia la profesionalización de los intérpretes en los servicios públicos y asistenciales españoles en el siglo XXI. *Cuadernos de ALDEEU, 25*, 109–131.

DeWan, G., & Mei, Z. (2005). Intercultural communication competence in the healthcare context. *Intercultural Journal of Intercultural Relations, 29*, 621–634.

Instituto Nacional de Estadística. (2023). Estadística continua de población. ECP. Datos provisionales 01/10/2023. https://www.ine.es/dyngs/INEbase/es/operacion.htm?c=Estadistica_C&cid=1254736177095&menu=ultiDatos&idp=1254735572981

Ostrach, B. (2012) 'Yo no sabía…' – Immigrant women's use of national health systems for reproductive and abortion care". *Journal of Immigrant and Minority Health, 15(2)*, 262–272.

Pena Díaz, C. (2018). Ethics in theory and practice in Spanish healthcare community interpreting. In V. Montalt (Ed.), *Retos actuales y tendencias emergentes en traducción médica* (pp. 93–115). Universitat d'Alacant.

Schouten, B., Manthey, L., & Scarvaglieri, C. (2023) Teaching intercultural communication skills in healthcare to improve care for culturally and linguistically diverse patients. *Patient education and counseling, 115*, 107890. https://doi.org/10.1016/j.pec.2023.107890

Valero-Garcés, C., & Wahl-Kleier, L. (2014) Desencuentros culturales en el ámbito de la salud: las voces de los profesionales sanitarios y los pacientes extranjeros. *Panace@, 15(40)*, 315–328.

Wiseman, R. L. (2002) Intercultural communication competence. In W. Gudykunst & B. Moody (Eds.), *Handbook of international and intercultural communication* (pp. 207–224). Thousand Oaks.

Development and assessment of an automatically creative and flexible use of medical English as a lingua franca – terminological awareness in healthcare communication

Alexandra Zimonyi-Bakó[1]

ABSTRACT

Medical English as a Lingua Franca (MELF) communication is highly dynamic, as, due to the increased chance of interlocutors' linguistic and cultural (linguacultural) backgrounds differ, more negotiation over meaning is necessary. Further complications are presented by the challenges of healthcare communication, precise information exchange, and providing support to patients. Accordingly, there is a need for terminological awareness (TA) ensuring automatically effective language use so that conscious efforts can be focused on providing quality patient care. To develop this language use, regular engagement with terminological consciousness (TC) is required, refining schemata responsible for effective healthcare communication. Tasks designed specifically to improve TC and thus develop TA can be included in English for Medical/Healthcare Purposes (EMP/EHP) classes. However, the assessment of MELF language use and improvement in TA/TC pose several challenges. The strategies used to exploit and adapt communicative and language resources in MELF interactions are not always clearly detectable and it is also hard to assess strategies that are used automatically. Therefore, optimally controlled environments are necessary to elicit real-life-like communicative behavior and reduce assessment bias, and a reflection element is needed to gain insight into the perceived effectiveness of the interaction and to explore the extent of learners' automatized strategic language use.

Keywords: Medical English as a Lingua Franca (MELF), healthcare communication, English for Medical/Healthcare Purposes (EMP/EHP), communicative strategies, terminological awareness

1. Introduction

In international healthcare communication a large number of interactions are between native speakers of English (NSs) and non-native speakers (NNss) or between NNss whose shared language is English (Bosher & Stocker, 2015; Keresztes, 2009; Martin, 2015; Oliver, 2015; Sobane, 2015; Tweedie & Johnson, 2019), with a dominance in the latter (cf. Graddol, 2006; Jenkins,

---

[1] Semmelweis University, Institute of Languages for Specific Purposes

2016). Such use of English is considered communication in English as a Lingua Franca (ELF), as for the interactants English is the selected mediating language, "the communicative medium of choice, and often the only option" (Seidlhofer, 2011, p. 7). This form of English language use in a healthcare setting was termed Medical English as a Lingua Franca (MELF) by Tweedie & Johnson (2018).

To determine how to prepare healthcare providers for MELF encounters and how to assess their capability to effectively engage in MELF communication, it is necessary to identify the challenges MELF communication may pose, the markers of successful MELF communication, and the means to achieving successful MELF communication.

1.1. Characteristics of MELF communication

Healthcare communication is special in the respect that any barriers in communication largely influence not only the quality of patient care but the safety of both patients and healthcare providers involved (Cooke et al., 2000; Deumert, 2010; Elderkin-Thompson, Silver, & Waitzkin, 2001; Hull, 2022; Martin, 2015; Schyve, 2007; Sobane, 2015; Waxman & Levitt, 2000) Furthermore, in medical encounters, conveying information precisely is critical, as providers must follow certain protocols while adhering to legal frameworks and working under time pressure (Tweedie & Johnson, 2022).

However, differing linguacultural backgrounds, i.e., different linguistic and cultural backgrounds (Baker, 2018; Jenkins, 2015; Pölzl & Seidlhofer, 2006; Landmark et al., 2017; Mauranen, 2018; Seidlhofer, 2018) of MELF communicative situations may pose several challenges to smooth communication, that is, without non-understandings or misunderstandings, since the interactants may differ not only in their degree of English proficiency, but, in all likelihood, their perception and knowledge of the world, and their experiences in health care (cf. Kaur 2011a; Roberts et al., 2005; Schouten & Meeuwesen, 2006).

The challenges of MELF communication often result in a more goal-oriented discourse, with less small talk (Bagheri, Ibrahim, & Habil, 2015). This heightened focus on the exchange of information may limit other crucial aspects of medical encounters, such as expressing support and providing hope (van Servellen, 2009). While these emotional aspects may not be the priority in certain high-stake situations, their omission can otherwise constitute a lack of proper communication, even to the extent of decreasing patient satisfaction and compliance, and thus the effectiveness of the treatment (Pilling, 2011).

Accordingly, healthcare providers must be prepared to engage in MELF encounters with increased flexibility and adaptiveness, that is, they need to display non-routine forms of communication and language use (cf. Pitzl, 2012, 2018). This also entails that healthcare providers need to establish temporary norms, together with their interlocutors, for the time of the interaction (Seidlhofer, 2011), which naturally requires a larger degree of cooperation (Cogo & House, 2018).

1.2. Preparing healthcare providers for successful MELF communication

Language use in these complex and dynamic MELF interactions relies on a plethora of factors rendering it difficult to capture or predict. This raises several issues in determining what should be taught and learnt on EMP/EHP classes. Nevertheless, since ELF "is not a variety of English but a variable way of using it" (Seidlhofer, 2011, p. 77), the focus of EMP/EHP classes should be drawn to how English can be used in a way that it facilitates MELF interactions.

Therefore, the fundamental approach to preparing healthcare providers for MELF interactions must be centred on the processes aiding the achievement of communicative goals, and the processes of making meaning (Widdowson, 2007) during medical encounters in international settings. The procedural ability necessary for solving problems in communication is a capability (Seidlhofer, 2011; Seidlhofer, 2015; Seidlhofer & Widdowson, 2017; Widdowson, 2003) responsible for processing the information and exploiting any possible resources – e.g., interactants' language use, nonverbal communication, previous experiences – during the interaction with the aim of making meaning to achieve communicative goals. This entails that the capability in question relies on mental structures (Illés, 2020) and it is these mental structures ruling the processes executed in the minds of healthcare providers that must be developed, improved, and refined in order to optimize the providers' effectiveness in MELF communication.

Furthermore, it must be kept in mind that the goal of healthcare communication is the provision of quality care, and providers' use of language is only a tool to reach this goal. Henceforward, providers must be capable of exploiting resources during the interaction with ease, even if they have to step out of pattern-driven communicative behavior so that their conscious focus can be devoted to providing patient care, as the mind is capable of allocating conscious effort to only one mental process, to one activity at a time (Kahneman, 2011). In other words, the provider must function with terminological awareness and an automatically effective use of language in exchanging information, such that they are able to effortlessly select medical terms to make meaning in the medical encounter (Bakó, 2022).

As for the development of terminological awareness, it is of utmost importance that healthcare providers engage in interactions where they need to select the appropriate medical terms consciously, that is, with terminological consciousness (Bakó, 2022), as in order to automatize flexible and adaptive language use, ample experience must be gained in solving communication problems characteristic of MELF interactions. In EMP/EHP classes, simulated MELF encounters can be practiced without any risk of harming patients, and with special focus on ensuring conscious exploitation and adaptation of communicative resources, especially language use. Moreover, a step-by-step development of terminological awareness can be achieved whereby various tasks prepare learners for the challenges of MELF interactions, simulated or real-life. Tasks should be designed to raise awareness of variable ways of expressing medical terms or concepts, for instance, by asking students to find synonyms or short descriptions for the same concept. Learners' adaptability can be improved if they are asked to reformulate the same information to different imaginary patients who come from various linguacultural backgrounds. Furthermore, reflections on the appropriateness of language use or effectiveness of communication can be elicited from learners with the aim of focusing their conscious attention on how challenges of MELF encounters can be addressed. (For further details, see Bakó, 2022.)

1.3. Assessment of language use in MELF communication

While the development of terminological awareness can be ensured with sufficient practice in solving communicative discrepancies in simulated or real-life MELF interactions, assessing healthcare providers' capability of doing so is a more challenging undertaking. As has been discussed in the previous section, the capability of using language appropriately and effectively is reliant on mental processes, and these are hard to capture, especially when they reach the level of automatization. Therefore, detectable traces of terminological awareness must be identified that can be used as the basis for estimating healthcare providers' level of expertise in MELF communication.

As Vettorel (2019) underlines, communication strategies "can be seen as underlying tools that speakers strategically employ in meaning co-construction" (p. 188), that is, while they are being used to creatively and effectively exploit language resources to reach a communicative goal (Tarone, 2016). This strategic capability is required in all communication, but usually to a higher degree in ELF communication due to the increased need for negotiation of meaning (Widdowson, 2003). Svennevig et al. (2019), analyzing emergency calls involving NNSs of English, also underline that the use of strategies results in fewer misunderstandings.

(M)ELF communication is characterized by the use of strategies such as comprehension checks, confirmation checks, and clarification requests (Björkman, 2014); pre-emptive strategies such as reformulation, simplification, left-dislocation, decomposition (breaking down complex concepts into less complex concepts), and self-initiated repair (Cogo & House, 2018; Cogo & Pitzl, 2016; Kaur, 2011b; Svennevig et al., 2019); proactive strategies such as repetition and paraphrasing to prevent misunderstandings (Ritala, 2022; Ting & Cogo, 2022); co-construction of meaning; discourse markers (*oh, well, you know, I mean, etc.*) and back-channeling; and using multilingual resources (Cogo & House, 2018). Besides compensatory strategies aimed at solving challenges due to language difficulties, much information can be gained from nonverbal cues, such as the use of gestures (Ting & Cogo, 2022), and looking at patients' visible symptoms or measurable parameters, which are equally important in making meaning (Blommaert, 2010; Canagarajah, 2018).

By focusing on the use of strategies in MELF communication, healthcare providers' adaptability (i.e., their ability to cope with the challenges of communicative situations) can be highlighted and thus assessment can shift away from evaluating NNSs' language use in comparison to NS norms (Harding, 2014). In other words, the aims of assessment should be to test whether the interactants' communicative goals are achieved (Jenkins & Leung, 2013; Chopin, 2015) and how effective their communication is (Harding & McNamara, 2018). Hence, assessment can become user-centred and norm-defocused (Newbold, 2015).

Nevertheless, detecting these strategies remains a highly challenging task, especially as an instructor or examiner aiming to assess healthcare providers' communicative capability and terminological awareness, as opposed to a researcher working with recordings and transcriptions. First of all, it must be ensured that the simulated MELF interactions exhibit enough discrepancies for the interactants so that negotiation of meaning can take place. As Harding (2015) proposes, the task should be interactive and goal-oriented; it should anticipate breakdowns in communication; and it should elicit negotiation of meaning by a minimum of two interlocutors. Secondly, assessors must determine what defines the various strategies under consideration, and how they should be detected. Thirdly, a framework must be created that is capable of assessing how effectively the strategies are used in achieving communicative goals.

2. Materials and methods

2.1. Data collection

Data collection was carried out as part of my PhD research (Zimonyi-Bakó, 2024). In the present study, a group of third-year (BSc) physiotherapy students were involved (N = 11, all female and native Hungarian speakers) at Semmelweis University, Budapest in November 2019 at the end of their 10-week-long course in English for Healthcare Purposes, which focused on physiotherapist-patient communication in English, in 90-minute weekly sessions. A prerequisite was a minimum B2-level English language exam certificate. The course material was specifically designed to improve their terminological awareness by including tasks in their lessons that involved conscious exploitation of their language resources, such as finding synonyms for medical terms *(humerus, articulation, etc.)* or learning how to describe the same notion to various patients in English; engagement in simulated physiotherapist-patient encounters where the learners simulating patients were told to create specific challenges in the interaction; and provision of feedback to one another after simulations.

On the final oral test, and after gaining learners' oral consent, an audio recording was made of the two parts of the tests. In the first part of the test, students were given a MELF situation randomly from a pile of cards explaining their task (in Hungarian) regarding what patient they were meeting and in what context. For example, on one card it was written that "you meet a 65-year-old patient for the first time in post-operative cardiac rehabilitation – tell him about post-op precautions and instruct him to carry out some exercises" (translated by the author). All the situations required professional knowledge that the students were familiar with, and the situations touched upon topics covered in the course material. Students were allowed 20-30 seconds to read the situation card and prepare their thoughts. Then, they were required to engage in the simulation as a physiotherapist, while the instructor (the author of this paper) simulated the patient – who was always a NNS of English – and created various communicative challenges, such as expressing non-understanding, using very simple (and not always grammatically correct) English, misunderstanding certain words, and displaying emotions, such as fear. Students had the opportunity to touch the simulated patient, for example, when examining a painful wrist or shoulder, and students' instructions on movements were carried out by the simulated patient. The simulated interactions were 4-7 minutes long.

The second part of the test was a retrospective (post-simulation) reflection, when they were asked to reflect on the effectiveness of the interaction and how they tried to be successful in communication. These reflections were conducted in the students' mother tongue, Hungarian, and were 2-5 minutes long.

2.2. Data analysis

The audio recordings were anonymized – students were assigned a number as ph_01, ph_02… – and transcriptions were created manually for further analysis. The simulated interactions and the reflections were studied separately, and strategies used by learners were identified. In the simulated interactions, the strategies that the physiotherapy students applied while engaging in the interaction were detected by the author. As for the reflections, those strategies that the students explicitly claimed they used in the simulated interaction were noted. Samples of strategies identified in both the simulations and reflections are listed in Figure 1 in Section 3.

3. Results

Altogether nine groups of strategies could be identified: using lay language, using simple language, using description, using synonyms, accommodation to patient's accent or language use, relying on feedback, using gestures, slowing down, and using repetition. Figure 1 provides samples of these strategies both in the simulations and the reflections, where applicable.

	simulation	reflection*
using lay language	-	"I tried not to use technical terms" (ph_04)
using simple language	"your bones are OK, but your joint is not" (ph_05)	"I tried saying basic things" (ph_05), "I tried to use everyday words" (ph_10)
using description	"you know what this cuff is? … I'll put it on your arm … for taking your blood pressure" (ph_09)	"I explained what the word scoliosis means" (ph_03)
using synonyms	"I can see you have pulmonary disease… asthma" (ph_01); "because of your sedentary lifestyle … because of your sitting lifestyle" (ph_03)	"if the words I used weren't clear, I tried them differently" (ph_02)
accommodation to patient's accent or language use	the student took over Italian words used by the patient; e.g., infiammazione, and used a more articulated pronunciation (ph_11)	"I'll palpate your knee… palpare" (ph_11)
relying on feedback	"you feel dizzy?" (ph_08) after the 'patient' stood up and leaned on the table for support	"he could follow my instructions" (ph_01); "I was trying to look at her reactions" (ph_02)
using gestures	"do this!" (ph_05), "let me show you how to do it" (ph_09)	"if I show it to her, it's the most straightforward because then she can see it, too" (ph_06)
slowing down	slow pace was detected if student's interaction with the simulated patient felt slower than the student's Hungarian talk during the reflection	"I talked slow to her … I mean not too slow, but not too fast… in Hungarian I talk much faster." (ph_06)
using repetition	"Patient: It's burning. Physio: It's a burning pain? P: It's warm. Ph: It's warm." (ph_02)	-

Figure 1. *Samples from the audio recordings for each group of strategies used*
*Note. The reflection is translated from Hungarian.

As the data analysis suggests, two strategies were detected almost exclusively by researcher; namely, using repetitions and slowing down, indicating that these strategies, when applied, are used automatically, with little conscious control. Meanwhile, the use of simple language, lay language, or synonyms were reported in certain cases by the students when the author did not detect these strategies. This may be due to the multiple factors determining whether terms used are considered lay versions or simple language use, thus making it hard to assess. When students claimed they used lay or simple words, they determined these in relation to their overall vocabulary range, which can only be assumed by an assessor. With regards to the detection of gestures, the audio recordings set some limitations, especially in cases where the use of gestures were not reflected upon or were not verbalized in the interaction.

As for the effectiveness and success of the communication, only the students were asked to evaluate their simulated interactions. The analysis concluded that most students found their interaction to be successful and those students who were not satisfied with their interaction also expressed how they tried to cope with the challenges of the situation.

4. Discussion

The findings of this study point at the necessities that assessments of MELF encounters must take into consideration. When planning tests to assess healthcare providers' capability to communicate with terminological awareness, the challenges of the simulated MELF encounters must be controlled and optimized, the detection of strategies used must be unified, and the measures regarding the effectiveness of communication must be introduced.

While this study sought to maintain an equal challenge for each student by having the same examiner in all the simulations, a more controlled environment can be created by using patient scenarios in the simulated interactions (Eklics et al., 2019; Takács-Czar, 2021). With the help of a list of patient characteristics to prepare a person to simulate the patient's role, it can be ensured that each student is presented with similar challenges and thus provided with approximately the same opportunities for activating strategies. Furthermore, using professional actors to play the simulated patient roles, as in the project of Eklics et al. (2019), can achieve greater authenticity while reducing examination stress. Moreover, additional aspects related to differences in cultural backgrounds or health beliefs can be incorporated in the simulations with the help of pre-written scenarios.

The strategies applied by the students represented all the types of strategies found in the literature. Students relied on feedback from the simulated patient in order to ensure comprehension. They extensively used pre-emptive strategies by reformulating and simplifying their language use, although many times these strategies were put to use only when they perceived misunderstanding or non-understanding. Proactive repetitions were applied less consciously, but some students made several attempts to use them. Multilingual resources were also drawn on, for example, when Italian words were added in the interaction. Moreover, visual clues from gestures or the simulated patient's behavior were deployed as sources of information. Adding more objective signs or parameters would probably make the interaction more authentic, but this is an aspect which is hard to include in classroom practice or in an exam setting; nevertheless, it is important to simulate certain symptoms or a near-realistic physical status, such as appearing weak or dizzy, or in pain.

Analysis of simulations and reflections showed that when detecting strategies, both resources are vital, as there were strategies mentioned by students in their retrospective reflections, but not detected by the instructor-researcher during analysis of the simulated interactions, and vice versa. The strategies not mentioned by the students can be considered automatized strategic language use and it is paramount to track these as well, since they show an automatically effective language use, i.e., terminological awareness. Those strategies that were not detected by the researcher were subsequently identified as coping mechanisms, which are hard to assess due to their relative nature. Therefore, certain measures must be introduced in MELF assessments that make these strategies, such as the use of lay or simple language, comparable.

In order to ensure both an emic and an etic perspective in the assessment, a second assessor should be included so that the assessments that have been carried out in the research investigation can be conducted in classroom environment as well. As for research purposes, the use of video recordings would highly increase the value of the data collected, as in the research of Ting & Cogo (2022). Most significantly, a detailed checklist for assessment would greatly benefit the precision of the assessment. Although general lists of what should be assessed in ELF interactions have been proposed (cf. Harding & McNamara, 2018), there is a pressing need for a MELF-specific checklist which incorporates those aspects of the interaction necessary for successful medical encounters in international settings.

For the assessment of effectiveness and success in MELF communication, soliciting students' reflections may not be sufficient. Indeed, all data gained from this inquiry is ultimately an expression of their strategic goals, the perception of which may even be distorted. Accordingly, it would be beneficial to gain feedback not only from the student, but from the simulated patient as well, in order to be able to estimate their mutual intelligibility (Marshall & Bakó, 2022). In the meantime, it must be considered that although both patients and providers tend to accommodate one another's language use in MELF encounters, it is the healthcare providers' responsibility to find ways of communicating that are understandable to their patients, as Johnson et al. (2022) and Rudd et al. (1999) also underline.

5. Conclusion

The present paper offered insights into the challenges of assessing effective language use in MELF encounters by analyzing in-class oral tests of Hungarian physiotherapy students. The focus was on provider-patient interactions, which is the main territory of MELF communication. It has been proposed that in order to successfully negotiate meaning in MELF, healthcare providers must possess terminological awareness, an automatically effective exploitation and adaptation of language use. This capability can best be captured by strategies used to exploit and adapt resources in communication; e.g., language use. Nevertheless, when designing assessment tools for MELF communication, it must be considered that the detection of strategies used by healthcare providers must be reinforced from multiple sources, that is, from both their interaction and retrospective reflection, and that multiple assessors should be involved. Furthermore, it has been highlighted that merely exploring providers' strategies does not yield sufficient information on the effectiveness of their language use; hence, information must be sought from both providers and simulated patients regarding the perceived effectiveness and success of the MELF encounter.

References

Bagheri, H., Ibrahim, N. A., & Habil, H. (2015). The structure of clinical consultation: a case of non-native speakers of English as participants. *Global journal of health science*, 7(1), 249.

Baker, W. (2018). English as a lingua franca and intercultural communication. In J. Jenkins, W. Baker, & M. Dewey (Eds.), *The Routledge handbook of English as a lingua franca (ELF)* (pp. 25–37). Routledge.

Bakó, A. (2022). Preparing healthcare providers for communication with patients in ELF contexts – a methodological framework of developing terminological awareness. In M. G. Tweedie & R. Johnson (Eds.), *Perspectives on Medical English as a Lingua Franca* (pp. 27–48). Cambridge Scholars Press.

Björkman, B. (2014). An analysis of polyadic English as a lingua franca (ELF) speech: A communicative strategies framework. *Journal of Pragmatics*, 66, 122–138. https://doi.org/10.1016/j.pragma.2014.03.001

Blommaert, J. (2010). *The sociolinguistics of globalization*. Cambridge University Press.

Bosher, S., & Stocker, J. (2015). Nurses' narratives on workplace English in Taiwan: Improving patient care and enhancing professionalism. *English for Specific Purposes*, 38, 109–120. https://doi.org/10.1016/j.esp.2015.02.001

Canagarajah, S. (2018). The unit and focus of analysis in lingua franca English interactions: In search of a method. *International Journal of Bilingual Education and Bilingualism*, 21(7), 805–824.

Chopin, K. (2015). Chapter 11. Reconceptualizing norms for language testing: Assessing English language proficiency from within an ELF framework. In. Y. Bayyurt & S. Akcan (Eds.), *Current Perspectives on Pedagogy for English as a Lingua Franca* (pp. 193–204). De Gruyter Mouton. https://doi.org/10.1515/9783110335965.193

Cogo, A., & House, J. (2018). The pragmatics of ELF. In J. Jenkins, W. Baker, M. Dewey (Eds.), *The Routledge handbook of English as a lingua franca (ELF)* (pp. 210–224). Routledge.

Cogo, A., & Pitzl, M.-L. (2016). Pre-empting and signalling non-understanding in ELF. *ELT Journal*, 70(3), 339–345. https://doi.org/10.1093/elt/ccw015

Cooke, M. W., Wilson, S., Cox, P., & Roalfe, A. (2000). Public understanding of medical terminology: non-English speakers may not receive optimal care. *Journal of Accident & Emergency Medicine, 17*(2), 119–121. https://doi.org/10.1136/emj.17.2.119

Deumert, A. (2010). "It would be nice if they could give us more language" – serving South Africa's multilingual patient base. *Social Science & Medicine (1982), 71*(1), 53–61. https://doi.org/10.1016/j.socscimed.2010.03.036

Eklics, K., Kárpáti, E., Cathey, R. V., Lee, A. J., & Koppán, Á. (2019). Interdisciplinary Medical Communication Training at the University of Pécs. In J. Domenech et al. (Eds.), *5th International Conference on Higher Education Advances (HEAd'19)* (pp. 695–703). Editorial Universitat Politècnica de Valencia:. https://doi.org/10.4995/HEAD19.2019.9443

Eklics K., & Fekete J. (2020). The role of simulation practices in acquisition or activation of medical terminology. *Porta Lingua*, 103–109.

Elderkin-Thompson, V., Silver, R. C., & Waitzkin, H. (2001). When nurses double as interpreters: A study of Spanish-speaking patients in a US primary care setting. *Social Science & Medicine (1982), 52*(9), 1343–1358. https://doi.org/10.1016/s0277-9536(00)00234-3

Graddol, D. (2006). *English next (Vol. 62).* British Council.

Harding, L., & McNamara, T. (2018). Language assessment – The challenge of ELF. In J. Jenkins, W. Baker, & M. Dewe (Eds.), *The Routledge handbook of English as a lingua franca* (pp. 74–79). Routledge.

Harding, L. (2014). Communicative language testing: current issues and future research. *Language Assessment Quarterly, 11*(2), 186–197.

Harding, L. (2015). Adaptability and ELF communication: The next steps for communicative language testing? In. J. Mader & Z. Urkun (Eds.) *Language testing: Current trends and future needs.* IATEFL TEASIG.

Hull, M. (2022). Medical language, a lingua franca of a different sort. In M. G. Tweedie & R. C. Johnson (Eds), *Perspectives on Medical English as a Lingua Franca* (pp. 169–199). Cambridge Scholars Publishing.

Illés, É. (2020). *Understanding context in language use and teaching: An ELF perspective.* Routledge.

Jenkins, J., & Leung, C. (2013). English as a lingua franca. In. A. Kunnan (Ed.), *The companion to language assessment* (pp. 1607–1616). John Wiley & Sons.

Jenkins, J. (2015). Repositioning English and multilingualism in English as a lingua franca. *Englishes in Practice*, *2*(3), 49–85. https://doi.org/10.1515/eip-2015-0003

Jenkins, J. (2016). International tests of English: are they fit for purpose? In H-H. Liao (Ed.), *Critical reflections on foreign language education: Globalization and local interventions* (pp. 3–28). Shulin Publishing Co. Ltd.

Kahneman, D. (2011). *Thinking, fast and slow*. Penguin Books.

Kaur, J. (2011a). Intercultural communication in English as a lingua franca: Some sources of misunderstanding. *Intercultural Pragmatics*, *8*(1). https://doi.org/10.1515/IPRG.2011.004

Kaur, J. (2011b). Raising explicitness through self-repair in English as a lingua franca. *Journal of Pragmatics*, *43*(11), 2704–2715. https://doi.org/10.1016/j.pragma.2011.04.012

Keresztes, Cs. (2009). English as the lingua franca of medicine. In M. Silye (Ed.), *Porta Lingua* (pp. 53–64). SZOKOE.

Landmark, A. M. D., Svennevig, J., Gerwing, J., & Gulbrandsen, P. (2017). Patient involvement and language barriers: Problems of agreement or understanding. *Patient Education and Counseling 100*(1092–1102). https://doi.org/10.1016/j.pec.2016.12.006.

Marhsall, B., & Bakó, A. (2022). Methodological considerations in teaching intercultural communication to healthcare professionals. In. R. M. Nistor & C. Teglaş (Eds.), *Limbajele specializate în era digitală: abordări metodologice și practice*, (pp. 155–164). Cluj-Napoca, Románia: Presa Universitară Clujeană.

Martin, G. (2015). "Sorry can you speak it in English with me?" Managing routines in lingua franca doctor-patient consultations in a diabetes clinic. *Multilingua: Journal of Cross-Cultural and Interlanguage Communication*, *34*(1), 1–32. https://doi.org/10.1515/multi-2013-0053

Mauranen, A. (2018). Conceptualising ELF. In J. Jenkins, W. Baker, & M. Dewey (Eds.), *The Routledge handbook of English as a lingua franca*. Routledge.

Newbold, D. (2015). Chapter 12. Engaging with ELF in an entrance test for European university students. In Y. Bayyurt & S. Akcan (Eds.), *Current Perspectives on Pedagogy for English as a Lingua Franca* (pp. 205–222). Berlin, München, Boston: De Gruyter Mouton. https://doi.org/10.1515/9783110335965.205

Oliver, S. (2015). English as a lingua franca in public health care services: The Spanish challenge. *Journal Of Intercultural Communication*, 39. https://www.immi.se/intercultural/nr39/oliver.html

Pilling, J. (2011). *Medical communication*. Medicina.

Pitzl, M.-L. (2018). *Creativity in English as a lingua franca*. In *Creativity in English as a Lingua Franca*. De Gruyter Mouton.

Pitzl, M.-L. (2012). Creativity meets convention: idiom variation and remetaphorization in ELF. *Journal of English as a Lingua Franca*, 1(1), 27–55. https://doi.org/10.1515/jelf-2012-0003

Pölzl, U., & Seidlhofer, B. (2006). In and on their own terms: The "habitat factor" in English as a lingua franca interactions. *International Journal of the Sociology of Language*, 177, 151–176. https://doi.org/10.1515/IJSL.2006.009

Ritala, M. (2022). Perspectives on ELF from Finnish nurses. In M. G. Tweedie & R. C. Johnson, (Eds), *Perspectives on Medical English as a Lingua Franca*. Cambridge Scholars Publishing.

Roberts, C., Moss, B., Wass, V., Sarangi, S., & Jones, R. (2005). Misunderstandings: a qualitative study of primary care consultations in multilingual settings, and educational implications. *Medical education*, 39(5), 465–475.

Schouten, B. C. & Meeuwesen, L. (2006). Cultural differences in medical communication: a review of the literature. *Patient education and counseling*, 64(1–3), 21–34.

Schyve, P. M. (2007). Language differences as a barrier to quality and safety in health care: The Joint Commission perspective. *Journal of General Internal Medicine*, 22(Suppl 2), 360–361. https://doi.org/10.1007/s11606-007-0365-3

Seidlhofer, B. (2011). *Understanding English as a lingua franca – Oxford Applied Linguistics*. Oxford University Press.

Seidlhofer, B. (2017). English as a lingua franca and multilingualism. In J. Cenoz, D. Gorter, & S. May (Eds.), *Language Awareness and Multilingualism. Encyclopedia of Language and Education*. Springer, Cham. https://doi.org/10.1007/978-3-319-02240-6_22

Seidlhofer, B. (2018). Standard English and the dynamics of ELF variation. In J. Jenkins, W. Baker, & M. Dewey (Eds.), *The Routledge Handbook of English as a Lingua Franca (ELF)*. Routledge.

Seidlhofer, B., & Widdowson, H. G. (2017). Competence, capability and virtual language. *Lingue e Linguaggi*, 24, 23–36.

Sobane, K. C. (2015). Communication challenges experienced in Lesotho clinics where physicians limitedly speak both the community language and lingua franca. *Journal of Social Sciences*, 43(3), 277–284. https://doi.org/10.1080/09718923.2015.11893445

Svennevig, J., et al. (2019). Pre-empting understanding problems in L1/L2 conversations: Evidence of effectiveness from simulated emergency calls. *Applied Linguistics*, 40(2), 205–227. https://doi.org/10.1093/applin/amx021.

Takács, T.. & Czar, D. (2021). Enhancing professional communication skills in teaching English for specific purposes. *International Journal of Second and Foreign Language Education*, 1(2), 48–59. https://doi.org/10.33422/ijsfle.v1i2.123

Tarone, E. (2016). Learner language in ELF and SLA. In M-L. Pitzl & R. Osimk-Teasdale (Eds.), *English as a Lingua Franca: Perspectives and prospects* (pp. 217–225). Mouton de Gruyter.

Ting, S. S. P., & Cogo, A. (2022). Repetition and rephrasing in English as a lingua franca medical consultations in Hong Kong. In M. G. Tweedie & R. C. Johnson (Eds.), *Perspectives on Medical English as a Lingua Franca* (pp. 1–26). Cambridge Scholars Publishing.

Tweedie, M. G., & Johnson, R. C. (2019). Research directions in medical English as a lingua franca (MELF). *Language and Linguistics Compass*, 13(3). https://doi.org/10.1111/lnc3.12312

Tweedie, M. G., & Johnson, R. C. (2018). Listening instruction and patient safety: Exploring Medical English as a lingua franca (MELF) for nursing education. *Journal of Belonging, Identity, Language, and Diversity* 2(1), 75–100.

Tweedie, M. G., & Johnson, R. C. (2022). *Medical English as a Lingua Franca*. De Gruyter Mouton.

Van Servellen, G. (2009). *Communication skills for the health care professional: Concepts, practice, and evidence*. Jones & Bartlett Publishers.

Vettorel, P. (2019). Communication strategies and co-construction of meaning in ELF: Drawing on "Multilingual Resource Pools". *Journal of English as a Lingua Franca, 8,* 179–210.

Waxman, M. A., & Levitt, M. A. (2000). Are diagnostic testing and admission rateshigher in non-English-speaking versus English-speaking patients in the emergency department? *Annals of Emergency Medicine, 36*(5), 456–461. https://doi.org/10.1067/mem.2000.108315

Widdowson, H. G. (2003). *Defining issues in English language teaching.* Oxford University Press.

Widdowson, H. G. (2007). *Discourse analysis* (Vol. 133). Oxford University Press.

Zimonyi-Bakó, A. (2024). *Raising health science students' terminological awareness with the aim of improving the effectiveness of healthcare communication in ELF contexts.* (ELTE PPK Doctoral School of Education, PhD Program in Language Pedagogy). (doctoral thesis).

"Doctor, I have not seen for three months / Docteur, je ne vois rien depuis trois mois": A comparative lexicological analysis of words and expressions related to the body and its (dys)functions in the English and French common languages

Pascaline Faure[1]

ABSTRACT

While caregivers are asked to avoid using medical jargon when talking with their patients, a separate source of confusion may be found in the lay words and expressions that refer to the body and its (dys)functions. These words and expressions, which have been grouped together under the term *patientese* for practical reasons, can be especially confusing when used in allophone contexts. Over the last 20 years, there has been a huge increase in the number of foreign physicians, many of whom practice in a non-native language and subsequently may face serious language barriers. In this paper, I propose a lexicological analysis of lay words and expressions mentioned in lexicons and textbooks aimed at foreign healthcare professionals in English and in French. I show that in both languages, *patientese* exhibits similar features (e.g., persistence of archaisms) and often resorts to the same conceptual tropes (metaphor, analogy, metonymy, euphemism, clipping, and onomatopoeia) because they are entrenched in shared physical experience, culture and history. I conclude on the necessity of integrating *patientese* within education programs for teaching language for medical purposes so that instructors can in turn teach it to their students.

Keywords: English for medical purposes, French for medical purposes, lay language, conceptual tropes, archaisms, misconceptions

Prelude

Some time ago, one of my doctor friends told me how one day, a patient presented to her general practice complaining about "not having seen for three months". Feeling somewhat skeptical, the doctor advised her patient to consult an ophthalmologist, to which the patient, flustered, retorted that she was afraid she might have fallen pregnant.

---

[1] Sorbonne University, Medical English Department

1. Introduction – Linguistic barriers in medical communication

In the current era of globalization, caregivers have to deal with patients with various cultural, linguistic, and socio-economic backgrounds. Meanwhile, modern Western medicine encourages patient empowerment and advocates for shared decision making. Speaking the patient's language is of paramount importance in building an effective relationship (Ferguson & Candib, 2002). Yet, due to increasing demographic mobility and changing socioeconomic circumstances, growing numbers of caregivers face the challenge of communicating across linguistic barriers.

Language barriers can have several origins: caregivers using medical jargon, caregivers and patients having different native languages or different regional accents and expressions, caregivers and patients not sharing the same culture, or patients having poor health literacy or presenting with cognitive impairments.

Extensive research has been devoted to patients' health literacy and how the language used by physicians during medical consultations can have an impact on perception of disease and adherence to treatment (Ogden & Parkes, 2013; Tailor & Ogden, 2009; Tayler & Ogden, 2005; Williams & Ogden, 2004; Tanguy et al., 2011). These studies consistently confirm that patients have difficulty comprehending medical jargon and that the vocabulary gap is a substantial barrier to health information access for laypersons (Zeng-Treitler & Tse, 2006). Other more recent studies demonstrate that patients achieve better health outcomes when they can communicate with their caregivers in the same language (Piyush, 2020; Seale et al., 2022) and that patients with lower language proficiencies were more likely to experience more negative interactions with their physicians (Aelbrecht et al., 2019).

Yet, to my knowledge, hardly any research has focused on physicians' understanding of the lay words and expressions used by their patients, especially when the physicians are not native speakers of their patients' language. A seemingly obvious reason would be that "doctors are bilingual: they speak their native everyday language, but they are also fluent in medical language" (Ong et al., 1995, p. 910). However, even in the case of caregivers who are native speakers of their patients' language, Roger Shuy (1983, p. 190) warns that "the patient may also have a medical, social, or regional vocabulary that is at odds with that of the physician".

Over the last 20 years, there has been a huge increase[2] in the number of foreign physicians, many of whom practice in a language that they are not native speakers of. And if the technical language, often referred to as *medicalese*, is translingual, the language used by patients and which I will call *patientese* – a term borrowed from Dirckx (1983) – differs greatly. However, as language for medical purposes (LMP) instructors, we tend to focus on the technical language because it is usually the language that we find most difficult. Yet, the misunderstandings that non-native English- or French-speaking caregivers may be faced with rarely arise from a lack of knowledge of the technical language but rather that of the lay language that patients use during interview. In a study exploring perception and use of everyday language and medical terminology among international medical graduates in a medical ESP course in Australia, Maria Dahm (2011, p. 1) states:

> Language and communication skills are among the greatest challenges that non-native-English speaking international medical graduates (IMGs) face in English medical consultations. Especially when patients use unfamiliar everyday expressions or attach different meanings to medical terminology, the communicative burden on doctor-patient communication may be increased.

Not only may everyday language deficits among foreign caregivers place successful medical communication at risk, but they may also pose a threat to the patient's life, as was the case in 2006 in the UK where a patient died because his French GP only spoke "Shakespearean English" (Campbell, 2006).

2. Methods and materials

This paper focuses on *patientese* and more precisely, on confusing lay words and expressions that might hinder communication between a caregiver and their patient. The examples provided come from task-based course material used with French medical students. The analysis concludes with the necessity

---

[2] The number of foreign doctors joining the NHS in England has almost doubled since 2018. In the US, 1 in 5 physicians was born and educated abroad. In France, the number of foreign physicians has increased by 60% since 2007 and they now account for 10% of all practicing physicians.

of integrating *patientese* within LMP teacher education, such that instructors can in turn teach *patientese* to their students.

For analysis, content was used from popular textbooks and lexicons dealing with English and French for medical purposes and aimed at foreign healthcare professionals. While the examples in this paper are extracted from the English language and the French language, the "*medicalese* versus *patientese*" issue is to be found in all languages. Examples of culturally-bound or idiomatic language were selected based on their likelihood to challenge medical communication. The examples were checked to confirm their continued currency using the Corpus of Contemporary American English and The British National Corpus for the English language, and of Le Corpus d'Étude pour le Français Contemporain for the French language.

3. Archaisms

While medical research has made much progress over the centuries, some lay words and expressions commonly used today are directly traceable to the past. Many of these archaisms originate from the Hippocratic humoral theory, which explains why they are similar in English and in French. The humoral theory held that health depended on the balance between the body's four basic substances called "humors": yellow bile (from the gall-bladder), black bile (from the spleen), blood (from the liver) and phlegm (from the lungs). Several words related to temperament derive from this theory: *melancholic* (Fr. *mélancolique*), *choleric* (Fr. *colérique* and *coléreux*), *phlegmatic* (Fr. *flegmatique*), *bilious* (Fr. *bilieux*), *sanguine* (Fr. *sanguin*), etc. Hence, the French lay expressions *se faire de la bile* (literally to 'have bile') and *se faire du mauvais sang* (literally to 'have bad blood') express anguish, while the English version *full of bile* designates anger (Faure, 2015).

The words *rheumatism* in English and *rhumatisme* in French (from the Greek verb *rhein* 'flow') are no longer acknowledged in the technical language[3] but are still common in the lay language. The Greek verb *rhein* also gave rise to the French word *rhume*, which designates a common cold in the lay language. Also descending from a Greek verb (*apoplessein* 'strike down,

---

[3] *Rheumatoid arthritis* in English and *polyarthrite rhumatoïde* in French are still acknowledged as part of the professional medical terminology.

incapacitate'), *apoplexy* in English and *apoplexie* in French are synonyms for *cerebrovascular accident* in the lay language.

Another interesting example is the word *angina*, which derives from the Greek *ankhone* 'strangling' and which, in English, indicates the crushing pain one may feel in their chest (e.g., *angina pectoris*). Yet, in French[4], *angine* designates the inflammation of the tonsils, thus leading to ambiguity since the word also stands for *chest pain* in the French medical language (e.g., *angine de poitrine*). In Latin, *angina* is used to define 'any inflammation of the throat making swallowing difficult'; however, with the progress made in medicine, the medical language now tends to be more specific with terms like *laryngitis* (fr. *laryngite*), *pharyngitis* (fr. *pharyngite*), and *tonsillitis* (fr. *amygdalite*), depending on the site of inflammation.

As shown in the table below, infectious diseases illustrate the double "archaic versus modern" nomenclature. For example, the lay word for *variola* is *smallpox* in English and *petite vérole* in French. In English, the word *pox* emerged in Old English as *pocc* 'pustule, blister, ulcer' from the Germanic **puh(h)-* 'swell up' and can be found in the lay names of many other diseases that entail skin lesions (also called *pockmarks*) such as *monkeypox, black pox, whitepox, milkpox, canarypox,* etc. In French, the word *vérole* was used to designate all eruptive diseases that were characterized by pustules. As in English, in which *smallpox* was opposed to *great pox*, in French *petite vérole* was used to distinguish *variola* from *grande vérole* or *syphilis*. In English, *measles*, which descends from the Indo-European root **smē-* 'smear', is a synonym for *rubeola*, whereas *German measles*, which was so called because the disease was first described in 1740 by a German physician, Friedrich Hoffmann (1660-1742), designates *rubella*. In French, the translation of *rubeola* is *rougeole*, and that of *rubella* is *rubéole*, with both words descending from the Indo-European root **reudh-* 'red, ruddy' (both diseases cause a rash) and containing the diminutive suffix *-ole* (Eng. *-ola*) of Latin descent (Faure, 2012a, 2012b). These "Eng. *rubeola* / Fr. *rougeole*" and "Eng. *rubella* / Fr. *rubéole*" pairs may be extremely confusing in an English-French patient-doctor interview.

---

[4] Except in Quebec, where *angine* only stands for 'chest pain', under the influence of English.

Table 1. *Infectious diseases*

Infectious diseases	Eng. medical term	Eng. lay term	Fr. medical term	Fr. lay term
	varicella	chickenpox	la varicelle	
	variola	smallpox	la variole	la petite vérole
	rubeola	measles	la rougeole	
	rubella	German measles	la rubéole	
	mononucleosis	glandular fever	la mononucléose	la grande vérole
	syphilis		la syphilis	
	acute parotitis	mumps	les oreillons	
	yersinia pestis	the plague	la peste	

4. Greco-Latin versus National languages

Often, words that are used to designate body parts and diseases pertain to at least two different languages: Greco-Latin and the national language. This 'doublet' phenomenon can be found in most Indo-European languages but even more so in those which do not originate from Latin or Greek. For example, in many Indo-European languages, the abdomen has two words, the medical one and the lay one: e.g., in Russian, *брюшная полость* lit. 'abdominal cavity' and *живот*; in Danish, *abdomen* and *maven*; in Swedish, *abdomen* and *buken*; in German, *Abdomen* and *Bauch*; etc. (Faure, 2021).

This phenomenon is particularly ubiquitous in the designation of body parts: e.g., in English, *umbilicus* and *navel* (from the Old English *nafela* 'the hub of a wheel'); *uterus* and *womb* (from the Germanic **wambo* 'belly, uterus'); *caecum* (from the Latin 'blind' because this part of the intestine ends in a cul-de-sac) and *blind gut*; *trachea* (from the Greek *trakheia*, in *trakheia arteria* literally 'rough artery', which is so called because of the rings of cartilage that form the trachea) and *windpipe*; *larynx* (from the Greek *laimos* 'throat') and *voice box*; *alveolus* (from the Indo-European root **aulo-* 'small cavity', which gave *alvus* in Latin 'belly, stomach' and *aulos* in Greek 'pipe, flute, hollow tube') and *air sac*; *blepharon* (from the Greek) and *eyelid*; or *maxilla(e)* (from the Latin 'jaw') and *mandible* (from the Latin *mandere* 'chew') and respectively *upper jaw(s)* and *lower jaw* (Faure, 2022).

In modern French, very few Gaulish (the language spoken by the Gauls, a Celtic people that inhabited France before the Roman conquest) and Germanic words (imported by the Franks in northern France, the Burgundians in the Rhône valley and the Visigoths in the Aquitaine region) remain, and most of the lexicon is of Latin origin. The few examples of doublets all descend from Latin: e.g., *abdomen* versus its lay version, *ventre* (from the Latin *venter, ventris* 'belly, stomach, womb', which referred to a large aera starting below the chest), and *ombilic* versus its lay version, *nombril* (both from Latin *umbilicus*), the second stemming from the agglutination of the indefinite article *un* and the popular dissimilation of the [l] sound into the [r] sound.

5. Tropes

When describing their body and its (dys)functions, patients frequently use a variety of tropes. This section refers to the Cognitive Trope Theory by Charles Forceville (2019), itself derived from the ground-breaking Conceptual Metaphor Theory by George Lakoff and Mark Johnson (1980 [2003]).

According to George Lakoff and Mark Johnson (2003, pp. 3-14), "metaphor is pervasive in everyday life" and has "a basis in our physical and cultural experience". The fact that all human beings share the same kind of body and therefore experience the same physical sensations explains why the same metaphors are to be found in most languages. The metaphorizing process allows human beings to conceptualize and thus grasp the meaning of otherwise overly abstract notions such as love and evil. But it is also a way for humans to act on a certain reality. For instance, many languages resort to the conceptual metaphors HEALTH IS UP AND SICKNESS IS DOWN. These two physically-based metaphors (e.g., when someone is ill, they are usually bed-ridden) are the core of numerous expressions such as *feel up, rev up, lift up / pick up, be looking up* with the meaning of 'recover/feel better', and *back on one's feet* in English, and *se relever d'une maladie* (literally 'get back up from a disease') and *(se) remettre sur pieds* (literally 'put back on one's feet'), in French.

Tropes can be fairly simple (e.g., the metonym *cot death* for *sudden infant death syndrome*) or more elaborate (e.g., the metaphonymic blend *my baby is passing cold with her bowels*[5]). Yet, when the caregiver is not familiar with

---

[5] "My baby has diarrhea".

them, awkward situations may result, like the use of the verb *voir*[6] in French. Indeed, the expression *Je ne **vois** rien depuis trois mois* (literally 'I have not seen for three months') can mean that the patient has not had her period for three months. For practical reasons, trope-based words and expressions are presented in tables.

5.1. Metaphor

Analysis of the corpora shows that most metaphors encountered in lay language are related to the 'megametaphor' THE HUMAN BODY IS A MACHINE. This originates in 17th century thinking, in which the human body was seen as a mechanism. This is why for example, in English, the heart can be called an *engine* and the urinary system one's *waterworks*. One metaphor that derives from this megametaphor is OUR SYSTEMS ARE TUBES, which explains why so many of our organs are referred to as *tubes* and *pipes*, and why these tubes can leak, run, be blocked or be opened. THE HUMAN BODY IS A MACHINE has also generated the metaphor OUR ORGANS ARE CONTAINERS illustrated by the use of words like *box*, *bag* or *sack* in English, and *buffet*, *caisse* or *bidon* in French (Faure, 2017a, 2017b).

Another interesting metaphor is MENSTRUATION IS ANGER, which underlies idioms like *mad cow disease* or *granny grunts* in English, and *avoir ses ours* (literally 'have one's bears'), *faire du boudin*, a phrase meaning 'sulk', or *avoir ses ragnagnas*, an onomatopoeic term, in French.

Table 2. *Metaphor*

Metaphor			
THE BODY IS A MACHINE	the heart	the engine	le palpitant
		the ticker	le battant
	the urinary system	plumbing/waterworks	la tuyauterie
	defecate	open one's bowels/have one's bowels opened	

---

[6] The use of *voir* with this meaning is considered to be either obsolete or regional (https://www.cnrtl.fr/definition/voir).

OUR SYSTEMS ARE TUBES	the lungs	the tubes	
	the uterine tubes	the tubes	
	the trachea	the windpipe	le tuyau
	the larynx		le gosier
	the vagina	the birth canal	
	the urethra	the pipe	
	the (o)esophagus	the food pipe	
		the gullet	
	incontinence	urinary leakage	des fuites urinaires
	rhinitis	a runny/running nose	le nez qui coule
		a blocked nose	le nez bouché
OUR ORGANS ARE CONTAINERS	the larynx	the voice box	
	the lungs	the bellows	
	the abdomen	the belly	le bidon, la bedaine, le buffet
	the scrotum	the bag	le paquet
		the sac	
		the package	
	the alveolus	the air sac	
	the head	the brain box	le caisson
	the thorax	the chest	le coffre, la caisse
		the barrel	le baquet
MENSTRUATION IS ANGER		mad cow disease, granny grunts, have a visit from granny, have a visit from Aunt Frieda / Aunt Rose / Grandma George	avoir ses ours, faire du boudin, avoir ses ragnagnas

5.2. Analogy

If the essence of a metaphor is understanding one thing in terms of another, the essence of an analogy is to use one feature that belongs to a source domain (in the examples below, a non-human animal) and apply it to a target domain (in the examples below, a human-being) while both domains remain distinct. Analogies are deeply embedded in human history; accordingly, many use animals that have been in contact with human-beings since prehistoric times like the dog (fr. *chien*), the horse (fr. *cheval*), the ox (fr. *bœuf*), the wolf (fr. *loup*), the bear (fr. *ours*), the bird (fr. *oiseau*), or the mole (fr. *taupe*).

Table 3. Analogy

Analogy			
ANIMALS	sickness	as sick as a dog	être malade comme un chien
	pain		avoir un mal de chien
	fever		avoir une fièvre de cheval
	hunger	hungry as a hog, hungry as a bear	avoir une faim de loup
	poor appetite		avoir un appétit d'oiseau
	breathlessness		souffler comme un bœuf, souffler comme un phoque
	myopia	blind as a bat	être myope comme une taupe
	nudity		être nu comme un ver
	sweating		suer comme un bœuf
	redness		être rouge comme une écrevisse
	psychosis	mad as a box of frogs	

5.3. Metonymy

In cognitive linguistics, metonymy is defined as inferential and comprises one domain from which both target and source are extracted. Therefore, metonymy is a mapping within one functional domain in which source and target are linked by a pragmatic function. One example is the link between menstruation and the red color (the color of blood).

Many idioms derive from this metonymic link, and some of them form blends such as, in French, *avoir ses Anglais* (literally 'have one's English people'), or *les Anglais ont débarqué* (literally 'The English have landed'), a metonymic relationship with the red color of the uniform English soldiers wore during the Napoleonic wars.

Indeed, some of the metonymies can only be rightly deciphered if one is familiar with the culture they are embedded in, such as *Carrie* that relates to the famous horror movie adapted from Stephen King's novel, and *bloody Mary* that is associated with the tomato juice cocktail, itself named after

Mary Tudor. Other colors are the white color used in relation to leukorrhea and the green color associated with nausea.

There are also numerous metonymic idioms in which the sources are movement (e.g., digestion and death) and regularity (e.g., menstruation).

Table 4. *Metonymy*

Metonymy			
COLOR RED	menstruation	red flag, surfing the crimson tide/wave, bloody Mary, shark week, red badge of courage, red wedding, Carrie, red baron, checking into the Red Roof Inn, flashing the red flag, have the painters in, red-letter day, code red	avoir ses Anglais, les Anglais ont débarqué, avoir ses coquelicots, écraser des tomates, avoir la mer rouge, avoir sa semaine de ketchup, alerte rouge
COLOR WHITE	leukorrhea	the whites	
COLOR GREEN	nausea	green around the gills	les pertes blanches
REGULARITY	menstruation	periods, monthlies, time of the month, monthly bill, monthly visitor, moon time, have one's moons	ses règles, ses périodes, ses lunes
MOVEMENT	diarrhea	the runs, the trots Aztec two-step, quickstep, loose motions	avoir la courante
	vomiting	throw up, bring up, hull up, cough up (blood) turn one's stomach	retourner l'estomac, rendre, gerber
	defecation	have a bowel movement	
	dying	pass out, check out, pass away, slip away	partir, quitter, s'en aller

5.4. Euphemism

Another common trope is euphemism and more precisely MORE VAGUE IS MORE ACCEPTABLE. Indeed, when designating taboo issues, lack of preciseness usually follows a desire for the explicit term to remain inexplicit. For example, referring to the genitals can be embarrassing for many patients, and they may instead use various vague terms. To refer to the genital area, female patients may use expressions like *down below* or *down there* in English, and *en bas* 'down' in French. Likewise, male patients may designate their genitals with words such as *parts*, *privates*, *groin*, *crotch*, and *loins* in English, and *parties* and *entrejambe* (literally 'between the legs') in French.

Other sources of embarrassment will be the vagina otherwise referred to as *front passage* in English and *devant* 'front' in French; the anal area called *back passage* in English; and the buttocks named *bottom*, *behind*, *rear* or *backside* in English and *derrière* 'backside' in French.

Table 5. *Euphemism*

MORE VAGUE IS MORE ACCEPTABLE	the female genitals	down below/down there	en bas
	the male genitals	the parts the privates the groin the crotch the loins	les parties l'entrejambe
	the vagina	the front passage up inside	devant
	the anus	the back passage	
	the buttocks	the bottom the behind the rear the backside	(le) derrière
	the breasts	the top part bust bosom	la poitrine le buste
	urine	water	
	the amniotic liquid	waters	les eaux
	the intestines	the innards/inside	les entrailles
	menstruation	thingies the thing the other women's troubles lady business	ses trucs ses histoires ses affaires ses choses ses machins
	the menopause	the change	le retour d'âge
	gonorrh(o)ea and syphilis	a double event/a full house	
	gonorrh(o)ea	a dose	
	AIDS	the complete package	

5.5. Clipping

Another trope worth examining here is clipping, which is also commonly used in lay language to denote taboo issues. There are several types of clipping. For example, apocope such as *mis* for *miscarriage* in English, apheresis such as *bortie* for *abortion* in English, initialism such as *STD* in English and *MST* (*Maladie Sexuellement Transmissible* 'sexually transmissible disease') in French for *venereal diseases*, and more complex clipping such as *la totale* for *total hysterectomy* in French and *the big M* for *menopause* in English.

What can be inferred from the table below is that clipped words often denote embarrassing diseases (usually venereal, digestive or psychiatric). For example, mononucleosis, herpes, chlamydia, trichomoniasis, syphilis, gonorrhoea, gastroenteritis, schizophrenia and paranoia.

Table 6. *Clipping*

LESS OF FORM IS LESS OF CONTENT	miscarriage	a mis	une IVG
	abortion	bortie	
	menopause	the big M	
	total hysterectomy	total hys	la totale
	menstruation	AF	
	cancer	the big C	
	venereal disease	an STD	une MST
	chlamydia	chlam / the c(h)lam	
	herpes	herp	
	syphilis	syph	
	blennorrhagia	(the) clap[7]	blenno
	trichomoniasis	trich	
	the contraceptive pill	the pill	la pilule
	sanitary towels	STs	
	mononucleosis	mono	
	gastroenteritis		gastro
	paranoia		parano
	schizophrenia	schizo	schizo

---

[7] From Old French *clapoire*, originally 'rabbit burrow', a slang extension to *brothel*.

5.6. Onomatopoeia

One last trope identified in this paper's corpora is onomatopoeia, defined here as the naming of a body part or a physiological process by a vocal imitation of the sound actually or supposedly associated with it.

Table 7. *Onomatopoeia*

urinate	pee	faire pipi
vomiting	a visit from Uncle Ralph, puke	
	hiccup	
singultus	squat a grumpy	hoquet
defecate	willy	
genitalia		zizi, zézette

Whether in English or French, patients' language is quite full of imagery to try and express what is sometimes difficult to verbalize.

6. Misconceptions

Lay language is sometimes based on a lack of knowledge and understanding of human anatomy and physiology (Dirckx, 1983, p. 132). For instance, when English-speaking patients complain about *heartburn*, they do not refer to heart problems but to gastric acid reflux. Likewise, French-speaking patients may say they have *mal au cœur* (literally 'a heart pain'), *le cœur au bord des lèvres* (literally 'the heart on the verge of one's lips'), or *le cœur qui se soulève* (literally 'the heart that lifts up') when they feel nauseated. In French, the expression *avoir mal à* is often non-specific. It only gives information about the site of the pain: e.g., *avoir mal à la tête* 'have a headache'; *avoir mal au ventre* 'have a bellyache', which usually expresses gastro-intestinal problems rather than pain; *avoir mal au dos* 'have a backache'; *avoir mal aux reins* (literally 'have kidney pain'), which actually designates low back pain; etc. In English, *have stomach-ache* rarely concerns the stomach but rather the whole abdomen whereas in French *avoir mal à l'estomac* is more specific. Inversely, *avoir mal aux yeux* (*yeux* is the plural of sg. *œil* 'eye') is non-specific and may mean the patient is suffering from photophobia or blurred vision whereas *avoir mal à l'oeil* refers to the organ and almost necessarily implies pain. Likewise, *avoir mal aux oreilles* (pl. 'ears') means the patient is presenting with some hypersensitivity to noise whereas *avoir mal à l'oreille* (sg. 'ear') will probably guide the doctor's diagnosis towards otitis as it almost always conveys the idea of pain.

In French, *crise de foie* (literally 'liver crisis') is synonym for *indigestion*, and *tour de rein* (literally 'twist of the kidney') is synonym for *lumbago*. *Bouton de fièvre* (literally 'fever spot') has little to do with fever but more with the immune system as it is due to labial herpes. *Avoir la tête qui tourne* (literally 'have the head that turns') is synonym for *dizziness*. *Avoir un point de côté* designates a type of abdominal pain that usually occurs on exertion. *Water(s)* in English and *eau(x)* in French refer to the amniotic fluid: e.g., *my water(s) broke* in English and *j'ai perdu les eaux* (literally 'I have lost the waters') in French.

In French, the word *ulcère* 'ulcer' only refers to gastric ulcers whereas in English, it stands for all sorts of ulcerative processes. Likewise, in French, the word *hernie* 'hernia' only defines inguinal or abdominal hernia, that is to say the protrusion of an organ through the wall of the abdomen. Consequently, whenever they wish to refer to other types of hernia, French patients need to add an adjective: e.g., *discale* 'disc', *hiatale* 'hiatal', etc.

Although it means an inflammation of the appendix, in the French everyday language, the word *appendicite* 'appendicitis' is often incorrectly used to refer to the surgery itself. Whenever the lymphoid nodes on either side of the neck tend to swell due to a throat infection, French patients will often wrongly say they have *ganglions* 'nodes', meaning their glands are swollen. Whether in French or in English, to say *have a temperature* (Fr. *avoir de la temperature*) when expressing a rise in the body temperature is very common.

In French, many patients use the word *schizophrénie* 'schizophrenia' (from the Greek *skhizein* 'split' and *phren* 'mind') to refer to multiple personalities when the term actually designates a split personality. Still in the field of psychiatry, the word *manie* 'mania' (from the Greek *mania* 'madness') is often erroneously used by patients to refer to their "little ways" rather than to a state of abnormally elevated or irritable mood. Likewise, *hystérie* 'hysteria' (from the Greek *hystera* 'womb') is often used with the sense of 'wild, exalted' in lay French while it is being progressively abandoned for *somatization disorder* due its inaccuracy in medical French.

7. Integrating *patientese* in an LMP course

The textbooks aimed at foreign healthcare professionals in English and in French used as corpora for this analysis mention some of the most common lay terms and expressions. Based on my investigation, I recommend integrating a comprehensive and systematic study of *patientese* within an LMP course in a comparative and reflexive perspective. This would first require an updated and reliable conceptual trope-based lexicological analysis. Secondly, LMP students' need to be made aware of (1) what a trope is, (2) when it may be used (e.g., when referring to genitals), (3) why it may be used (e.g., to avoid embarrassment), (4) by whom it may be used (e.g., *zizi* is used by children), (5) to what register it belongs (e.g., *gerber* is popular whereas *rendre* is formal),

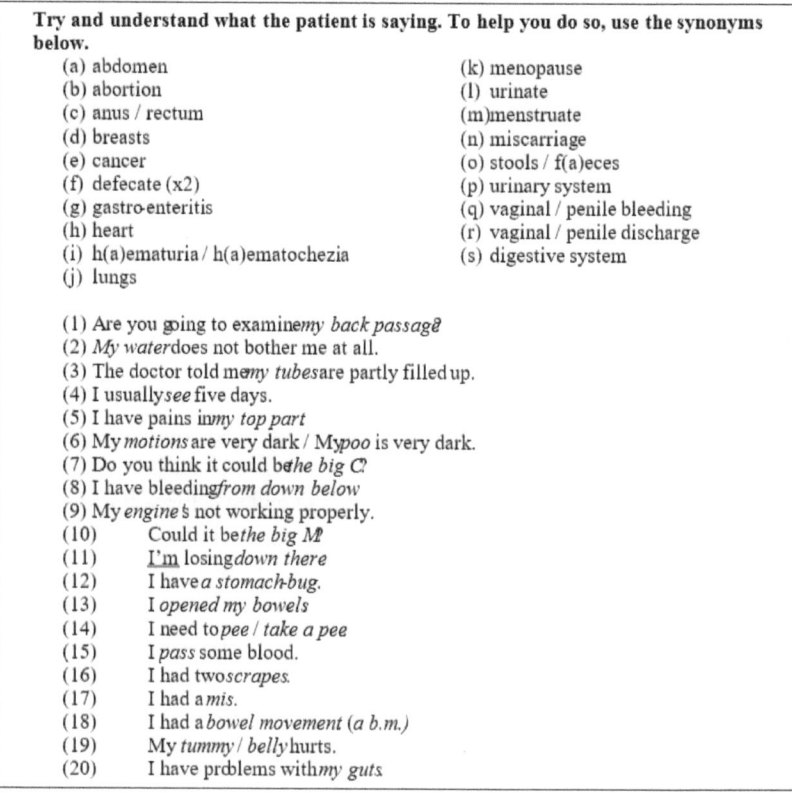

Figure 1. *Matching activity*

A COMPARATIVE LEXICOLOGICAL ANALYSIS

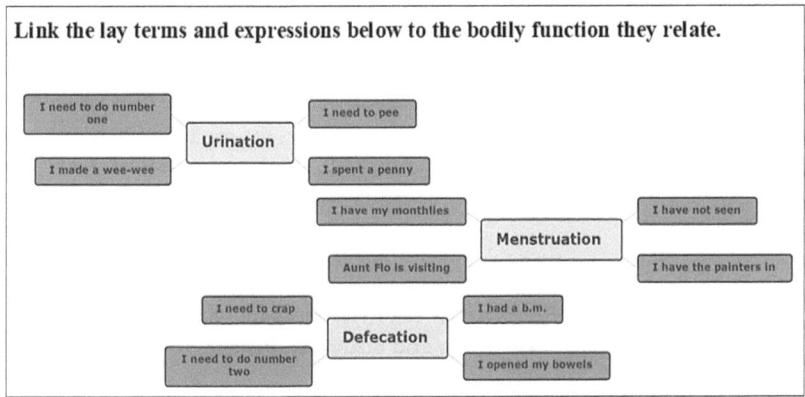

Figure 2. *Mind-mapping activity*

(6) to what region it may be peculiar (e.g., *"Je ne vois rien"* is known to be common in the Normandy region), and (7) whether the same trope may be found in their own language to refer to the same body-part or bodily function. Finally, and in accordance with the aforementioned points, course materials should be designed that are stimulating, meaningful, and effective in achieving the objective of raising students' awareness of this language and its potential issues. Below in Figure 1 and Figure 2 are two examples of task-based activities (matching and mind mapping) designed for French medical students.

8. Conclusion – Pedagogical implications

In the present study, I have examined common lay words and expressions that designate the body and its (dys)functions in English and French and that I have grouped together under the term *patientese* for practical reasons. I have shown that in English and in French, *patientese* exhibits similar features (e.g., persistence of archaisms) and often resorts to the same conceptual tropes. Yet, while English is of Germanic origin, French is a Latin language, which means that patients' mastery of basic medical terms, most of which are of Greco-Latin origin, will differ from one language to another. In addition, popular medical TV series have introduced medical jargon into everyday language, thus blurring its frontiers with the technical language. But, at a time when caregivers are asked to favor plain language when communicating with non-expert patients and at a time when more and more caregivers are non-native speakers of their patient's language, it is essential that *patientese* be part of the teaching and learning of languages for medical purposes.

References

Aelbrecht, K., Hanssens, L., Detollenaere, J., Willems, S., Deveugele, M., & Pype, P. (2019). Determinants of physician–patient communication: The role of language, education and ethnicity. *Patient Education and Counseling 102*(4),776–781.

Campbell, A. (2006). Patient died because GP only spoke French. *Metro*.

Dahm, M. (2011). Exploring perception and use of everyday language and medical terminology among international medical graduates in a medical ESP course in Australia. *English for Specific Purposes 30*(3), 186–197.

Dirckx, J. (1983). *The Language of Medicine, its evolution, structure and dynamics*. Praeger.

Faure, P. (2022). *Réussir sa consultation en anglais*. Medline.

Faure, P. (2021). *Les langues de la médecine: analyse comparative interlingue*. Peter Lang.

Faure, P. (2017a). Metaphors we suffer by. In J.-M. J.-M., & E. Navarro (Eds.), *Langues, diversité et stratégies interculturelles* (pp. 270–286). Michel Houdiard Éditeur.

Faure, P. (2017b). Euphemism as a core feature of patientese: A comparative study between English and French. In M. Gotti, & F. Salager-Meyer (Eds.),*The teaching of medical discourse in Higher Education. Language Learning in Higher Education* (Special Issue) (pp. 167–184). De Gruyter Mouton.

Faure, P. (2015). La langue du patient, de l'archaïsme à l'orthonyme: analyse comparative français/anglais. *Les Cahiers de Lexicologie 106*, 213–228.

Faure, P. (2012a). Maux et mots ou la dénomination des maladies: Étude comparative anglais/français. *Neologica 6*, 191–207.

Faure, P. (2012b). *L'anglais médical et le français médical: analyse linguistico-culturelle et modélisations didactiques*. Editions des Archives Contemporaines.

Ferguson, W., & Candib L. (2002). Culture, language, and the doctor-patient relationship. *Family Medicine 34*(5), 353–361.

Forceville, C. (2019). Developments in multimodal metaphor studies: A response to Górska, Coëgnarts, Porto & Romano, and Muelas-Gil. In I. Navarro I Ferrando (Ed.), *Current Approaches to Metaphor Analysis in Discourse Applications of Cognitive Linguistics* (pp. 367–378). De Gruyter Mouton.

Lakoff, G., & Johnson, M. (2003 [1980]). *Metaphors we live by*. The University of Chicago Press.

Ogden, J., & Parkes, K. (2013). "'A diabetic' versus 'a person with diabetes': The impact of language on beliefs about diabetes". *European Diabetes Nursing* 10(3), 80–85.

Ong, L., de Haes, H., Hoos, A., & Lammes, F. (1995). Doctor-patient communication: A review of the literature. *Social Science and Medicine* 40(7), 903–918.

Piyush, R., Kumari, A., & Arora, C. (2020). The value of communicating with patients in their first language. *Expert Review of Pharmacoeconomics & Outcomes Research 20*, 559–561.

Seale, E. et al. (2022). Patient–physician language concordance and quality and safety outcomes among frail home care recipients admitted to hospital in Ontario, Canada. *Canadian Medical Association Journal 194*(26), 899–908.

Shuy, R. (1983) Three types of interference to an effective exchange of information in the medical interview. In S. Fisher, & A. Todd (Eds.), *The social organization of doctor–patient communication* (pp. 189–202). Center for Applied Linguistics.

Tanguy, L. et al. (2011). Caractérisation des échanges entre patients et médecins: approche outillée d'un corpus de consultations médicales. *Corpus*. http://corpus.revues.org/2058

Tailor, A., & Ogden, J. (2009). Avoiding the term "obesity": An experimental study of the impact of doctors' language on patients' beliefs. *Patient Education and Counseling, 76*(2), 260–274.

Tayler, M., & Ogden, J. (2005). Doctors' use of euphemisms and their impact on patients' beliefs about health: an experimental study of heart failure. *Patient Education and Counseling 57*(3), 321–326.

Williams, N., & Ogden, J. (2004). The impact of matching the patient's vocabulary: a randomized control trial. *Family Practice 21*(6), 630–635.

Zeng-Treitler, Q., & Tse, T. (2006). Exploring and developing consumer health vocabularies. *Journal of the American Medical Informatics Association 13*(1), 24–29.

Bouché, P. (1994). *Les mots de la médecine*. Belin.

Sources

Fassier, T., & Talavera-Goy, S. (2008). *Le français des médecins.* Presses Universitaires de Grenoble.

Glendinning, E., & Holmström, B. (2004). *English in Medicine.* Cambridge University Press.

Glendinning, E., & Howard, R. (2007). *Professional English in use: Medicine.* Cambridge University Press.

McCullagh, M., & Wright, R (2008). *Good practice.* Cambridge University Press. 2008.

Mourlhon-Dallies, F. (2004). *Santé-médecine.com*. CLE International.

Parkinson, J. (1999 [1969]). *Manual of English for the overseas doctor.* Elsevier/Churchill Livingstone.

Quérin, S. (2007). *Dictionnaire des difficultés du français médical*. Maloine.

Sales, D. (2004). *Medical IELTS: A workbook for international doctors and PLAB candidates.* Radcliffe Publishing.

Culturally aware healthcare providers: training future physicians and midwives to work with trained interpreters

Tinka Reichmann[1] – Luciana Carvalho Fonseca[2] – Danjela Brückner[1] – Daisy Rotzoll[3] – Henrike Todorow[4] – Anne Tauscher[1] – Larissa Evers[3]

ABSTRACT
The *Teaming in Translation* initiative was developed in response to the growing need for improved training in both professional interpreting and healthcare delivery, particularly in the context of cross-cultural communication. The program, implemented at Leipzig University, aims to raise awareness among medical, midwifery, and interpreting students about the cultural barriers that can arise in healthcare settings. By integrating interprofessional education and simulation-based learning models, the program provides a unique, hands-on opportunity for students to engage in simulated patient-physician and patient-midwife encounters, specifically within the domain of maternal health. This immersive experience is designed to foster a deeper understanding of the challenges that arise in multicultural medical environments and improve communication skills in these high-stakes scenarios. This paper presents the results of an online questionnaire distributed to 82 students in total, measuring their overall satisfaction with the respective training modules. In addition, the paper includes an analysis of the text-based feedback collected from participants, offering valuable insights into the strengths and areas for improvement of the program. The course has been effective in developing interprofessional skills, raising awareness about the roles of every participant in the triadic communication and their interaction, as well as fostering awareness of cultural barriers among students.

Keywords: culturally competent care, cultural barriers in healthcare, healthcare interpreting, interprofessional training, public service interpreting

1. Introduction

The World Migration Report of 2022 highlights a significant increase in global migration over the past 50 years, with Germany emerging as the second

---

[1] Leipzig University, Institute of Applied Linguistics and Translatology, IALT
[2] University of São Paulo, Department of Modern Languages, DLM
[3] Leipzig University, Medical Faculty, Institute for Interprofessional Simulation in Medicine, IISIM
[4] Leipzig University, Medical Faculty, Institute for Midwifery Science and Interprofessional Perinatal Medicine Leipzig University, University Hospital Leipzig, Department of Women and Child Medicine, Clinic and Polyclinic for Obstetrics

most prominent destination, hosting nearly 16 million migrants (McAuliffe & Triandafyllidou, 2021). This influx positions Germany as the European country with the largest foreign-born population (DESTATIS 2022). Due to communication barriers, foreign-language speakers have more difficulties accessing healthcare than German speakers. This results in worse health outcomes for this group, including lower vaccination rates and higher maternal mortality (Mösko et al., 2016). Studies since the 1980s have emphasized the pivotal role of interpreters in mitigating health disparities, as flawed communication, in the absence of an interpreter, can lead to inadequate care and adverse events (Glenn et al., 2003; Hoang et al., 2009).

Against the backdrop of these challenges, the *Teaming in Translation* (*TeamTra*) program was initiated at Leipzig University, with the aim of enhancing the training of both interpreters and healthcare providers. The pilot project, which ran from 2022 to 2024, involved the creation of an interprofessional teaching program aimed at medical, midwifery and interpreting students. Students participated in simulated bilingual patient-physician and patient-midwife encounters; i.e., the patient and the healthcare professional did not speak the same language. Maternal health was deliberately focused upon due to its profound societal impact: Effective communication in this field not only influences individuals but society as a whole, given the crucial life events involved (Susam-Saraeva & Fonseca, 2021). Furthermore, a midwifery program had recently been established at Leipzig University, which made it possible to involve the three groups (medical, midwifery, and interpreting students) on an interprofessional level.

Translation and Interpreting (T&I) play a crucial role in integrating migrants into national healthcare systems. However, policy approaches worldwide vary, and assimilation is often prioritized over pluriculturalism (Dahinden & Bischoff, 2010), with less political will to create or support a language assistance system (Antonini et al., 2017). A central pillar of such a system would be a carefully planned and effective public service interpreting scheme. Although trained interpreters are available, a general reluctance to determine cost responsibilities results in infrequent hiring (Bahadır, 2010; Slapp, 2004), with the result that public service interpreting in Germany is primarily carried out by untrained interpreters (Kalina, 2001; Sauerwein, 2006). This does not come without significant challenges both for healthcare professionals and patients, since strained or flawed communication may lead to misunderstandings, incorrect diagnoses, poor compliance, increased complications, prolonged hospitalizations, and reduced patient satisfaction (Brisset et al., 2013; Krystallidou et al., 2018).

At the same time, article 1(3) of the German Basic Law expressly prohibits discrimination based on various factors, including language. The German Civil Code reinforces healthcare professionals' obligation to provide information and secure informed consent (German Civil Code, Sections 630c, 630e), safeguarding patient human rights: "The treating party is obliged to explain to the patient in comprehensible terms at the beginning of the treatment, and where necessary in the course of the treatment, in particular the diagnosis, the anticipated health development, the therapy and the measures to be taken in addition to the therapy and subsequent to it." (German Civil Code, Section 630c, Para. 2, Clause 1. Federal Republic of Germany 2021).

The apparent contradiction indicated above stems from a lack of specific regulations, as there is no legislation governing the use of interpreters in healthcare. Consequently, the healthcare interpreting landscape in Germany exhibits significant heterogeneity (Slapp, 2004). While some clinics have opted to establish their own interpreting services (UKE n.d.) and some local governments provide interpreters to a limited extent (Stadt Leipzig n.d.), these instances remain isolated. The majority of migrant healthcare service users lack access to trained interpreters, who are crucial to successful communication in healthcare settings, and therefore, in maintaining and improving health (Jaeger et al., 2019; Rosenberg et al., 2008). Furthermore, the role of healthcare interpreters extends beyond linguistic communication, encompassing significant contributions to understanding cultural nuances (Dahinden & Bischoff, 2010; ISO 13611 2014). Cultural differences in healthcare include communication styles, compliance, pain management, and obtaining informed consent, among others (Kassenärztliche Bundesvereinigung, 2015). Health literacy aspects, such as breaking down medical terms into understandable language, can be addressed by sensitized interpreters and healthcare providers together (Hsieh, 2013).

The intersections between T&I and maternal care are complex and multi-layered (Susam-Saraeva & Fonseca, 2021). Fair et al. (2020) postulate four areas of difficulty for migrant women navigating healthcare systems, namely: general orientation, addressing communication challenges, being treated with respect, and acknowledging broader needs beyond pregnancy.

The authors conclude that "professional interpreters should be provided at each appointment/care encounter to enable [healthcare providers] to listen to women and build a friendly, trusting relationship with women." (Fair et al., 2020: s.p.). In this complex context, *TeamTra* strives to bridge a crucial gap in upholding the healthcare rights of the non-German speaking population by raising awareness of language and cultural barriers in healthcare and imparting the skills required to address them.

While previous publications have addressed earlier stages of the project (Reichmann et al., 2023; Reichmann et al., 2024a; Reichmann et al., 2024b), this paper will report on selected results of the project, drawing on student feedback obtained through an online evaluation questionnaire.

2. TeamTra

2.1. Program Overview

TeamTra was integrated into simulation teaching at LernKlinik Leipzig (Rotzoll, 2016), the skills and simulation center at the Medical Faculty of Leipzig University. Interpreter training at Leipzig University is currently available for the following language combinations: Arabic-German, English-German, French-German, and Spanish-German. Of the four languages, Arabic and Spanish were selected as program languages to create a higher degree of immersion, challenge, and authenticity, as the German-speaking medical and midwifery students were less likely to speak these languages.

TeamTra focuses on two primary objectives. Firstly, the program aims to foster awareness of cultural and language barriers within the healthcare system. Secondly, it seeks to create a deeper understanding among and between participants (interpreting students, medical students, and midwifery students) regarding the intricacies of triadic collaboration. The program is designed to enhance trainee interpreters' knowledge of institutionalized healthcare settings and to concurrently improve future healthcare professionals' comprehension of interpreting practices.

In total, around 80-90 students participated over the course of three semesters (2022-2024). The interpreting students were mainly in the second year of their Master's in Conference Interpreting, while the midwifery students were in the second year of their Bachelor's in Midwifery. The medical students were in the sixth year of their Human Medicine Program, which is the

Praktisches Jahr (residency), which meant that they had clinical experience. As the maternal health ward at University of Leipzig Medical Center had a limited pool of medical students, also students from pediatrics and anesthesiology were recruited for the simulation trainings.

The program operates within Leipzig University's LernKlinik – a modern skills and simulation laboratory serving dentistry, pharmacy, medical, and midwifery students. With 23 specialized training rooms, it offers hands-on training covering medical procedures, device operation, and crucial communication skills. To heighten realism, the LernKlinik hires amateur and professional actors as simulated patients and devises scripts for scenario-based learning.

Each semester of the program featured a consistent framework, comprising seven 90minute sessions, including an introductory workshop and one simulation training repeated six times to account for student numbers, as each simulation session was limited to a maximum of 20 students. Students participated in up to three sessions, one per semester. In the following, a brief overview of these sessions shall be provided.

2.2. Introductory Workshop

The introductory workshop aimed to sensitize all participating students to the challenges faced by foreign-language speakers in German hospitals. Its aims were to familiarize medical and midwifery students with interpreting practices, introduce interpreting students to the medical professions, establish specific learning goals for each group (such as choosing the appropriate strategy for interpreting or optimizing communication within the team), and discuss positive outcomes and challenges.

2.3. Simulation

The simulation phase featured one of three scripted scenarios, with one scenario being taught per semester and repeated six times to account for student numbers. The individual 90-minute simulation sessions were split into three segments:

(a) Welcome: Students were briefed on the scenario, session objectives, and their individual learning goals. Students were then divided into role-playing participants and observers, and were equipped with tools for effective feedback. The students played their own respective roles (i.e., one trainee interpreter assumed the role of a trained interpreter, one midwifery student that of a trained midwife and one medical student that of a trained physician). The remaining students and instructors observed the scenario from an adjacent room, separated from the simulation room by one-way glass.

(b) Simulation: During this phase, the scripted scenarios were enacted. Each session featured one simulation with an amateur actor playing the role of a foreign-language speaking pregnant woman and one representative from each student group. Scenario one, for instance, involved a pregnant woman who believed her waters had broken, prompting a hospital visit. The interprofessional team then collaborated to diagnose, conduct tests (e.g., CTG 'cardiotocography'), and decide on potential admission to the labor and delivery room. Similar scripts guided scenarios two and three. Both the midwife and physician relied on the interpreter to communicate with the patient, emphasizing the interpreter's indispensable role.

(c) Feedback: Observations made by both the role-playing students and the observers were discussed during the subsequent feedback session. This comprehensive feedback loop was intended to enrich the learning experience, allowing for in-depth analysis and constructive insights from various perspectives.

3. Data and Methods

Students were recruited in the three courses of study (medical, midwifery and conference interpreting programs) and the simulated patients in the interpreting programs (Arabic or Spanish native speakers), who were hired by the LernKlinik as amateur actors. Each session concluded with participants contributing to an online survey that consisted of a quantitative and a qualitative part. The survey was conducted using EvaSys®, a survey and examination software[5] used by Leipzig University's Quality Management for evaluating its courses of study. The questions of the survey were elaborated by the TeamTra organizers and distributed to all participants (15% medical, 57% midwifery, 28% interpreting students) via a QR-code right after each simulation session. The quantitative part involved 10 questions by which

---

[5] https://evasys.de/en/

students were asked to rate the session on a six-point Likert scale ranging from "strongly agree" to "strongly disagree":

1. The learning objectives for the entire course group for working in a team are clear to me.
2. The subject-specific learning objectives for my profession are clear to me.
3. The materials used in the course (presentation, task sheets) were helpful for my learning process.
4. The simulation person(s) used in the course was/are helpful for my learning process.
5. How well did the course build on your previous knowledge?
6. Attending the course was helpful in developing my team communication skills.
7. Attending the course was helpful in developing my profession-specific technical skills.
8. I found the overall structure of the course useful.
9. In conclusion, how would you evaluate the course? (School grade 1 (best) to 6 (worst))
10. "Take Home Message": How would you rate the benefits of the joint course with the other professions for your future practical work?

The qualitative part involved 5 questions inviting students to share any additional insights through free-text responses (cf. annex for the 3 questionnaires). Responses to the online questionnaire were compiled by the project team and analyzed accordingly.

4. Results

In this chapter, a selection of answers is presented (cf. annex for a full list of answers). The responses (n = 82) to Question 9 of the quantitative part ("In conclusion, how would you evaluate the course?") indicate overall satisfaction with the course. Using a six-point scale from 1 (excellent) to 6 (fail), students evaluated the training with a mean value of $m = 2.0$ (SD = 0.95). Figure 1 illustrates the statistical distribution of grades given by students.

As regards the qualitative part of the survey, students shared insights gained from the course in response to the question: "State 1-3 insights that

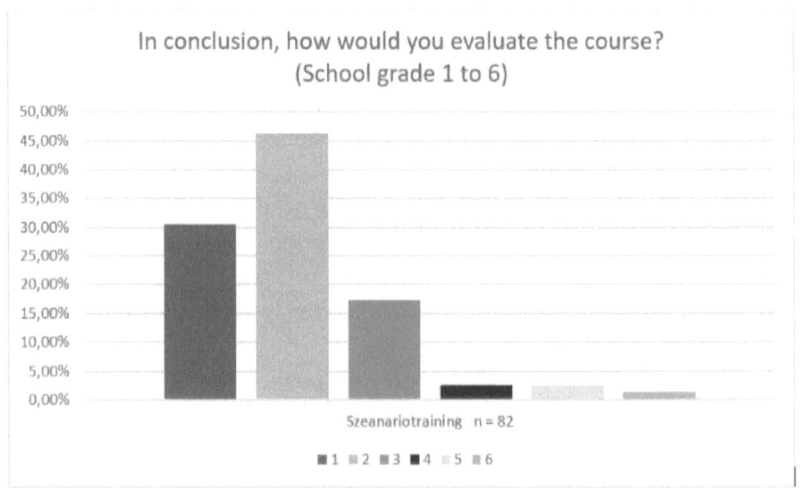

Figure 1. *Overall satisfaction with the TeamTra course*

you have gained from the session." With $n = 92$[6] free-text responses, the responses were subdivided by topic into six groups by two members of the project team, a midwife and an interpreting scholar. The groups were: (i) skills related to interpreting situations, (ii) skills related to interprofessionalism, (iii) empathy, (iv) skills and insights related to feedback, (v) skills related to health literacy, and (vi) others. Figure 2 presents the distribution of responses for each category.

Examples of student feedback included recognizing the importance of keeping the patient at the center of the conversation, the essential role of effective interprofessional consultation for optimal patient care, and the use of non-verbal communication to enhance empathy. The need for trained medical interpreters in clinics was also emphasized.

In response to the question "What did you particularly like about the 'TeamTra' project?" with $n = 65$ free-text responses, responses were subdivided by topic into three groups: (i) interprofessionalism, (ii) simulation training, and (iii) feedback. Figure 3 illustrates the distribution of responses for each category.

---

[6] This difference in number of responses collected is due to the fact that students could share 1-3 insights in response to this specific question.

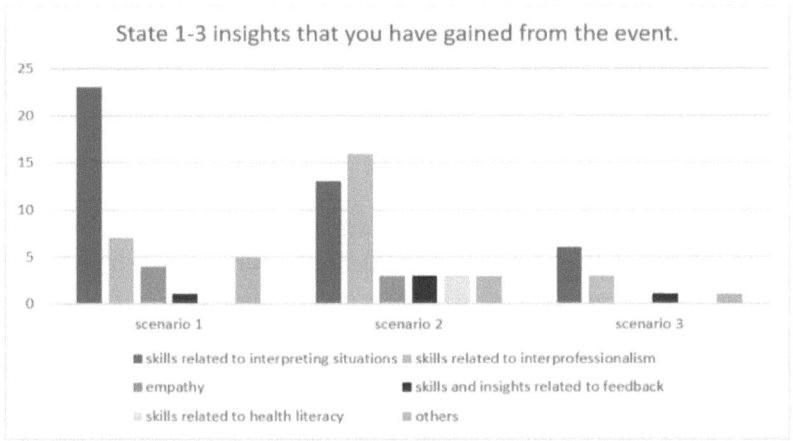

Figure 2. *Distribution of responses for each category*

Students expressed appreciation for the exchange between professions, providing a better understanding of others' perspectives, realistic simulation reflecting real-life situations, and constructive feedback rounds for reflection. This analysis indicates that the *TeamTra* program achieved its main goal of

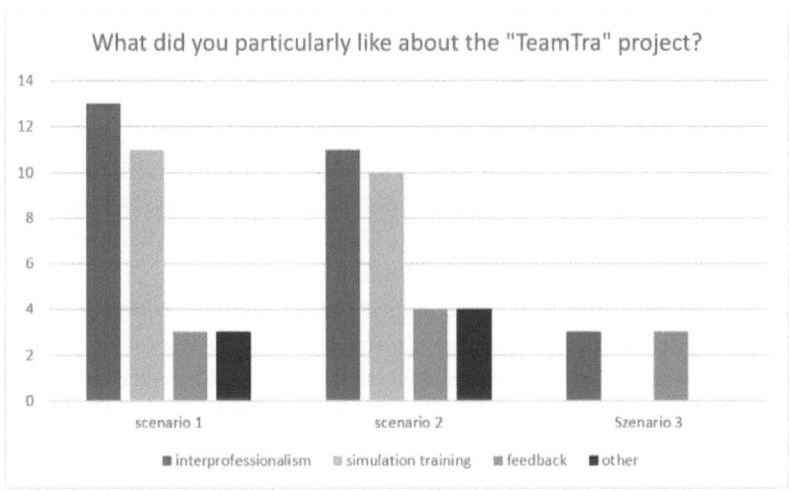

Figure 3. *Distribution of responses for each category*

creating awareness among students about the challenges and opportunities of medical interpreting, providing valuable insights for interprofessional collaboration and simulation training.

5. Discussion

The course evaluation, with an average rating of m = 2.0, reflects the students' overall satisfaction with the training. The breakdown of free-text responses into categories (Figure 2, Figure 3) offers insights into the specific learning outcomes achieved by students. Proficiency in interpreting situations, promoting interprofessional collaboration, nurturing empathy, mastering feedback-giving, and addressing health literacy differences all emerged as pivotal skills acknowledged by the participants. Notably, students reported that they acquired new skills related to interpreting situations, such as maintaining eye contact and directly engaging with patients. The articulated need for trained interpreters in real-world healthcare scenarios, as highlighted by some students, underscores the tangible relevance and impact of the program. In conclusion, the results affirm the efficacy of the chosen approach in fostering a culturally competent healthcare workforce.

Regarding limitations, the *TeamTra* program encountered several challenges, primarily stemming from its status as a pilot project. A fundamental hurdle involved the need for ongoing adjustments, relying heavily on observations and feedback from both instructors and students. The recruitment of volunteers, particularly among medical students, was another challenge. The maternal health ward at University of Leipzig Medical Center had a limited pool of medical students, which led to the project being extended to include students from pediatrics and anesthesiology. These students, lacking prior experience in maternal health settings, sometimes felt overwhelmed by the unique challenges presented in the simulation.

The findings mentioned above suggest that the course has been effective in developing interprofessional skills and fostering awareness of cultural barriers among students. The positive response from students has prompted the project team to integrate the training into the regular curriculum of the programs involved. Looking forward, the *TeamTra* program could serve as a practical model for other universities interested in offering similar training.

Funding: *TeamTra - Teaming in Translation: Gesundheitsberufe und Dolmetschen* Project received funding from the Stiftung Innovation in der Hochschullehre - Freiraum 2022. Luciana Carvalho Fonseca's participation was funded by grant #2023/02812-4, awarded by the São Paulo Research Foundation (FAPESP).

References

Antonini, R., Cirillo, L., Rossato, L., & Torresi, I. (2017). Introducing NPIT studies. In R. Antonini, L. Cirillo, L. Rossato, & I. Torresi (Eds.), *Non-professional Interpreting and Translation. State of the art and future of an emerging field of research* (pp. 1–26). John Benjamins.

Bahadır, Ş. (2010). *Dolmetschinszenierungen*. SAXA.

Brisset, C., Leanza, Y., & Laforest, K. (2013). Working with interpreters in health care: A systematic review and meta-ethnography of qualitative studies. *Patient Education and Counseling 91*(2), 131–140. https://doi.org/10.1016/j.pec.2012.11.008.

Dahinden, J., & Bischoff, A. (2010). Integration unter den Bedingungen gesellschaftlicher Vielfalt und Transnationalität – einige Reflexionen. In J. Dahinden & A. Bischoff (Eds.), *Dolmetschen, Vermitteln, Schlichten – Integration oder Diversität?* (pp. 7–34). Seismo.

DESTATIS (Statistisches Bundesamt). (2022). *Gut jede vierte Person in Deutschland hatte 2021 einen Migrationshintergrund. Pressemitteilung.* https://www.destatis.de/DE/Presse/Pressemitteilungen/2022/04/PD22_162_125.html.

Fair F., Raben L., Watson H., Vivilaki V., van den Muijsenbergh M., & Soltani H., ORAMMA team. (2020). Migrant women's experiences of pregnancy, childbirth and maternity care in European countries: A systematic review. *PLoS One 15*(2). https://doi.org/10.1371/journal.pone.0228378.

Federal Republic of Germany. (2024). *Basic Law (GG)*. https://www.gesetze-im-internet.de/englisch_gg/englisch_gg.html.

Federal Republic of Germany. (2021). *German Civil Code (BGB)* https://www.gesetze-im-internet.de/englisch_bgb/.

Glenn, F., Laws M. B., Mayo, S. J., Zuckerman, B., Abreu, M., Medina, L., & Hardt, E. J. (2003). Errors in medical interpretation and their potential clinical consequences in pediatric encounters. *Pediatrics, Official Journal of the American Academy of Pediatrics 111*(1), 6–14. https://doi.org/10.1542/peds.111.1.6.

Hsieh, E. (2013). Health literacy and patient empowerment: The role of medical interpreters in bilingual health communication. *Reducing health disparities: Communication intervention 6*, 35–58. https://elainehsiehphd.net/download/Hsieh2013-Dutta%20Chapter.pdf.

Hoang, H, Le, Q., & Kilpatrick, S. (2009). Having a baby in the new land: A qualitative exploration of the experiences of Asian migrants in rural Tasmania. *Rural and Remote Health 9*(1), 1–11. https://doi.org/10.22605/RRH1084.

International Organization for Standardization. (2014). *Interpreting. Guidelines for community interpreting* (ISO Standard No. 13611:2014). https://www.iso.org/standard/54082.html.

Jaeger, F. N., Pellaud, N., Laville, B., & Klauser, P. (2019). The migration-related language barrier and professional interpreter use in primary health care in Switzerland. *BMC Health Services Research 19*(1), 429. https://doi.org/10.1186/s12913-019-4164-4

Kalina, S. (2001). Zur Professionalisierung beim Dolmetschen. Vorschläge für Forschung und Lehre. In A. Kelletat (Ed.), *Dolmetschen. Beiträge aus Forschung, Lehre und Praxis* (pp. 51–64). Peter Lang.

Kassenärztliche Bundesvereinigung. (2015). *Kultursensibilität*. https://www.kbv.de/media/sp/4.20_Kultursensibilitaet_in_der_Patientenversorgung.pdf.

Krystallidou, D., Van De Walle, C., Deveugele, M., Dougali, E., Mertens, F., Truwant, A., Van Praet, E., & Pype, P. (2018). Training 'doctor-minded' interpreters and 'interpreter-minded' doctors. The benefits of collaborative practice in interpreter training. *Interpreting 20*(1), 126–144. https://doi.org/10.1075/intp.00005.kry.

McAuliffe, M., &. Triandafyllidou, A. (2021). *World Migration Report 2022*. International Organization for Migration. Geneva. https://publications.iom.int/system/files/pdf/wmr-2022_0.pdf.

Mösko, M., Demet, D., Penka, S., Vardar, A., Schulz, H., Koch, U., Heinz, A., & Kluge, U. (2016). Prevalence of mental disorders and health service utilization among individuals with Turkish migration backgrounds in Germany: A study protocol for an epidemiological investigation. *Open Journal of Psychiatry 6*(3), 237–252. http://dx.doi.org/10.4236/ojpsych.2016.63029.

Reichmann, T., Fonseca, L. C., & Brückner, D. (2023). TeamTra: Joint training of interpreting, medical and midwifery students at Leipzig University. In C. Valero Garcés, (Ed.), *Traducción e interpretación en los servicios públicos (TISP) en transición / Public Service Interpreting and Translation (PSIT) in Transition* (pp. 157–170). Editorial Universidad de Alcalá.

Reichmann, T, Fonseca, L. C., Brückner, D., Rotzoll, D., Todorow, H., & Tauscher, A. (2024a). Teaming in Translation: training interpreting, medical, and midwifery students in simulated birth settings. *FITISPos International Journal, 11*(2), 112–132. https://doi.org/10.37536/FITISPos-IJ.2024.11.2.365.

Reichmann, T, Fonseca, L. C., Brückner, D., Rotzoll, D., Todorow, H., Tauscher, A., & Evers, L. (2024b). Dolmetschen in der Geburtshilfe: Gesprächssteuerung, Fachsprache und interprofessionelle Zusammenarbeit. In M. Adams (Ed.), *Internationalisierung neu denken?! Fachkommunikation und Studienerfolg im Fokus* (pp. 213–239). Frank&Timme.

Rosenberg, E., Seller, R., & Leanza, Y. (2008), Through interpreters' eyes: Comparing roles of professional and family interpreters. *Patient Education and Counseling 70*(1), 87–93. DOI: 10.1016/j.pec.2007.09.015.

Rotzoll, D. (Ed.) (2016). *Das Skillslab ABC. Praktischer Einsatz von Simulatorentraining im Medizinstudium.* De Gruyter.

Sauerwein, F. S. (2006). *Dolmetschen bei polizeilichen Vernehmungen und grenzpolizeilichen Einreisebefragungen.* Peter Lang.

Slapp, A. M. (2004). *Community Interpreting in Deutschland. Gegenwärtige Situation und Perspektiven der Zukunft.* Meidenbauer.

Stadt Leipzig: *Vielfalt leben. Gesamtkonzept zur Integration von Migrantinnen und Migranten.* https://static.leipzig.de/fileadmin/mediendatenbank/leipzig-de/Stadt/02.1_Dez1_Allgemeine_Verwaltung/18_Ref_

Migration_und_Integration/Gesamtkonzept_zur_Integration/Broschure_VIELFALT_LEBEN.pdf.

Susam-Saraeva, Ş., & Fonseca, L. C. (2021). Translation in maternal and neonatal health. In. S. Susam-Saraeva, & E. Spišiaková (Eds.), *The Routledge Handbook of Translation and Health* (pp. 348–368). Routledge.

UKE (Universitätsklinikum Hamburg-Eppendorf): *Aufenthalt.* https://www.uke-io.de/de/ablauf-kosten/aufenthalt.html.

Communication as language use in consultations: methodological considerations

Sarah Bigi[1]

ABSTRACT

In this contribution, I present an approach to the analysis of medical consultations aimed at highlighting and describing some of the communication processes that might then be linked to proximal and intermediate outcomes, leading to clinical outcomes. The contribution takes into consideration aspects of language use in medical interactions, developing a description of medical consultations as one kind of activity type in which 'advice giving' is the focal discourse type. This approach enables the description of the various linguistic strategies adopted by participants as strategies aimed at co-constructing advice seeking and giving through a complementary distribution of the interactional work that shapes cooperative communication projects within the dialogue. The approach is exemplified through the analysis of one extract from a real-life consultation. In the conclusion, advantages and implications of the proposed approach are highlighted.

Keywords: activity type, healthcare communication, advice giving, asymmetry, decision making

1. Introduction

In a seminal paper published in 2013, Richard Street reflected methodologically on studies in healthcare communication, observing that usually, there is no direct impact of communication on clinical outcomes. More frequently it is possible to describe different pathways that lead indirectly from communication to outcomes (Street, 2013). For example, effective argumentation can improve patients' motivation to self-care; this, in turn, can improve their commitment to treatment and, ultimately, result in better quality of life (QoL), if not healing. In this sense, argumentation (a communication process) does not impact *directly* on QoL or healing, but does so in a mediated way; i.e., by impacting on a proximal outcome, such as 'motivation'. Street's (2013) arguments rest on the premise that it is possible to identify and describe different communication processes, in order to then connect them consecutively to proximal, intermediate and clinical outcomes. This premise calls for the collaboration of the medical sciences with the linguistic sciences, as

---

[1] Catholic University of the Sacred Heart in Milan, Department of Linguistic Sciences and Foreign Literatures

argued by Rossi and Sarangi (Rossi, 2021): it is only when we think of communication as a science of interpretation and meaning-making, that we can bring into the picture disciplines such as philosophy of language, linguistics, pragmatics, rhetoric, etc., and thus foster a thorough understanding of the various phenomena and factors at play in verbal interactions (Rossi, 2021). It is this broad understanding that allows the description of the pathways from communication to outcomes suggested by Street (2013). It also facilitates the planning of interventions and the updating of medical students' training so that the profession can face the challenges posed by new technologies and changing societies.

In this contribution, I present an approach to the analysis of medical consultations that offers theoretical and methodological tools for highlighting and describing some of the communication processes that might then be linked to proximal and intermediate outcomes. The contribution is organized as follows: I will first argue for the usefulness of considering consultations through the concept of *activity type*, a construct that enables the highlighting of typical features of dialogues in institutional settings. I will then characterize consultations as activity types in which 'advice giving' is the focal discourse type and in which professionals can play the role of knowledge 'translators', helping to adapt specialized knowledge to the specific circumstances of patients' lives. I will finally discuss the implications of this approach, both at a theoretical and analytical level.

2. Consultations as instances of activity types

The concept of *activity type* (AT) was first proposed by Levinson (1979) with the intention to describe and understand the ways in which structural features of an interactional event impact on the functions of the linguistic structures used within that same event. In his definition, ATs are:

> any culturally organized activity, whether or not that activity is coextensive with a period of speech or indeed whether any talk takes place in it at all […] I take the notion of activity type to refer to a fuzzy category whose focal members are goal-defined, socially constituted, bounded events with *constraints* on participants, setting, and so on, but above all on the kind of allowable contributions. Paradigm examples would be teaching, a job interview, a jural interrogation, a football game, a task in a workshop, a dinner party and so on. (Levinson 1979, p. 368)

ATs can be highly organized and planned (e.g., a religious rite), but also unstructured and improvised (e.g., greetings in the street). Moreover, language plays different roles in different ATs: while some can be realized *only* through verbal communication (e.g., a phone call), others need very few words to happen (e.g., a tennis match). There are three features in particular that Levinson (1979) considers typical of ATs: structure, orientation towards a goal, and inferential schemata.

The first two features are clearly connected, in the sense that the structure of an AT is determined and develops around the goal that the AT serves. The structure of an AT can be described and observed from two different but complementary perspectives. The first takes into account the development throughout the AT of topical trajectories that generate "thematic episodes", understood as "islands of partially shared understanding" (Linell, 1998). In other words, it is possible to observe the ways in which single topics are brought up for discussion and developed throughout the interaction by means of various interactional strategies (e.g., repetitions, interruptions, use of synonyms, etc.).[2] The second perspective considers the structure of ATs as a chain of communicative projects, aimed at solving local interactional problems, such as the need to agree on an assessment, to arrive at mutual understanding, to decide on a course of action etc.[3]. In this perspective, projects can be collective and cooperative, provided the asymmetry of roles presupposes a complementary distribution of the tasks foreseen by the AT; in other cases, the projects can derive from the specific functions of certain roles within the dialogue, so that they can be individual or even in competition one with the other. In some cases, it is possible to describe a hierarchy among different projects, where some are more prominent, with others dependent on them.

The fact that ATs are structured in certain ways and that 'interactional patterns' are visible within them are what leads Levinson (1979) to highlight the third point; i.e., the link between ATs and the inferential patterns that participants activate to interpret the functions of utterances. Indeed, the definition of an AT includes a description of *which* verbal contributions are admissible within its 'boundaries', not so much in the sense of the 'form' utterances may take, but in the sense of the functions that can be attributed to these utterances

---

[2] On this aspect, see also Roberts & Sarangi,2005; Duffin & Sarangi,2018.
[3] See also the notion of "coordination problem" in Clark, 1996; Linell, 1998.

(Levinson, 1979). In other words, any AT generates a set of 'inferential schemata' that derive from the structural properties of the activity in question, in the sense that the functions of utterances are inferred by participants based on their knowledge of the AT itself and based on the collocation of the utterance within the AT's structure. This particular aspect highlights something that can be of interest also for our discussion: indeed, it implies that utterances within ATs can play the most unexpected functions, not only thanks to their structure, but also due to the expectations that participants have regarding what may or may not happen within the boundaries of a certain AT. This observation allows reconnecting the macro-analytic level of analysis – which includes general inferential principles such as the Principle of Cooperation or Gricean maxims – to the micro-analytic level, where it is possible to account for inferences triggered by the specific features of a certain interactional activity (Sarangi, 2000; Linell & Thunqvist, 2003; Culpeper, Crawshaw & Harrison, 2008).

To make these considerations more applicable for analysis, Sarangi (2000) introduced the construct of *discourse type* (DT) to indicate the "forms of talk" (Sarangi, 2000, p. 2) used within a certain AT. So, while the AT is used to describe the context of the interaction (e.g., a medical encounter), the DT is used to account for the various ways in which dialogue develops in a specific context (e.g., the anamnesis in a consultation, but also the question-answer sequences within a counter-interrogation).

Based on this general description of ATs, consultations show all the features of those ATs used to manage an epistemic imbalance: typical cases are all interactions with professionals of any kind (lawyer, architect, doctor, but also plumber, tailor, cobbler, etc.), but the category also includes cases of interactions between peers, in which one is considered more knowledgeable regarding a certain topic and is thus bestowed the role of 'advice-giver'(Riccioni, Bongelli & Zuczkowski, 2014). Such ATs usually revolve around a specific topic of interest (in our case, health); often happen in dedicated places (it is not the same if health care professionals provide their advice at a birthday party); and often use 'official' channels for the provision of the advice (e.g., electronic records; more recently, channels used for telemedicine). In the case of interactions with professionals, these ATs also feature different social roles: the more knowledgeable persons regarding the topic at issue can perform certain actions with an institutional value (e.g., prescriptions) and are also legally liable for their acts and words.

If, as also argued elsewhere (Bigi, 2018), consultations can be considered as instances of ATs used to manage an epistemic imbalance, it is reasonable to consider *advice-giving* as the focal discourse type in these ATs[4]. The word *advice* is intended here in a broad sense, to indicate any of the 'acts' that medical professionals perform in response to a query by a patient or a caregiver and aimed at improving patients' wellbeing[5]. In this sense, the word will be used in this contribution to include not only recommendations, diagnosis, prescriptions or patient education and counseling sessions, but also any instance of expert opinion, which may include breaking bad news, assessing a lay diagnosis offered by patients, providing opinions regarding symptoms or parameters deriving from exams prescribed by others, etc.

Next to the epistemic imbalance, these interactions also feature an imbalance regarding roles, where a distinction should be made between *discourse roles* and *activity roles* (Halvorsen & Sarangi, 2015). Discourse roles are defined in relation to what is said; thus, it is possible to describe participants in terms of 'counselor', 'informer', 'advice giver', or 'addressee' or 'hearer'. Activity roles instead are defined in relation to the activity type, so, for example, 'doctor', 'patient', 'caregiver', 'nurse', etc. This is an important distinction when considering potential interactional difficulties that can be attributed to the epistemic imbalance between participants. Indeed, activity roles are usually predefined by social structures and conventions and are seldom explicitly contested. On the contrary, discourse roles can be acknowledged and explicitly agreed upon, for the interaction to run more smoothly. A nice example of this is the case of caregivers, who often find themselves without a clear legitimization during the consultation. The lack of clarity regarding their discourse role is often what causes them to 'construct' a role for themselves, which however is not always aligned with the goals of the consultation or the goals that the healthcare professional is trying to achieve (Bigi, 2021).

In consideration of the description of ATs provided above, this characterization of roles can also be useful in redefining the respective 'room for action' that participants appear to have during consultations. Indeed, if ATs can be conceptualized as a chain of communicative projects aimed at reaching local interactional goals, the difference in roles can be construed as

---

[4] See also: Pilgram, 2009; Walton, 1985.
[5] Consider also Dingwall & Pilnick, 2020.

an "asymmetrical division of labor in the pursuit of common goals" (Linell, 1998, p. 258). This kind of reading of interactions in the medical context opens the possibility for a different understanding also of those situations in which problems arise that can be clearly attributed to the asymmetry of roles. Perhaps the problems are not generated by the fact that there are asymmetrical roles, but by the 'incompetence' of the participants in managing their own role. This kind of incompetence should be understood as that kind of communicative incompetence arising when interactants are not aware of certain implicit conversational rules or conventions in a certain context, or when they do not share the same understanding of what words mean. Indeed, the asymmetry in the consultation can be so significant that it seems possible to construe consultations as special cases of 'intercultural interactions'.

2.1. Consultations as opportunities for knowledge translation and cultural brokerage

Regardless of the different disciplinary perspectives from which consultations are considered, they are interactions in which experts and non-experts meet to solve a problem.

From this point of view, and in consideration of the differences that characterize the roles of 'healthcare professional (of any kind)' and 'patient', it is possible to analyze dialogue in these interactions in the same way as dialogue is analyzed in interactions between participants who do not share the same language and/or the same cultural background. In the literature, there are studies in which this intuition is already present; for example, in McWhinney (1989):

> the physician tries to enter the patient's world, to see the illness through his or her eyes. In the traditional doctor-centered method, physicians try to bring the patient's illness into their world and to interpret the illness in terms of pathology. The transformed method will, of course, include this process, but it will no longer have the dominance it now enjoys. (McWhinney, 1989, p. 34)

A similar perspective is shared by those who have proposed to consider clinicians as bilinguals; i.e., competent in both everyday language and medical language (Bourhis, Roth & MacQueen, 1989; Ong et al., 1995; Williams & Ogden, 2004), or by those who have noticed the presence of different 'voices' in medical encounters (Mishler, 1984; Cordella, 2004). A more linguistic trend of studies also supports this notion by defining "special languages" as a variety of a language, described with reference to a certain knowledge domain or specialized activities, mostly used by a group within the wider community of speakers of a language to achieve the communicative needs of that specific domain (Cortelazzo, 1994; Pierini, 2014; Donadio, 2019). It is in particular the lexical level that distinguishes special languages from the 'standard' variety, making them difficult to understand for non-experts (Serianni, 2005; Gualdo & Telve, 2021).

What this interpretation of consultations implies is a different approach to their analysis. Indeed, the awareness of having little in common changes the dynamics of communication, as shown by studies in the field of intercultural pragmatics (Kecskes, 2023b). Interactions between individuals who are not equally competent in a language and do not share the same common ground[6] typically rely more on the language created *ad hoc* and less on prefabricated, conventional protocols or linguistic structures available in the language. There is also greater attention to recipient design, in the sense that speakers are more careful about how they say things, verifying often for the addressee's understanding and uptake. From an analytic point of view, this implies placing more attention on discourse than on the production of single utterances (Kecskes, 2014; Bigi & Rossi, 2023; Kecskes, 2023a), and on phenomena such as repetitions, reformulations, cohesion strategies, and the organization of information rather than singling out short turn sequences and assessing them as representatives of a communicative style or behavior.

This approach allows one to describe the various linguistic strategies adopted by participants as strategies aimed at co-constructing advice seeking and giving through a complementary distribution of the interactional work that shapes cooperative communication projects within dialogues in which common ground cannot be taken for granted. In this sense, it constitutes an expansion of the description of consultations in terms of activity types: indeed, the lack of common ground between participants is a structural

---

[6] Common ground can be further specified as *core common ground* and *emergent common ground*: the former "is composed of common sense, cultural sense, and formal sense, and mainly derives from the interlocutors' shared knowledge of prior experience", while the latter "is composed of shared sense and current sense, and mainly derives from the interlocutors' individual knowledge of prior and/or current experience that is pertinent to the current situation" (Kecskes & Zhang, 2009).

element in consultations, and it can impact heavily on the inferential schemata responsible for meaning interpretation. Observed in this perspective, consultations can be understood also as particularly appropriate moments in which professionals can realize the tasks of knowledge translation and 'cultural brokerage'. By 'knowledge translation' I refer to the adaptation of specialized knowledge to non-specialized kinds of texts and registers: this is, for example, what healthcare professionals do when they are explaining to patients 'how their illness works'. 'Cultural brokerage' means helping non-experts understand specialized knowledge or concepts in relation to their own lives: healthcare professionals can provide a general explanation in lay terms of why smoking is not good for anybody's health, and this would correspond to knowledge translation; but they can also provide examples of why it is not good for a particular patient, in relation to their particular profile and health conditions. This means providing criteria to assess the gravity of a certain behavior in the context of own's own life, interests and priorities. From an analytical point of view, the ways in which these communicative functions are realized through linguistic strategies can be revealing of how the specific activity type represented by consultations modifies cooperativeness and politeness in view of the institutional goals of the interaction (Caffi, 1999). In the next section, an example of analysis in the light of this perspective is described.

2.1.1. Using asymmetry to convey recommendation and advice

The following extract is taken from a follow-up encounter in a diabetes outpatient clinic[7]. The patient is a woman in her early 70s; in this encounter, she is meeting with the nurse for a routine check to assess how her diabetes is being managed and whether she needs to see the dietician or the diabetologist in the following months.

In the typical structure of these encounters (Bigi, 2022), there are two main parts: in the first part, nurses check patients' parameters; i.e., blood pressure, weight, results from any previous exams, any glycaemia values recorded in the

---

[7] The encounter is part of a larger collection of transcripts of video recordings of doctor-patient, nurse-patient and dietician-patient encounters, collected between 2012-2014 in a diabetes outpatient clinic in Northern Italy (Bigi, 2014). The extract discussed here is taken from encounter P_5-2.

diary or in the glucometer, and, if necessary they perform the 'foot check' to assess whether patients are developing a nerve condition common in diabetes called neuropathy; the second part of the encounter is usually devoted to scheduling the next encounters and planning the necessary routine exams.

The extract presented and discussed is taken from the first part of the encounter, when the nurse suggests that the patient be more careful in measuring and recording her measurements[8]:

> 1 N: *you know what, madam? You have already told me that your measurements have not been so 2 good because of the situation with your husband*
> 3 P: *yes yes*
> 4 N: *but to understand better, I would need that you tried to do it a bit more rationally, I mean*
> 5 P: *every day?*
> 6 N: *well, we can divide it, not every day but by couples. I mean, I should measure before the meal*
> 7 P: *yes*
> 8 N: *and two hours after your meal*
> [...]
> 9 N: *if we never measure glycemia values the way I told you we can never understand. It's what* 10 *I was telling you before. Maybe you start the day with a very good glycemia but then what*
> 11 *happens after your breakfast? Today we realized you were over 200*
> 12 P: *yes basically*
> 13 N: *so I need you to measure in a more rational way*
> 14 P. *ok*
> 15 N: *structured like I told you*

In this short sequence, the discourse roles are those of 'advice-giver' and 'advice-receiver', while the activity roles are the ones predefined by the activity type, so 'nurse' and 'patient'. The activity roles are conventionally defined as to their functions, but the ways in which these functions are realized are

---

[8] The original dialogue is in Italian. The translation proposed here aims at maintaining the meaning of the turns exchanged but is not an attempt at rendering the dialogical features of the exchange.

less fixed. In the case of this extract, the nurse needs to achieve an important goal; i.e., motivating the patient to perform her measurements in a more useful way. The whole encounter shows that the patient understands what 'glycemia' means and also that she is well aware of the fact that diabetes and eating habits are directly correlated. However, during the months previous to this encounter she did not measure her glycemia values. The nurse puts forward her recommendation in a mitigated way: in other words, she takes advantage of her activity role and of the patient's knowledge regarding how these encounters develop and what is usually discussed to put forward a recommendation in a way that saves the patient's 'face', at the same time creating a space for repeating instructions that might have been forgotten or not well understood previously. Strategies that allow mitigating the directive force of the recommendation in this example are, first, the fact that the nurse recalls the account offered by the patient to explain the lack of measurements, thus showing that she accepts it as legitimate and does not intend to reproach the patient; also, the use of the conditional mood of the verb in Italian ("I would need", *'mi servirebbe'*, "I should measure", *'dovrei farli'*), which conveys politeness and a friendlier, non-judgmental attitude; finally, the use of the first person plural or first person singular when referring to the things that actually only the patient should do: a strategy that expresses involvement and again, lack of judgment.

All of these strategies show a way of 'playing' the nurse role that allows the creation of a safe space for the patient in two different senses: on the one hand, this collaborative way of putting forward the recommendation presupposes some common ground built during previous consultations and fosters the patient's cooperation. On the other hand, the nurse creates for herself a 'dialogical space' to repeat instructions that might have been forgotten or not well understood, avoiding for the patient to feel that she is being patronized. In this repetition of instructions (especially, lines 9-11), she is performing at the same time the task of knowledge translation and of cultural brokerage (Section 2.1), because she is conveying technical information to the patient, but she does it by using a non-specialized language and by relating this information to the patient's life and condition. This also contributes to strengthening an existing common ground or creating a new one, in the event that instructions were not understood previously.

3. Discussion and conclusion

This contribution addresses the challenges posed by a generic understanding of 'communication' in relation to medical consultations. As has been highlighted by various scholars, this vagueness makes it difficult to relate specific communication processes to outcomes of interest in various medical settings. In this contribution, 'communication' is understood as 'language use' in a specific context of interaction and, as such, it is possible to analyze it by resorting to constructs developed for the analysis of dialogues, in particular the notion of *activity types*.

The concept of activity type is a way of describing language use in relation to (more or less) conventionalized social structures of interaction, generated to solve (more or less) routinized interactional problems (asking for advice, buying, selling, arguing, etc.). As such, it allows one to focus on the verbal part of communication (which includes implicit meaning, reconstructed through inferential schemata), considered in relation to one or more communicative goals, which can be achieved through a chain of local interactional projects.

In this perspective, consultations are understood as activity types generated by the need to solve health-related problems by resorting to expert opinion or advice. Thus, they are characterized by a significant epistemic imbalance, and advice giving can be considered as the focal discourse type. In relation to the epistemic imbalance, two considerations can be made: 1) participants acquire activity and discourse roles, which are not symmetrical and which serve the purpose of collaboratively reaching the intended communicative goal; 2) the participants with more specialized knowledge perform activities of knowledge translation and cultural brokerage every time they are able to convey specialized knowledge in ways that are understandable by non-experts and relatable to patients' everyday life and needs. As the example presented in Section 2.1.1 has shown, these activities can be achieved by various discursive strategies, that need to be considered within the overall structure of the single dialogue, considered as an instance of a certain kind of activity type.

There are various advantages of using this approach for the analysis of consultations. First, it orients the analyst to consider what happens dialogically in relation to the given institutional framework. This warrants more objectivity in the assessment of communicative behaviors, which can be considered more or less effective in relation to a communicative goal, rather than good or bad in a more subjective sense. A second advantage, connected to the first one, is that it allows one to reconsider the traditional paradigms of care mentioned in the literature, which can be described according to recurrent communicative behaviors of the participants in the interaction. At a more general level, the perspective proposed in this contribution may also stimulate reflections on what we mean when we refer to 'evidence-based research' in the domain of healthcare communication. Indeed, evidence in linguistic analysis is a very delicate topic, linguistic data being subjected to various levels of manipulation and interpretation before they can be analyzed (Sarangi, 2015). Are these 'intermediate' procedures on data being accounted for in healthcare communication studies that claim to be based on evidence?

Probably, studies on the quality and effects of communication in healthcare should be more explicit about what exactly they are measuring under the banner of 'communication' and in relation to which specific outcomes (Street, 2013), to allow for a clearer understanding of the factors at play in consultations, and for more effective training of healthcare professionals.

References

Bigi, S., & Rossi, M. G. (Eds.) (2023). *A pragmatic agenda for healthcare: Fostering inclusion and active participation through shared understanding* (Vol. 338). John Benjamins.

Bigi, S. (2022). *Le strutture interrogative nelle interazioni in contesto clinico.* Vita e Pensiero.

Bigi, S. (2021). Achieving shared understanding in chronic care interactions: The role of caregivers. *Working With Older People, 25*(3), 245–252.

Bigi, S. (2018). The role of argumentative practices within advice-seeking activity types. The case of the medical consultation. *Rivista italiana di Filosofia del Linguaggio, 12*(1), 42–52.

Bigi, S. (2014). Healthy reasoning: The role of effective argumentation for enhancing elderly patients' self-management abilities in chronic care. In G. Riva, P. Ajmone Marsan, & C. Grassi (Eds.), *Active Ageing and Healthy Living* (pp. 193–203). IOS Press.

Bourhis, R. Y., Roth, S., & MacQueen, G. (1989). Communication in the hospital setting: A survey of medical and everyday language use amongst patients, nurses and doctors. *Social Science & Medicine, 28*(4), 339–346.

Caffi, C. (1999). On mitigation. *Journal of Pragmatics, 31*(7), 881–909.

Clark, H. H. (1996). *Using Language*. Cambridge University Press.

Cordella, M. (2004). *The Dynamic Consultation*. John Benjamins Publishing.

Cortelazzo, M. (1994). *Lingue speciali. La dimensione verticale*. Unipress.

Culpeper, J., Crawshaw, R., & Harrison, J. (2008). 'Activity types' and 'discourse types': Mediating 'advice' in interactions between foreign language assistants and their supervisors in schools in France and England. *Multilingua, 27*, 297–324.

Deveugele, M. (2015). Communication training: Skills and beyond. *Patient Education and Counseling, 98*(10), 1287–1291.

Donadio, P. (2019). Special languages vs. languages for special purposes: What's in a name? *International Journal of Language Studies, 13*(4), 31–42.

Duffin, D., & Sarangi, S. (2017). Shared decision or decision shared? Interactional trajectories in Huntington's disease management clinics. *Communication & Medicine, 14*(3), 201–216.

Gualdo, R., & Telve, S. (2021). *Linguaggi specialistici dell'italiano*. Carocci.

Halvorsen, K., & Sarangi, S. (2015). Team decision-making in workplace meetings: The interplay of activity roles and discourse roles. *Journal of Pragmatics, 76*, 1–14.

Kecskés, I. (2014). *Intercultural pragmatics*. Oxford University Press.

Kecskés, I. (2023a). Face-to-face intercultural communication and mediated intercultural communication as related to health communication. In S. Bigi & M. G. Rossi (Eds.), *A Pragmatic agenda for healthcare: Fostering inclusion and active participation through shared understanding* (pp. 106–123). John Benjamins Publishing Company.

Kecskés, I. (2023b). *The Cambridge handbook of intercultural pragmatics*. Cambridge University Press.

Levinson, S. C. (1979). Activity types and language. *Linguistics, 17*, 365–399.

Linell, P. (1998). *Approaching dialogue: Talk, interaction and contexts in dialogical perspectives* (Vol. 3). John Benjamins.

Linell, P., & Thunqvist, D. P. (2003). Moving in and out of framings: Activity contexts in talks with young unemployed people within a training project. *Journal of Pragmatics*, *35*(3), 409–434.

McWhinney, I. (1989). The need for a transformed clinical method. Communicating with medical patients. In M. Stewart & D. Roter (Eds.), *Communicating with medical patients* (pp. 25–40). Sage Publications.

Mishler, E. (1984). *The discourse of medicine: Dialectics of medical interviews*. Ablex.

Ong, L. M., De Haes, J. C., Hoos, A. M., & Lammes, F. B. (1995). Doctor-patient communication: a review of the literature. *Social Science & Medicine*, *40*(7), 903–918.

Pierini, F. (2014). Definition and main features of business English with a special regard to differences with the language of economics. *ESP across Cultures*, *11*, 109–119.

Pilgram, R. (2009). Argumentation in doctor-patient interaction: medical consultation as a pragma-dialectical communicative activity type. *Studies in Communication Sciences*, *9*(2), 153–169.

Riccioni, I., Bongelli, R., & Zuczkowski, A. (2014). Mitigation and epistemic positions in troubles talk: The giving advice activity in close interpersonal relationships. Some examples from Italian. *Language & Communication*, *39*, 51–72.

Roberts, C., & Sarangi, S. (2005). Theme-oriented discourseanalysis of medical encounters. *Medical Education*, *39*(6), 632–640.

Rossi, M. G. (2021). Communication skills, expertise and ethics in healthcare education and practice: Interview - Srikant Sarangi. *Rivista Italiana di Filosofia del Linguaggio*, *15*(1), 106–122.

Sarangi, S. (2015). Communication research ethics and some paradoxes in qualitative inquiry. *Journal of Applied Linguistics & Professional Practice*, *12*(1), 94–121.

Sarangi, S. (2000). Activity types, discourse types and interactional hybridity: the case of genetic counselling. In S. Sarangi & M. Coulthard (Eds.), *Discourse and social life* (pp. 1–27). Routledge.

Serianni, L. (2005). *Un treno di sintomi. I medici e le parole: percorsi linguistici nel passato e nel presente*. Garzanti.

Street, R. L. (2013). How clinician–patient communication contributes to health improvement: Modeling pathways from talk to outcome. *Patient Education and Counseling*, 92(3), 286–291.

Taylor, K. (2009). Paternalism, participation and partnership – the evolution of patient centeredness in the consultation. *Patient Education and Counseling*, 74(2), 150–155.

Walton, D. N. (1985). *Physician-patient decision-making: A study in medical ethics*. Greenwood Press.

Williams, N., & Ogden, J. (2004). The impact of matching the patient's vocabulary: A randomized control trial. *Family Practice*, 21(6), 630–635.

PART IV

Metaphors in healthcare

How mothers think about postpartum mood disorders: A metaphor analysis of Hungarian online forums

Petra Bialkó-Marol[1]

ABSTRACT
This research is aimed at exploring the subjective experiences of Hungarian mothers regarding postpartum mood disorders and their expressions through conceptual metaphors. To this aim, qualitative research was conducted using the Metaphor Identification Procedure (MIP), analyzing data from online forums operated on the Hoxa.hu platform. Conceptual metaphor theory served as a theoretical framework for analyzing and interpreting the metaphorical language used on the forums. The study identified two groups of personified symptoms associated with postpartum mood disorders. The mood disorder itself was personified through various source domains, and non-personified structural metaphors also emerged related to these disorders. The main conclusion is that conceptual metaphors linked to losing control and to the healing process hold particular significance in the context of postpartum mood disorders.

Keywords: conceptual metaphor, postpartum mood disorder, depression, metaphor analysis

1. Introduction

Postpartum mood disorders, ranging from postpartum blues and depression to postpartum psychosis, significantly impact maternal and infant well-being, influencing early mother-infant relationships and child development (Félegyházy & Adler, 2013; Járfás et al., 2015; Beck, 2020a). Despite affecting an estimated 13-20% of mothers (Goyal et al., 2009), these disorders are underdiagnosed due to challenges in diagnosis (Bågedahl-Strindlund & Börjesson, 1998; Beck, 2002, 2020a). Mothers' hesitation to disclose symptoms of postpartum mood disorders, fueled by perceived stigma (Edhborg et al., 2005), contributes to the issue. There are three particular "taboo topics" within women's health that are often referred to as the "three Ms": menstruation, maternity, and menopause (Grandey et al., 2020, as cited in Kapoor & McKinnon, 2021). Societal attitudes, especially those surrounding motherhood, further complicate matters by creating a conflict between the reality of

---

[1] Corvinus University of Budapest, Doctoral School of Sociology and Communication Science

these disorders and the idealized image of motherhood (Kinloch & Jaworska, 2020; Latalova et al., 2014; Scambler & Hopkin, 1986). This stigma leads to increased shame, further hindering disclosure and open communication.

Health, illness, and their associated emotions are frequently described using metaphors (Demjén & Semino, 2017), such as describing cancer as a battle (*'fighting cancer'*) or depression as a heavy burden (*'carrying the weight of depression'*). In the context of health, conceptual metaphors shape schemas, mental models, and lay theories about how illnesses or complex health situations affect individuals' lives (Palmer-Wackerly & Krieger, 2015; Sopory, 2005, as cited in Lazard et al., 2016). Healthcare professionals and researchers often use metaphors to help the public better understand unfamiliar concepts, while patients and their families rely on them to express their experiences with illness (Gibbs & Franks, 2002, as cited in Harrington, 2012). Moreover, patients perceive physicians who incorporate analogies and metaphors into their explanations of illnesses as having stronger communication skills (Casarett et al., 2010, as cited in Harrington, 2012). By way of illustration, cancer patients often use metaphors to share aspects of their illness experiences, helping to bridge communication gaps (Bowker, 1996; Domino, et al., 1992; Gibbs & Franks, 2002, as cited in Harrington, 2012). In the relationship between healthcare professionals and patients, mutually understood metaphors can provide a common ground for communicating about the clinical reality and they can aid professionals in recognizing the severity of an issue (Semino et al., 2017). As McMullen observes (1996, p. 251, as cited in Tay, 2017), therapists and clients frequently "struggle to find words" to express hard-to-describe sensations, emotions, psychological states, and self-perceptions. In such contexts, metaphors can help to articulate these complex experiences.

The identification of metaphors used by mothers experiencing postpartum mood disorders can offer valuable insights, supporting healthcare providers in developing appropriate treatment strategies (Beck, 2020a). Despite the significance of metaphors in healthcare, there is a lack of research examining how mothers in Hungary discuss postpartum mood disorders through conceptual metaphors. This research seeks to bridge this gap by exploring how mothers in Hungary communicate about postpartum mood disorders using conceptual metaphors on online peer-to-peer forums. The paper first explores metaphors associated with depression before detailing the data collection process and methodology. This is followed by the results and discussion, leading to the conclusion.

2. Depression metaphors

The concepts of health and illness are shaped primarily by social and cultural factors, and their meanings can be partially understood through the analysis of metaphorical language (Benczes & Burridge, 2018). The term "conceptual metaphor" was introduced by Lakoff and Johnson (1980) in *Metaphors We Live By*. They argued that metaphors are not merely rhetorical ornaments but essential elements of our thinking and understanding of the world. Metaphors are an effective tool for describing a complex phenomenon by comparing them to something more concrete (Kövecses & Benczes, 2016). In the literature, they are typically represented in small capitals, with the target domain being placed in front of the source domain, for instance, LOVE IS A JOURNEY (KÖVECSES & BENCZES, 2016). In this case, the more concrete, tangible source domain (JOURNEY) provides a structured and coherent conceptual framework that we use to comprehend the more abstract target domain (LOVE). The metaphorical linguistic expressions are the linguistic realizations of conceptual metaphors, usually marked in italics to distinguish them from conceptual metaphors (Kövecses, 2022). Metaphors, serving as a means of conveying emotions, are particularly relevant when discussing depression (Lyddon et al., 2001). Individuals might rely on metaphors to effectively communicate their experiences of depression, especially when lacking familiarity with medical terminology (Charteris-Black, 2012; Beck, 2020b). To reveal the struggle embedded in general depression, researchers have identified common metaphors, such as DEPRESSION IS DARKNESS, WEIGHT, DESCENT and CAPTOR (McMullen & Conway, 2002). Charteris-Black (2012) identified two containment metaphors, distinct from McMullen and Conway's CAPTOR metaphor, describing depression either as an external container confining individuals to a physical space or individuals as containers of negative emotions. Beck (2020a) found that medical terminology falls short in capturing the experiences of mothers with postpartum depression. In contrast, metaphors, as identified in her study, such as POSTPARTUM DEPRESSION IS A THIEF or ERUPTIVE VOLCANO, provide powerful communication tools for mothers to express their experiences authentically.

3. Data collection and analysis

Mothers facing isolation often seek support in online peer-to-peer forums. To explore how mothers talk and think about postpartum mood disorders for the purpose of this study, it was necessary to identify Hungarian forums where this topic was discussed. The Hoxa.hu website, specifically its forums, was chosen for this purpose. Hoxa.hu is an online platform aimed at women, offering not only published articles but also forums for its registered users. In these interactive forums, users can engage in discussions on a wide variety of topics, including, but not limited to sports, health, motherhood, and relationships.

The forum feature of this website is highly popular, with certain forums preserving over a decade of user activity with archives of up to 100,000 comments. Within the forum feature, it is possible to filter by topic. The corpus was identified using Hoxa.hu's search engine, which filtered forums relevant to this research. Keywords commonly used in medical terminology to discuss postpartum mood disorders, such as *baby blues*, *'szülés utáni/ posztnatális/posztpartum depresszió'* (postpartum/postnatal depression), and *'szülés utáni/posztpartum pszichózis'* (postpartum psychosis), were searched for. Additionally, terms that might be more commonly used among mothers, such as *'szülés utáni szorongás'* (postpartum anxiety) and *'szülés utáni rosszkedv'* (postpartum low mood), were also explored. Only two of these keywords yielded results: the term *baby blues* returned one forum, while *'szülés utáni depresszió'* (postpartum depression) led to nineteen forums listed by the search engine.[2] The focus of the research was not on quantitative analysis but on understanding the qualitative aspects of the examined phenomenon and uncovering the conceptual metaphors of postpartum mood disorders. However, it is important to note the number of comments, which contributed to the analysis by demonstrating the diversity of experiences shared across the forums. In total, the twenty forums included 1.110 comments, of varying length. Some were brief responses to other forum users, while longer comments were typically used by mothers to provide detailed accounts of their condition. It is also important to note that contributions in these forums are posted under pseudonyms chosen voluntarily by the users (other details, such as the commenter's age, are not displayed). This anonymity allows mothers

---

[2] The translations are provided by the author.

to share postpartum stories and issues which they might avoid discussing in offline settings due to fear of stigma. The forum comments analyzed in this study were posted between 2006 and 2022, with the analysis being conducted in 2023. For the analysis, a Microsoft Excel document was created in which the comments from the twenty forums were copied and organized by forum. The corpus contained a total of 51,146 words. To further protect the participants' identities, the pseudonyms of the users were not transferred to the document.

The study aimed to identify conceptual metaphors related to postpartum mood disorders. Since most conceptual metaphors are made explicit through metaphorical expressions, it is particularly important to define the requirements that must be fulfilled for a linguistic expression to be considered metaphorical (Kövecses & Benczes, 2016). To identify metaphorical expressions used by forum users, the Metaphor Identification Procedure (MIP) was applied (Pragglejaz Group, 2007). Following the MIP steps, each forum comment from the twenty forums was read for a comprehensive understanding. The sentences of the forum comments were then divided into lexical units, and their contextual meanings were established. Each unit's basic contemporary meaning in other contexts was assessed. The online version of *A Magyar Nyelv Értelmező Szótára (The Explanatory Dictionary of the Hungarian Language)* was used to determine the basic meaning of each lexical unit. If the contextual meaning could be understood through similarity to the basic meaning, the linguistic unit was labelled as metaphorical.

4. Results and discussion

Following identification of metaphorical linguistic expressions and conceptual metaphors in the analyzed forum comments, a grouping principle was established based on how conceptual metaphors relate to each other thematically. The conceptual metaphors found in the forum comments suggest that the state of postpartum mood disorder manifests in two main symptom groups: a) thoughts that are personified and b) feelings that are also personified. The postpartum mood disorder itself was also personified in various source domains. In addition to personification, non-personified structural metaphors concerning these mood disorders were also identified.

4.1. Negative thought is a torturer

The tendency toward anthropomorphism is rooted in human cognition (Epley et al., 2007). Personification is considered one of the most fundamental types of conceptual metaphors (Galac, 2022), and involves the mapping of a human source domain onto a non-human target domain (Dorst et al., 2011). The following sentences metaphorically depict the experiences of mothers struggling with negative, compulsive thoughts, and personify these thoughts as a torturer:

> (1) [...] *agresszív* kényszergondolatok is *gyötörnek* és rettegek attól h [...] véletlenül bántom a kisbabám. ('[...] *aggressive* intrusive thoughts *torment me*, and I'm afraid that [...] I might accidentally harm my baby.')

> (2) Amikor itt vagyok és *kínoz* valami gondolat, írj bátran privit. ('When I'm here and some thought is *torturing you*, feel free to write a private message.')

In (1), the mother personifies her aggressive thoughts, characterizing them as if they were individuals displaying confrontational behavior. In (2), the linguistic expression *torture* personifies the thoughts, suggesting that seeking support and communicating about the negative thoughts can provide relief from the tormenter. The mappings include the thought as the tormentor, the mother as the victim, and liberation through communication. The fear of losing control and accidentally harming the child vividly portrays the mother's desperation.

4.2. Negative thought is an uninvited guest

The negative thoughts appeared not only as torturers but also as uninvited guests in the forum comments, as displayed in examples (3) and (4).

> (3) Minden okom megvan a boldogságra és *jönnek* ezek a hülye gondolatok és nem tudom *megszüntetni* őket. ('I have every reason to be happy, and these stupid thoughts **come**, and I can't *get rid of* them.')

> (4) De a rossz gondolatok folyton itt *ólálkodnak* körülöttem. ('But the negative thoughts are constantly *lurking around* me.')

The metaphorical expressions *come, get rid of,* and *lurking around* illustrate the conceptual metaphor NEGATIVE THOUGHT IS AN UNINVITED GUEST. These negative thoughts are metaphorically depicted as intrusive visitors who arrive unexpectedly and resist departure. This metaphor highlights the intrusive and unwelcome nature of the thoughts, with the mother serving as the host, and her consciousness as the location of the visitation. In example (3), the mother conveys frustration and a perceived inability to rid herself of these thoughts, suggesting a struggle to reestablish control over her cognitive processes. The plural form of the negative thoughts, paired with the singular status of the mother, establishes an asymmetrical power dynamic.

4.3. Negative feeling is an uninvited guest

The source domain UNINVITED GUEST extends to the target domain NEGATIVE FEELING, as shown in example (5).

> (5) […] tini korom óta fennállnak ezek a hangulatváltozások, és szülés után megint *rám törtek*. ('[…] these mood swings have been present since my teenage years, and after giving birth, they *intruded upon me* again.')

The conceptual metaphor NEGATIVE FEELING IS AN UNINVITED GUEST conveys the notion that negative emotions represent an external force beyond the mother's control, as expressed in the metaphorical statement *intruded upon me*. The metaphor facilitates an explanation of individuals' perceptions wherein negative emotions manifest as dominant forces.

4.4. Negative feeling is a social superior

The conceptual domain of SOCIAL SUPERIOR is accessible to the target domain of NEGATIVE FEELING in the example (6).

> (6) […] a császármetszésnek van köze a depimhez. […] Emiatt szégyenérzet és harag *kerített hatalmába*, hogy nem tudta azt produkálni a testem amit kell. ('[…] the caesarean section is connected to my depression. […] Because of this, shame and anger *overpowered me*, as my body couldn't produce what it should have.')

In example (6), the negative emotions of the mother, shame and anger, appear as a socially superior that has gained control, surpassing the mother's ability to maintain emotional balance. The metaphorical linguistic expression *overpowered me* suggests that the negative feelings have taken over, dominating the mother's emotional state. The mother is depicted as highly dependent on this overarching social superior, illustrating a dependency relationship between the mother and her negative feelings; she is not an active participant but a passive one. The caesarean section, which may have influenced the speaker's feelings related to depression, acts as a catalyst for this metaphorical power dynamic. This metaphor is a specific case of the conceptual metaphor EMOTION IS A SOCIAL FORCE presented by Kövecses (2003).

4.5. Anxiety is a companion

Anxiety is one of the indicators of postpartum mood disorders, both in the case of baby blues and postpartum depression (Beck, 2002), as displayed in example (7).

> (7) Az én szorongásom is itt van, *hűséges* hozzám nagyon, bár napról napra jobb.
> ('My anxiety is also here, very *loyal* to me, although it gets better day by day.')

The metaphorical use of *loyal* suggests that anxiety is personified as a constant companion in the mother's life. The conceptual metaphor ANXIETY IS A COMPANION creates dissonance between the positive connotations of a companion and the negative associations of anxiety. This dissonance highlights the complex relationship with anxiety, formed through personification. The second part indicates the mother's progress in managing anxiety, reflecting a challenging coexistence rather than a simple resolution.

4.6. Postpartum mood disorder is a criminal

Mothers not only anthropomorphized negative thoughts and feelings during postpartum mood disorders but also extended personification to the very concept of postpartum mood disorders. The conceptual metaphor POSTPARTUM MOOD DISORDER IS A CRIMINAL is exemplified in the following instance (8).

> (8) [...] ha időben *el van kapva* a betegség akkor jó eséllyel nem tart hónapokig.
> ('[....] if the illness *is caught* early, it likely won't last for months.')

In this case, the mother uses the term *illness* to describe postpartum mood disorders. The metaphor POSTPARTUM MOOD DISORDER IS A CRIMINAL personifies the disorder as a threat, emphasizing its negative and potentially harmful nature. The term *is caught* implies an urgent need for intervention, drawing parallels between apprehending a criminal and identifying the disorder early to prevent further harm. Recognition and timely intervention are portrayed as critical for minimizing both the duration and impact of the disorder.

4.7 Postpartum mood disorder is a kidnapper

The target domain POSTPARTUM MOOD DISORDER can be interpreted along the source domain KIDNAPPER, as seen in the following examples (9, 10).

> (9) [...] engem is *elkapott* a baby blues, kezdek *kikeveredni belőle*, de jó lenne beszélgetni erről másokkal! ('I also *got caught by* the baby blues. I'm starting to *get out of it*, but it would be good to talk about it with others!')

> (10) Ez "egyszerűen" egy betegség, amely *elkapja* azt aki hajlamos rá. ('This is "simply" an illness that *catches* those who are prone to it.')

This metaphor draws on a kidnapping scenario, where individuals are forcibly caught against their will. It conveys the sudden onset of mood disorders and the subsequent loss of agency for new mothers. According to the metaphorical correspondences, the kidnapper is the postpartum mood disorder, and the captive individual is the new mother. In example (9), *get out of* implies liberation from the kidnapper's captivity, as if the mother must navigate her way out of a labyrinth. Example (10) uses *simply* ironically, acknowledging the complexity of mood disorders. The metaphor conveys that susceptibility increases the likelihood of mood disorders catching mothers, making susceptibility a characteristic sought by the metaphorical kidnapper. This conceptual metaphor parallels McMullen and Conway's (2002) metaphor DEPRESSION IS A CAPTOR.

4.8. Postpartum mood disorder is a war

War metaphors are deeply embedded in both Western and Eastern cultures, influencing the way we talk about health and illness (Atanasova & Koteyko, 2020). Examples (11, 12) illustrate how the conceptual frame of WAR manifests in the context of postpartum mood disorders.

> (11) [...] a depresszió egy BETEGSÉG! És aki ezzel *küzd*, az nem tudja reálisan szemlélni a dolgokat szerintem. ('[...] depression is an ILLNESS! And someone *fighting with* it, in my opinion, cannot view things realistically.')

(12) Szerintem a depresszió kezelését általában érdemes szakemberre bízni [...]. De a legjobb talán az lenne, ha mindenki megtalálná az erőt magában, hogy *legyőzze*. ('In my opinion, it's generally advisable to entrust the treatment of depression to a professional [...]. But perhaps the best would be if everyone could find the strength within themselves to *win over* it.')

The metaphorical expressions *fight with* and *win over* within examples (11) and (12) imply the conceptual metaphor of POSTPARTUM MOOD DISORDER IS A WAR. Within this metaphorical framework, the adversarial force represents postpartum mood disorder, particularly a subtype – depression. The defending entity is the new mother, wielding either her intrinsic strength or the assistance of a professional as her weaponry. The duration of the battle corresponds to the duration of the healing process. It is crucial to note that the process of healing is much more prominent in this conceptual metaphor than in the previously mentioned personifications. Mothers engage in the battle with the hope of a successful recovery, and the victory represents the attainment of a healthy state, marking the end of the postpartum mood disorder.

4.9. Postpartum mood disorder is a journey

The conceptual frame JOURNEY is associated with the spatial movement depicted by the SOURCE-PATH-GOAL image schema. This spatial movement is also evident in the context of postpartum mood disorders (13, 14).

(13) Én is *végigjártam* ezt az *utat!* Már az, hogy klaviatúrát ragadtál és írsz erről a problémádról egy *első lépés afelé*, hogy jobban érezd magad! ('I*'ve been through* this *journey* too! Just the fact that you grabbed the keyboard and write about your problem is a *first step toward* feeling better!')

(14) Nem segítséget kérek itt hanem olyan anyukákkal beszélgetni akik ugyanezen *keresztül mennek/mentek*. ('I'm not asking for help here but to talk to moms who *are going/have gone through* the same thing.')

In examples (13, 14), metaphors such as *have been through*, *journey*, *first step toward* and *going through* collectively imply the conceptual metaphor POSTPARTUM MOOD DISORDER IS A JOURNEY. These linguistic expressions convey that communication functions as a metaphorical vehicle, supporting the healing progress for mothers (travelers) navigating through similar experiences on this journey. The metaphorical journey represents the path toward recovery from postpartum mood disorders, emphasizing the role of communication as a crucial tool in this healing process.

4.10. Postpartum mood disorder is a container

The conceptual frame JOURNEY sometimes partly merges with the conceptual frame CONTAINER (15, 16).

> (15) [...] *ki fogsz jönni belőle*, de segítség kell! Férjednek, anyukádnak is szólj. ('[...] you will *come out of* it, but you need help! Talk to your husband and your mom.')

> (16) Olyan anyukákkal szeretnék beszélgetni, akik *nyakig benne vannak* ebben az állapotban vagy már *kigyógyultak belőle*. ('I would like to talk to moms who *are neck-deep in* this condition or have already *emerged out of* it.')

Metaphors such as *come out of*, *deeply immersed in*, and *emerged out of* indicate the conceptual metaphor POSTPARTUM MOOD DISORDER IS A CONTAINER. In this case, the container represents postpartum mood disorder, within which the mother is situated. Getting out of the container can be facilitated through communication about the condition. In this interpretation, communication can restore the lost sense of control for mothers. The aspect of healing is also evident in this context.

4.11. Postpartum mood disorder is an abyss

The VERTICAL image schema provides the basis for the structural POSTPARTUM MOOD DISORDER IS AN ABYSS conceptual metaphor (17).

> (17) [...] amikor ő megszületett, *beleestem* a szülés utáni depresszióba. ('[...] when he was born, I *fell into* postpartum depression.')

The metaphorical expression *fall into* implies the conceptual METAPHOR POSTPARTUM MOOD DISORDER IS AN ABYSS. This downward motion indicates a sudden and involuntary fall into a negative emotional state. It portrays the experience of postpartum mood disorders as a rapid and uncontrollable descent. This metaphorical representation emphasizes the unexpected nature of postpartum mood disorders. The abyss also functions as an external container, implying a sense of confinement and the perception of being trapped in the depths of postpartum mood disorders.

5. Conclusion

Figurative language, such as metaphors, can be crucial in healthcare practice when a healthcare professional, such as a nurse, needs to recognize during a conversation with a new mother that the issue in question is not merely exhaustion or low mood, but a more serious problem. Furthermore, once the problem has been recognized, addressing the patient's needs becomes essential. From the patient's perspective, two key needs arise when visiting a doctor: the need to understand their medical condition and the need to feel understood by their doctor. However, if the patient presents with a condition that is considered taboo, these needs may not be fulfilled (Ong et al., 1995, as cited in Kapoor & McKinnon, 2021). Therefore, it is essential to pay close attention to the metaphors mothers with postpartum mood disorders use.

Metaphors are often referred to as "the language of change," and in therapy, they can be seen as "signposts" that convey the direction in which an individual is developing (Muran & DiGiuseppe, 1990; Levitt et al., 2000). By way of illustration, Levitt et al. (2000) compared the use of 'burden' metaphors by clients in dyads with both positive and negative outcomes, discovering that only the former group showed a gradual shift from metaphors of 'being burdened' to those of 'unloading the burden' (Tay, 2017). Another example comes from Sarpavaara and Koski-Jännes (2013, as cited in Tay, 2017), who explored how clients used the metaphor of change as a journey. They found that those who viewed themselves as playing an active role in reaching the destination (e.g., *the direction is correct, but still there's a need to continue the journey, to keep going in the same direction*) were more likely to recover compared to those who did not (e.g., *why try to change something so hard. When the time comes, one sort of finds his own path*) (Tay, 2017, p. 373).

A further point worth mentioning is that metaphors can have a 'reinforcing' effect. For example, if the therapist uses the depressed individual's own metaphor and reframes it in a way that empowers the patient, it can provide them with a greater sense of control over their illness (Coll Florit et al., 2021). Loftus (2011, as cited in Demjén & Semino, 2017) discusses metaphors not just as a way of expressing what one's pain feels like, but also as a way of understanding and managing it. The integration of metaphors into health communication strategies can facilitate a better understanding of postpartum mood disorders and enhance the effectiveness of doctor-patient communication, allowing for a more nuanced understanding of women's health concerns (Beck,

2020a). According to Beck (2020a), the metaphors used by mothers struggling with postpartum depression can provide valuable insights for health visitors in developing appropriate treatment strategies tailored to patients' specific psychological and emotional needs. For example, the conceptual metaphor POSTPARTUM DEPRESSION IS AN ERUPTING VOLCANO may suggest to a health visitor that issues related to anger management need to be addressed. Beck (2020a) argued that incorporating such metaphors into traditional screening methods, such as postpartum depression screening scales, could provide a deeper understanding of the emotions experienced by women.

The presence of conceptual metaphors in this study, related to the loss of control and the healing process, holds particular significance in the context of postpartum mood disorders. The metaphor of losing control reflects the overwhelming feelings and perceived lack of agency that individuals may experience. In the example of the conceptual metaphor THE NEGATIVE FEELING IS AN UNINVITED GUEST, the negative feelings overwhelmed the new mother. Building on the idea that metaphors can be seen as 'signposts' and can have a 'reinforcing effect,' if later on, the mother expresses that she 'managed to *get rid of* the negative thoughts,' it could indicate the regaining of control and the progress of the treatment. This shift in metaphor not only signifies improvement but also demonstrates the therapeutic potential of reframing and reshaping these metaphors during the healing process. Staying with the same conceptual metaphor, if the mother's own metaphor is reshaped and used in such a way that 'it's up to her whether she *lets* these feelings *in*,' the mother may feel that she has regained control over her negative feelings.

Acknowledgments

I would like to express my sincere gratitude to my Supervisor, Dr. Réka Ágnes Benczes, for her invaluable guidance and support throughout this research.

References

Atanasova, D., & Koteyko, N. (2020). Fighting obesity, sustaining stigma: how can critical metaphor analysis help uncover subtle stigma in media discourse on obesity. In Zs. Demjén (Ed.), *Applying Linguistics in Illness and Healthcare Contexts* (pp. 74–98). Bloomsbury Academic.

Bågedahl-Strindlund, M., & Börjesson, K. M. (1998). Postnatal depression: a hidden illness. *Acta Psychiatrica Scandinavica, 98*(4), 272–275.

Beck, C. T. (2002). Revision of the postpartum depression predictors inventory. *Journal of Obstetric, Gynecologic, & Neonatal Nursing, 31*(4), 394–402.

Beck, C. T. (2020a). Mother–infant interaction during postpartum depression: a metaphor analysis. *Canadian Journal of Nursing Research, 52*(2), 108–116.

Beck, C. T. (2020b). Postpartum depression: A metaphorical analysis. *Journal of the American Psychiatric Nurses Association, 28*(5), 382–390.

Benczes, R., & Burridge, K. (2018). Speaking of disease and death. In K. Allan (Ed.), *Oxford Handbook of Taboo Words and Language* (pp. 61–76). Oxford University Press.

Charteris-Black, J. (2012). Shattering the bell jar: Metaphor, gender, and depression. *Metaphor and Symbol, 27*(3), 199–216.

Coll-Florit, M., Climent, S., Sanfilippo, M., & Hernández-Encuentra, E. (2021). Metaphors of depression. Studying first person accounts of life with depression published in blogs. *Metaphor and Symbol, 36*(1), 1–19.

Demjén, Zs., & Semino, E. (2017). Using metaphor in healthcare: Physical health. In E. Semino & Zs. Demjén (Eds.), *The Routledge handbook of metaphor and language* (pp. 385–399). Routledge.

Dorst, A. G., Mulder, G. & Steen, G. J. (2011). Recognition of personifications in fiction by non-expert readers. *Metaphor and the social world, 1*(2), 174–200.

Edhborg, M., Friberg, M., Lundh, W., & Widström, A. M. (2005). "Struggling with life": Narratives from women with signs of postpartum depression. *Scandinavian journal of public health, 33*(4), 261–267.

Epley, N., Waytz, A., & Cacioppo, J. T. (2007). On seeing human: a three-factor theory of anthropomorphism. *Psychological review, 114*(4), 864–886.

Félegyházy, Z., & Adler, M. (2013). Hangulati betegségek és azok kezelése a terhesség alatt és a szülés után – áttekintés. *Neuropsychopharmacologia Hungarica, 15*(1), 40–48.

Galac, Á. (2022). Megszemélyesítő konceptualizációk a látás, hallás és szaglás fogalmi tartományában. *Jelentés és Nyelvhasználat, 9*(1), 155–183.

Goyal, D., Gay, C., & Lee, K. (2009). Fragmented maternal sleep is more strongly correlated with depressive symptoms than infant temperament at three months postpartum. *Archives of women's mental health*, 12, 229–237.

Harrington, K. J. (2012). The use of metaphor in discourse about cancer: A review of the literature. *Clinical Journal of Oncology Nursing*, 16(4), 408–412.

Járfás, V., Lipienné Krémer, I., & Hoyer, M. (2015). A szülés körüli történések hatása a gyermekágy során kialakuló anyai hangulatváltozásokra. *Egészségfejlesztés*, 56(4), 10–18.

Kapoor, A., & McKinnon, M. (2021). The elephant in the room: tackling taboos in women's healthcare. *Journal of Science Communication*, 20(1), 1–10.

Kinloch, K., & Jaworska, S. (2020). Using a comparative corpus-assisted approach to study health and illness discourses across domains: The case of postnatal depression (PND) in lay, medical, and media texts. In Zs. Demjén (Ed.), *Applying Linguistics in Illness and Healthcare Contexts* (pp. 74–98). Bloomsbury Academic.

Kövecses, Z. (2003). *Metaphor and emotion: Language, culture, and body in human feeling*. Cambridge University Press.

Kövecses, Z. (2022). A NEMZET fogalma – másként. *Magyar Nyelvőr*, 146, 137–164.

Kövecses, Z., & Benczes, R. (2016). *Kognitív nyelvészet*. Akadémiai Kiadó.

Lakoff, G., & Johnson, M. (1980). *Metaphors We Live By*. University of Chicago Press.

Latalova, K., Kamaradova, D., & Prasko, J. (2014). Perspectives on perceived stigma and self-stigma in adult male patients with depression. *Neuropsychiatric disease and treatment*, 10, 1399.

Lazard, A. J., Bamgbade, B. A., Sontag, J. M., & Brown, C. (2016). Using visual metaphors in health messages: A strategy to increase effectiveness for mental illness communication. *Journal of Health Communication*, 21(12), 1–9.

Levitt, H., Korman, Y., & Angus, L. (2000). A metaphor analysis in treatments of depression: Metaphor as a marker of change. *Counselling Psychology Quarterly*, 13(1), 23–35.

Lyddon, W. J., Clay, A. L., & Sparks, C. L. (2001). Metaphor and change in counseling. *Journal of Counseling & Development, 79*(3), 269–274.

McMullen, L. M., & Conway, J. B. (2002). Conventional metaphors for depression. In S. R. Fussell (Ed.), *The verbal communication of emotions* (pp. 167–181). Lawrence Erlbaum.

Muran, J. C., & DiGiuseppe, R. A. (1990). Towards a cognitive formulation of metaphor use in psychotherapy. *Clinical Psychology Review, 10*(1), 69–85.

Pragglejaz Group (2007). MIP: A method for identifying metaphorically used words in discourse. *Metaphor and Symbol, 22*(1), 1–39.

Scambler, G., & Hopkins, A. (1986). Being epileptic: coming to terms with stigma. *Sociology of health & illness, 8*(1), 26–43.

Semino, E., Demjén, Zs., Demmen, J., Koller, V., Payne, S., Hardie, A., & Rayson, P. (2017). The online use of Violence and Journey metaphors by patients with cancer, as compared with health professionals: a mixed methods study. *BMJ supportive & palliative care, 7*(1), 60–66.

Tay, D. (2017). Using metaphor in healthcare: Mental health. In E. Semino & Zs. Demjén (Eds.), *The Routledge handbook of metaphor and language* (pp. 371–384). Routledge.

Just war? Variation in COVID-19 metaphors in Hungarian public communication

Lilla Petronella Szabó[1] – *Réka Benczes*[1] – *Utku Bozdağ*[2]

ABSTRACT
In communicating the outbreak of the COVID-19 pandemic and the rapid measures taken to contain the spread of the virus, government communication frequently featured military metaphors, thus depicting pandemic management as a military struggle between nations and the coronavirus. Research has since indicated that increased public understanding of the dangers and risks of the virus over time makes the use of military metaphors unnecessary. However, very little is known about whether or how public discourse about the virus – in particular the reliance on the WAR metaphor – changed over the course of the successive waves of the pandemic. In this context, we investigated the use-frequency of the WAR metaphor by one Hungarian news portal in three different periods during the pandemic. Our results confirm that the use of the WAR metaphor showed a significant decrease over time, with a concurrent rise of alternative metaphors (such as JOURNEY and EXPLOSION). The observed evolution towards a variety of metaphorical domains calls into question the generally accepted dominance of the WAR metaphor in pandemic discourse and highlights how metaphorical frames are constantly negotiated to fit a dynamically changing context.

Keywords: COVID-19 pandemic, WAR metaphor, metaphorical variation, Hungarian public discourse, health communication

1. Introduction

The prevalent conceptualization of the coronavirus pandemic in public discourse revolved around the WAR metaphor (Musolff, 2024.; Piredda, 2022), depicting pandemic management[3] as a military struggle pitting nations against coronavirus as the enemy (Musolff, 2022). Furthermore, by using militaristic metaphors to evoke the image of a "just war" on COVID-19,

---

[1] Corvinus University of Budapest, Department of Communication and Media Science
[2] Corvinus University of Budapest, Doctoral School of Sociology and Communication Science
[3] Measures against the pandemic included wearing a face mask in public, the isolation of infected or exposed people, and social distancing (Cowling, 2020).

governments were able to justify restrictive measures which intruded on people's lives and civil liberties (Gillis, 2020). Military language prevailed in numerous countries among politicians, medical professionals, the media, and the general public (Hanne, 2022; Olza et al., 2021). In fact, by the middle of March 2020, leading politicians made it clear in their speeches that we were "at war" with coronavirus (Musolff, 2024).

WAR metaphors are ubiquitous in public discourse in general (Flusberg et al., 2018) and in the discourse about illnesses, such as cancer and AIDS, in particular (Benczes & Burridge, 2018; Sontag, 1978; Semino et al., 2017). However, the use of the military metaphor in the pandemic discourse is shown to be a double-edged sword. Its major advantage is in drawing attention to the seriousness and the urgency of the situation (Flusberg et al., 2018; Musolff, 2022; Roberts & Bolognesi, 2024; Semino, 2021). At the same time, a potential downside of WAR metaphors is the backgrounding of other possibilities of handling the pandemic, such as adapting to the current situation (Semino, 2021). A further concern is that military terms could legitimize autocratic and disproportionate measures under the label of "crisis management" (Hanne, 2022; Semino, 2021; cf. Gillis, 2020).

Hungarian political communication was not exempt from the use of war-related expressions in the wake of the Covid-19 pandemic, as vaccinations were referred to as "arms," medical workers as "soldiers," and the handling of the pandemic as a "battle" (Szabó & Béni, 2021). For example, Prime Minister Viktor Orbán, who acted as the main commentator on the unfolding pandemic in the country (Bene & Boda, 2021; Merkovity et al., 2021) made frequent use of the WAR metaphor in his radio interviews (Szabó, 2020; Szabó & Szabó, 2022) and on social media as well (Molnár et al., 2020; Simon et al., 2022; Szabó & Farkas, 2022). Furthermore, the language of war was also adopted by the Hungarian news media (Szabó & Béni, 2021).[4,5]

The Hungarian results cited above concern the first and second waves of the pandemic (the spring and fall of 2020, respectively), i.e., when the number of active cases was high. Subsequently, the number of cases dropped, and

---

[4] Apart from the Hungarian media, WAR metaphors appeared in Italy, France, Germany, Spain, the United Kingdom and the United States of America as well (Piredda, 2022).

[5] Research shows that the pandemic even altered the frequency of domains through which they conceptualize LIFE itself. A nationally representative survey among Hungarian adults showed that a higher ratio of respondents interpreted LIFE AS A STRUGGLE/WAR

COVID-19 restrictions were finally lifted in March 2022. Research indicates that increased public understanding of the dangers and risks of the virus – which can be expected after an extended period of exposure to the pandemic – makes the continued use of military metaphors unnecessary (Roberts & Bolognesi, 2024). However, very little is known whether or how public discourse about the virus – in particular the reliance on the WAR metaphor – changed in the various waves of the pandemic. Thus, in the present paper we investigate how Hungarian news discourse metaphorically conceptualized the virus, its spread, and its management when infection rates were at the extremes; that is, when they were at their highest and lowest levels. Following Roberts and Bolognesi (2024), we expected a decrease in the reliance on the WAR metaphor in subsequent waves of the pandemic, with a concomitant increase in less combative, alternative conceptualizations that foreground management and adaptation, rather than combat.

In what follows, we discuss the cognitive linguistic interpretation of the WAR metaphor in public discourse in Section 2. Section 3 lays out the corpus and the methodology, while Section 4 presents and discusses the results. Section 5 presents concluding remarks.

2. Politics and military metaphors

In the field of cognitive linguistics, the literature supports the view that metaphors are not merely ornaments of language but reside in our conceptual system and aid us in making sense of the world (Lakoff & Johnson, 1980/2003; Kövecses, 2010). Thus, when we interpret more abstract concepts, such as a POLITICAL CAMPAIGN,[6] we frequently draw on more concrete concepts (Bougher, 2012), such as STRUGGLE, by means of the POLITICAL CAMPAIGN IS A STRUGGLE metaphor (Benczes et al., 2022). Conceptual metaphors can be manifested in language use and thus, we speak about "election victories" and candidates "fighting" for votes. The same abstract concept can be interpreted through various other concepts. Thus, a specific form of the STRUGGLE domain, namely

---

at the time of the coronavirus pandemic, in comparison with the results of a survey conducted prior to its outbreak (Benczes et al., 2024).

[6] In line with cognitive linguistic conventions, we use small capitals to mark conceptual content.

SPORT, can also be used to speak about campaigns; for example, candidates may also "compete" to get votes.

Metaphors thrive in the language of politics, as they enable political actors to present complex issues which would otherwise require expert knowledge (e.g., economic policies, foreign policy, etc.), in a manner that is accessible to laypeople (Lakoff, 2014; Mio, 1997; Musolff, 2016.; Charteris-Black, 2011.; Benczes & Szabó, 2020). Research has attested that metaphors do have an effect on the way recipients view a specific political issue. According to Ottati et al. (2014), the activation of metaphor via a communication cue in politics can bring about images and storylines which are associated with the political event or the entity that is discussed. It is the activated metaphor which influences opinions about the given event or entity. Metaphors are thus at the disposal of political actors when communicating about public issues to non-expert citizens (Bougher, 2012). This was tested by Roberts and Bolognesi (2024), who created hypothetical news articles each representing COVID-19 in an alternative way, either as a battle or a journey. The texts containing the alternative metaphors were read by participants (n = 140) in the United Kingdom. The results show that BATTLE elicited higher scores of negative effects as compared to JOURNEY. Moreover, the same study also reported that respondents proposed more restrictive suggestions to contain the virus after reading the text which included the BATTLE metaphor. However, Schnepf and Christmann (2022) found a limited effect of the WAR metaphor among US speakers, questioning overall to what degree military language is in fact effective in the case of COVID-19 policies.

3. Corpus and methodology

To gain insight into the conceptualization of the pandemic, 364 articles were collected from the news site index.hu (the most widely read source about COVID-19 in May 2020; NMHH, 2020) from three distinct phases of the crisis between 4 March 2020, which marks the first confirmed case in Hungary, and 7 March 2022, when restrictions related to the pandemic were lifted in the country. The search was performed for the keyword *koronavírus* ("coronavirus") in domestic news texts, which constituted the corpus of the analysis. The aim was to give an insight into the conceptualization of the coronavirus when infection rates were at the extremes; that is, when they were at their highest and lowest levels. Accordingly, based on data obtained from the World Health Organization (World Health Organization. "Hungary: WHO Coronavirus Disease (COVID-19) Dashboard. https://covid19.who.int/region/euro/country/hu) about the spread of the virus in Hungary, the periods selected were 1) the month of June 2020, when the lowest number of confirmed cases in a month occurred; 2) December 2021, when the highest ratio of the weekly decrease of confirmed cases was identified; and 3) January 2022, which marked the month when the highest number of confirmed cases were reported in the country. Variation was expected in the use of WAR metaphors between June 2020 and December 2021 (as the number of cases was low in those months) and in January 2022 due to the surge in the number of cases. To assess the significant relationship between metaphor type and period, we used a negative binominal regression test (NBR) and Fisher's Exact Test to support the findings. We conducted all analyses using the R programming language (v4.4.1; R Core Team, 2024) with the ggplot2 R (Wickham, 2016.) and the MASS R (Venables & Ripley, 2002) packages.

Metaphorical expressions were identified and analyzed by means of the discourse dynamics approach to metaphor (Cameron et al., 2009; Cameron et al., 2010). Following a thorough reading of the articles, those expressions which could not be interpreted in their literal sense in the context of the pandemic were selected. These expressions were then categorized according to metaphorical concept. By way of illustration, Example (1) shows the concept of WAR.

> (1) Még mindig nem sikerült visszaszorítani a koronavírus *offenzíváját*. [The *offensive* of the coronavirus has not been forced back yet.], December 2021[7,8]

In this case, it is clear that *offensive* is part of the military lexicon, as it refers to a large-scale attack. Since viruses cannot literally launch military campaigns, the use of *offensive* was labelled as an example of the WAR metaphor.

---

[7] Each translation and emphasis in the examples are our own.
[8] https://index.hu/belfold/2021/12/06/meg-mindig-a-covid-az-ur-emelkedo-viruskoncentracio-szennyviz-adatok/

4. Results and discussion

The identification procedure yielded multiple metaphorical conceptualizations in terms of both the management of the pandemic and the virus itself. However, due to limitations in space, the discussion is restricted here to domains that appeared in at least two out of the three observed time periods.

The virus itself was conceptualized via two main domains, namely ENEMY (Example 2), and PERSON (Example 3).

> (2) nem volt magyarországi *áldozata* a vírusnak [the virus did not have a *victim* in Hungary], June 2020[9]

> (3) megjelent a vírus, és akkor még nem gondoltuk volna, hogy *eljön* Európába, [the virus appeared, and we would not have thought at that time that it would *come* to Europe], June 2020[10]

As Example (2) shows, the virus was conceptualized as an ENEMY that claims victims, while in the case of personification (Example 3), we encounter a less violent frame in the sense that the virus merely "came" to Europe.

The conceptualization of the spread of coronavirus was also analyzed, and three main metaphors were identified: THE SPREAD OF CORONAVIRUS IS AN EXPLOSION (Example 4); THE SPREAD OF CORONAVIRUS IS A FLOOD (Example 5); and THE SPREAD OF CORONAVIRUS IS A MILITARY ATTACK (Example 6).

> (4) Jön az *omikron-robbanás*, kerülni kell a zárt helyeket [The *omicron-explosion* is coming, closed spaces should be avoided], January 2022[11]

> (5) *Elsodorta* a koronavírus Ácson a zeneiskolát [The coronavirus *swept* the music school in Ács], June 2020[12]

---

[9] https://index.hu/belfold/2020/06/29/koronavirus_magyarorszagon_adatok_0628/
[10] https://index.hu/belfold/2020/06/17/koronavirus_operativ_torzs_sajtotajekoztato_junius_17./
[11] https://index.hu/belfold/2022/01/19/jon-az-omikronrobbanas-kacskovics-negyedik-oltas-otodik-hullam/
[12] https://index.hu/belfold/2020/06/26/koronavirus_onkormanyzati_tamogatas_megvonasa_acs_ritmus_zeneiskola/

(6) Már itthon is egyszerre *támad* az influenza és a koronavírus [Influenza and coronavirus *attack* jointly in Hungary as well], January 2022[13]

The results suggest that different levels of potential agency are assigned to authorities tackling the pandemic: while there is a possibility to defend the population or launch a counterattack against COVID-19 when its spread is conceptualized as a MILITARY ATTACK (Example 6), virtually no measure can be taken against an EXPLOSION (Example 4) and FLOOD (Example 5).

Finally, two prominent conceptual metaphors emerged in connection with the management of the virus; namely, VIRUS MANAGEMENT IS WAR and VIRUS MANAGEMENT IS A JOURNEY. The linguistic manifestations of these domains are demonstrated by Examples (7) and (8), respectively.

(7) Nemzeti egység alakult a járvány elleni *küzdelemben* [A national unity was formed in the *battle* against the virus], June 2020[14]

(8) A járvány vége felé *haladunk* [We are *heading to* the end of the pandemic], June 2020[15]

The alternative representations of pandemic management shown in Example (7) and Example (8) reveal distinct approaches: while the concept of war implies a more violent attitude, the journey concept corresponds to tackling coronavirus in a more cooperative and peaceful way, as "we" together as a nation head to the end of the crisis.

In the next step, the aim was to explore whether shifts in the metaphorical representation of the virus and its management correlated with the time of publication of the news articles. First, a frequency table of different metaphorical domains by year (Table 1) and a plot (Figure 1) are presented to visualize the data and highlight the overall trend. Second, the results of our negative binominal regression test (NBR) are presented to show that there is a significant association between metaphor type and time period.

---

[13] https://index.hu/belfold/2022/01/03/koronavirus-omikron-varians-jarvany-labor-influenza-pcr-teszt-covid-19/
[14] https://index.hu/belfold/2020/06/19/kasler_miklos_muller_cecilia_sajtotajekoztato/
[15] https://index.hu/belfold/2020/06/08/koronavirus_operativ_torzs_sajtotajekoztato_junius_8./

Third, Fisher's Exact Test is used to support these findings. All analyses were executed using the R programming language (v4.4.1; R Core Team, 2024) together with the ggplot2 R package (Wickham, 2016.) and the MASS R package (Venables & Ripley, 2002).

The frequency plot illustrates the distribution of different metaphors used in news articles during the COVID-19 pandemic across three turbulent periods: 2020, 2021, and 2022. In 2020, the WAR metaphor was dominant with 50 occurrences, followed by the VICTIM metaphor with 14 occurrences. In 2021, while the WAR metaphor remained significant with 27 occurrences, the VICTIM metaphor increased sharply to 34 instances. By 2022, the frequency of the WAR metaphor decreased to 17, and the VICTIM metaphor saw a decline to 7.

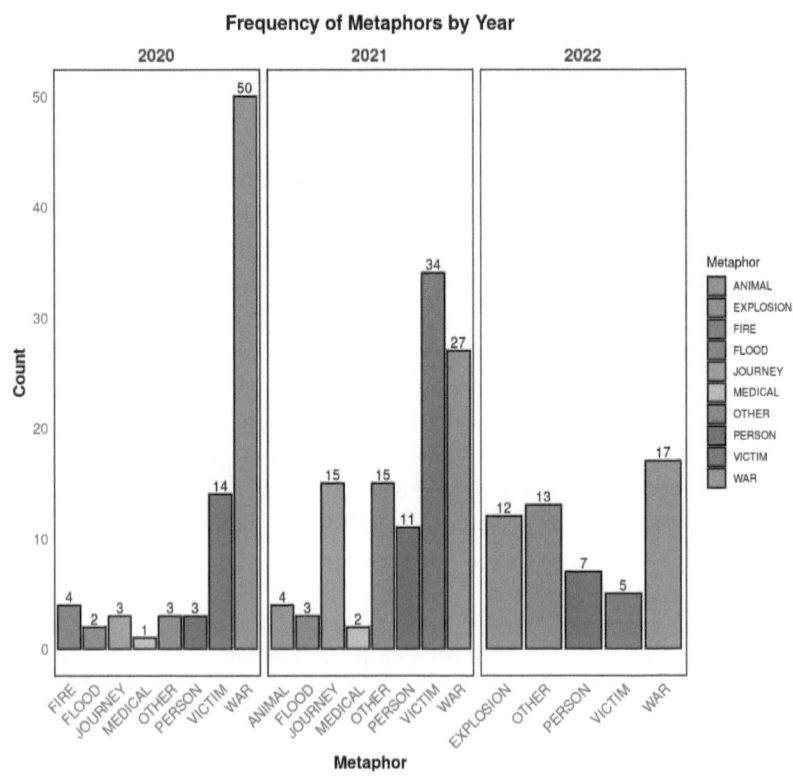

Figure 1. *Frequency of metaphors by year*

Other metaphors, such as ANIMAL and JOURNEY, showed smaller but notable variations across the years. This plot suggests shifting metaphor usage over time, with a clear decrease in war-related language.

Table 1. *Frequency Table of Metaphors by Year*

Year	Metaphor	Count	Percentage
2020	Fire	4	5.0
2020	Flood	2	2.5
2020	Journey	3	3.8
2020	Medical	1	1.3
2020	Other	3	3.8
2020	Person	3	3.8
2020	Victim	14	17.5
2020	War	50	62.5
2021	Animal	4	3.6
2021	Flood	3	2.7
2021	Journey	15	13.5
2021	Medical	2	1.8
2021	Other	15	13.5
2021	Person	11	9.9
2021	Victim	34	30.6
2021	War	27	24.3
2022	Explosion	12	22.2
2022	Other	13	24.0
2022	Person	7	12.0
2022	Victim	5	9.2
2022	War	17	31.4

Shown below, a negative binomial regression model (Table 2) was used to assess the association between Year, Metaphor types, and their interaction, with the frequency of metaphors used in news articles related to COVID-19. The model accounts for variations in total article counts by including an offset for the log of total articles, and the reference year is set to 2020, with the WAR metaphor as the reference category. Due to the nature the data, NBR was chosen, as it is more appropriate for count data and can adjust for overdispersion and the varying number of articles in each year.

The results confirm that the use of WAR metaphors (estimate = -0.81, p < .001) significantly declined over time, supporting the hypothesis that war-related language became less frequent as the pandemic progressed. At the same time, metaphors such as JOURNEY (estimate = 1.83, p < .01), OTHER (estimate = 1.19, p < .001), and PERSON (0.93, p < .01) became more prevalent in 2021 and 2022. These shifts indicate a move away from the initial combative framing of the pandemic (WAR) toward a broader framing. Meanwhile, interaction terms for FLOOD, MEDICAL, and VICTIM were not significant, indicating that their usage patterns did not vary significantly across the selected time periods. It should be noted that given the limited sample size of the articles (364), the findings should be interpreted with caution and further research with larger samples is necessary.

Table 2. *NBR results*[16]

Coefficient	Estimate	SE	z-stat	p-value
Intercept	1,655.4612261	362.8580955	4.5622827	p < .001 ***
War	−0.8198384	0.1795644	−4.5657073	p < .001 ***
Other	1.1953640	0.3283537	3.6404763	p < .001 ***
Flood	0.6268643	0.9523810	0.6582074	.51
Journey	1.8308371	0.6882560	2.6601107	p < .01 **
Medical	0.9145464	1.2544705	0.7290298	.46
Person	0.9382992	0.3597435	2.6082452	p < .01 **
Victim	0.2612248	0.2787267	0.9372076	.34

Our findings are supported by a statistically significant relationship between metaphor categories and the three distinct phases of the pandemic

---

[16] Null deviance: 167.949 on 20 degrees of freedom. Residual deviance: 13.616 on 4 degrees of freedom. AIC: 134.38, pseudo-R ≈ 0.919. Mean = 11.6. Variance = 152.3. The coefficients for interactions between Year and certain metaphors (ANIMAL, EXPLOSION, and FIRE) were not estimable, resulting in NA values. This is because these metaphors appeared only in one specific year, preventing the model from estimating how their frequency changed across the years. These metaphors are included in the model, but their interaction with Year could not be calculated due to lack of variation.

under investigation. The application of Fisher's Exact Test[17] yields a p-value of less than .001, providing strong evidence for an association between the temporal periods of the pandemic and the metaphorical domains employed in public discourse. Even considering the limitations of our dataset, this suggests that the observed shifts in metaphor usage across the investigated time frame are not attributable to random variation but are instead indicative of systematic changes in the metaphorical framing of COVID-19. In addition, pairwise correlations were applied to identify specific years when changes in metaphor usage were statistically significant (Table 1). The focus here is on the distinct concepts employed to comprehend the virus, rather than individualized conceptualizations of VIRUS, VIRUS SPREAD, and VIRUS MANAGEMENT.

Table 3. *Pairwise correlations by metaphorical domains*

Year Comparison	Categories with p > 0.05	Categories with p ≤ 0.05	Categories with p < 0.01	Categories with p < 0.001
June 2020 vs December 2021	EXPLOSION, FLOOD, PERSON	JOURNEY	-	WAR
June 2020 vs January 2022	FLOOD, JOURNEY	-	WAR	EXPLOSION
December 2021 vs January 2022	FLOOD, PERSON, WAR	-	JOURNEY	EXPLOSION

The findings in Table 2 show that the transition from June 2020 to 2021 was marked by a significant decrease in WAR metaphors (p < .001), reflecting a pivotal change in public discourse. This shift can be contextualized within the broader timeline of the pandemic. In June 2020, when COVID-19 was an emerging, unfamiliar threat, the usage of WAR metaphors was likely driven

---

[17] The choice of Fisher's Exact Test over the Chi-square test is justified by the small expected frequencies in the contingency table. The Chi-square test expects that no more than 20% of the expected counts are less than 5, which is not the case in our dataset. Fisher's Exact Test is more appropriate for tables with small sample sizes or where the assumptions for the Chi-square test are not met. Therefore, we progressed with Fisher's Exact Test over the Chi-square.

by a collective sense of confronting an unknown enemy. Such metaphors fostered a narrative of unity and resilience in the face of adversity.

However, in December 2021, the narrative began to change, as the country started to adapt to the 'new normal'; that is, a set of restrictions to tackle the pandemic, including limited business and service operations, 100-person caps on private events, and travel bans (Crisis, 2021). Furthermore, advancements in the development and distribution of vaccines contributed to a more nuanced understanding of the pandemic by the general public. This transition from acute crisis management to a phase of sustained mitigation is arguably reflected in the language used in public discourse. Hence, the decrease in militaristic metaphors might indicate a collective shift towards viewing the pandemic through a lens of management and adaptation, rather than combat.

There was a slight increase in the number of VIRUS MANAGEMENT IS WAR in January 2022. However, the pairwise correlations demonstrate a lack of significant difference in the use of WAR metaphors between December 2021 to January 2022. This could be interpreted as the public becoming more accustomed to living with the virus, where the initial urgency and combativeness have given way to a more balanced, albeit cautious, approach to pandemic management. The re-emergence of these metaphors, albeit at a lower frequency, could also be attributed to specific events or developments in the pandemic's trajectory, such as the emergence of new variants or vaccination drives, which may have temporarily reignited a sense of urgency.

Furthermore, the findings reveal a number of metaphorical categories with notable significance, requiring further examination to understand the shifts in metaphor usage. For instance, the change in the usage of VIRUS MANAGEMENT IS A JOURNEY and THE SPREAD OF CORONAVIRUS IS AN EXPLOSION throughout the selected periods further illustrates the evolution of public discourse in response to the pandemic's trajectory. As argued, VIRUS MANAGEMENT IS A JOURNEY, which became more prominent in December 2021, may suggest a conceptualization of the pandemic as a path with challenges to overcome and an eventual end, resonating with the public's perception of progress through the pandemic's timeline. Thus, this metaphorical domain could serve to substitute a sense of collective endurance as the nation navigates through the crisis. In contrast, the surge in THE SPREAD OF CORONAVIRUS IS AN EXPLOSION, notably in January 2022, corresponds with a critical phase in the pandemic characterized by a rapid increase in COVID-19 cases. The sudden emergence of this metaphorical domain captures the abruptness of the virus's spread. The use of THE SPREAD OF CORONAVIRUS IS AN EXPLOSION arguably served as a linguistic strategy to convey the severity and immediacy of the situation, and potentially aimed at reigniting public alertness and response in the face of an escalating threat. This metaphorical choice can be viewed as a response to the changing dynamics of the pandemic, and an attempt to encapsulate the urgent nature of the evolving health crisis in a manner that is immediately graspable.

The observed decline in the use of WAR metaphors over time, and the concurrent rise of metaphors such as JOURNEY and EXPLOSION, indicates a broadening of the metaphorical repertoire in news discourse. This diversification suggests that communicators were seeking new linguistic tools to articulate the complexities of the pandemic as it progressed. The transition towards a variety of metaphorical domains reflects an ongoing search for novel ways to describe and make sense of the pandemic's constantly changing phases. Hence, it highlights how public discourse adapted to the dynamically changing context that the evolution of the pandemic created.

5. Concluding remarks

The conceptualization of a dynamically evolving crisis alters as it develops (Benczes & Benczes, 2018). This paper explored whether the use of WAR, a dominant metaphor of the COVID-19 pandemic, fluctuated as the pandemic progressed. While military language can be effective when reacting to sudden crises due to the strong and life-threatening images associated with it, as the population learns more about the "enemy", namely, the virus, and adapts to the measures (e.g., mandatory face masks and social distancing) taken against it, the relevance of the WAR metaphor may alter (Roberts & Bolognesi, 2024).

The findings in this research confirm this trend, as they reveal a decline in war-related language use over time. Moreover, the research highlighted representations of the virus and the management of the pandemic, which painted a less combative image. While our research faces limitations in terms of the number of sources and the restricted time period it investigated, it can serve as a basis for further investigations on larger samples with regards to the dynamic evolution of health communication in general and pandemic discourse in particular.

Shifts in metaphorical language use are indicative of how metaphors serve not only to describe the crisis but also to engage with and influence public discourse. This aligns with Lakoff and Johnson's (Lakoff & Johnson, 1980/2003) proposition that metaphors are not merely rhetorical devices, but powerful tools that shape our conceptualization and response to events. In the context of the COVID-19 pandemic, the evolving metaphors reflect a linguistic adaptation to the changing realities, serving as a tool for public understanding. Metaphor variation is critical in shaping the interpretation of the pandemic, and it influences how the crisis is perceived, experienced, and acted upon by the public.

References

Benczes, I., & Benczes, R. (2018). From financial support package via rescue aid to bailout: Framing the management of the Greek sovereign debt crisis. *Society and Economy*, *40*(3), 431–445. https://doi.org/10.1556/204.2018.40.3.9

Benczes, R., Benczes, I., Ságvári, B., & Szabó, L. P. (2024). When life is no longer a journey: the effect of the COVID-19 pandemic on the metaphorical conceptualization of life among Hungarian adults–a representative survey. *Cognitive Linguistics*, *35*(1), 143–165. https://doi.org/10.1515/cog-2023-0050

Benczes, R., & Burridge, K. (2018). Speaking of disease and death. In K. Allan (Ed.), *The Oxford handbook of taboo words and language* (pp. 61–76). Oxford University Press. https://doi.org/10.1093/oxfordhb/9780198808190.013.4

Benczes, R., & Szabó, L. P. (2020). Brussels–boss, bully or the big brother? Framing CONFLICT in contemporary Hungarian political rhetoric. *Jezikoslovlje*, *21*(3), 345–369. https://doi.org/10.29162/jez.2020.11

Benczes, R., Szabó, L. P., & Virág, Á. (2022). It's showtime: The POLITICS IS A SHOW metaphor in the 2022 election campaign of Fidesz. *Médiakutató*, *23*(3–4), 109–121.

Bene, M., & Boda, Zs. (2021). Hungary: Crisis as usual—Populist governance and the pandemic. In G. Bobba & N. Hubé (Eds.), *Populism and the politicization of the COVID-19 crisis in Europe* (pp. 87–100). Springer.

Bougher, L. D. (2012). The case for metaphor in political reasoning and cognition. *Political Psychology, 33*(1), 145–163. DOI: 10.1111/j.1467-9221.2011.00865.x

Cameron, L., Maslen, R., Todd, Z., Maule, J., Stratton, P., & Stanley, N. (2009). The discourse dynamics approach to metaphor and metaphor-led discourse analysis. *Metaphor and Symbol, 24*(2), 63–89. DOI: 10.1080/10926480902830821

Cameron, L., Maslen, R., & Low, G. (2010). Finding systematicity in metaphor use. In L. Cameron, & R. Maslen (Eds.), *Metaphor analysis: Research practice in applied linguistics, social sciences and the humanities* (pp. 116–146). Equinox.

Charteris-Black, J. (2018). *Analysing political speeches: Rhetoric, discourse and metaphor.* Bloomsbury Publishing.

Cowling, B. J., & Aiello, A. E. (2020). Public health measures to slow community spread of coronavirus disease 2019. *The Journal of infectious diseases, 221*(11), 1749–1751. https://doi.org/10.1093/infdis/jiaa123

Crisis. (2021, December 16). Hungary: Authorities extend COVID-19 state of emergency through to June 1 2022 /update 35. *Hungary: Authorities Extend COVID-19 State of Emergency Through to June 1 2022 /Update 35 | Crisis24.* https://crisis24.garda.com/alerts/2021/12/hungary-authorities-extend-covid-19-state-of-emergency-through-to-june-1-2022-update-35

Flusberg, S. J., Matlock, T., & Thibodeau, P. H. (2018). War metaphors in public discourse. *Metaphor and Symbol, 33*(1), 1–18. from https://doi.org/10.1080/10926488.2018.1407992

Gillis, M. (2020). Ventilators, missiles, doctors, troops… the justification of legislative responses to COVID-19 through military metaphors. *Law and Humanities, 14*(2), 135–159. https://doi.org/10.1080/17521483.2020.1801950

Hanne, M. (2022). How we escape capture by the "war" metaphor for COVID-19. *Metaphor and Symbol, 37*(2), 88–100. DOI: 10.1080/10926488.2021.1935261

Kövecses, Z. (2010). *Metaphor: A practical introduction* (2nd ed.). Oxford University Press.

Lakoff, G., & Johnson, M. (1980/2003). *Metaphors we live by.* University of Chicago Press.

Lakoff, G. (2014). *The all new don't think of an elephant!: Know your values and frame the debate*. Chelsea Green Publishing.

Merkovity, N., Bene, M., & Farkas, X. (2021). Hungary: Illiberal crisis management. In. D. Lilleker, I. A. Coman, M. Gregor, & E. Novelli (Eds.), *Political communication and COVID-19: Governance and rhetoric in times of crisis* (pp. 269–279). Routledge.

Mio, J. S. (1997). Metaphor and politics. *Metaphor and symbol, 12*(2), 113–133. DOI: 10.1207/s15327868ms1202_2

Molnár, A., Takács, L., & Jakusné Harnos, É. (2020). Securitization of the COVID-19 pandemic by metaphoric discourse during the state of emergency in Hungary. *International Journal of Sociology and Social Policy, 40*(9/10), 1167–1182.

Musolff, A. (2016). *Political metaphor analysis: Discourse and scenarios*. Bloomsbury Publishing.

Musolff, A. (2022). "War against Covid-19": Is the pandemic management as war metaphor helpful or hurtful? In A. Musolff, R. Breeze, K. Kondo, & S. Vilar-Lluch (Eds.), *Pandemic and crisis discourse: Communicating COVID-19 and public health strategy* (pp. 307–320). Bloomsbury Publishing.

Musolff, A. (2024). War metaphors and conspiracy theories. In M. Romano (Ed.), *Metaphor in socio-political contexts: Current crises* (pp. 159–176). De Gruyter Mouton.

Nemzeti Média- és Hírközlési Hatóság [National Media and Infocommunications Authority] (NMHH). (2020). *A lakosság médiahasználati és hírfogyasztási szokásai a koronavírus-járvány első szakaszában [The media usage and news consumption habits of the population during the first period of the coronavirus-pandemic]*. https://nmhh.hu/dokumentum/213415/NMHH_PSYMA_COVID_JELENTES_fin.pdf

Olza, I., Koller, V., Ibarretxe-Antuñano, I., Pérez-Sobrino, P., & Semino, E. (2021). The# ReframeCovid initiative: From Twitter to society via metaphor. *Metaphor and the Social World, 11*(1), 98–120. DOI: 10.1075/msw.00013.olz

Ottatti, V., Renstrom, R., & Price, E. (2014). The metaphorical framing model: Political communication and public opinion. In M. J. Landau,

M. D. Robinson, & B. P. Meier (Eds.), *The power of metaphor: Examining its influence on social life* (pp. 179–202). American Psychological Association.

Piredda, P. (2022). War metaphors during the COVID-19 pandemic: Persuasion and manipulation. In P. Blumczynski & S. Wilson (Eds.), *The languages of COVID-19: Translational and multilingual perspectives on global healthcare* (pp. 48–62). Routledge.

R Core Team. (2024). *R: A language and environment for statistical computing. R Foundation for Statistical Computing.* https://www.R-project.org/

Roberts, I. M., & Bolognesi, M. M. (2024). The influence of metaphorical framing on emotions and reasoning about the COVID-19 pandemic. *Metaphor and Symbol, 39*(1), 55–74. DOI:10.1080/10926488.2023.2273301

Schnepf, J., & Christmann, U. (2022). "It's a war! It's a battle! It's a fight!": Do militaristic metaphors increase people's threat perceptions and support for COVID-19 policies?. *International Journal of Psychology, 57*(1), 107–126. DOI: 10.1002/ijop.12797

Semino, E. (2021). "Not soldiers but fire-fighters"–metaphors and Covid-19. *Health communication, 36*(1), 50–58. DOI: 10.1080/10410236.2020.1844989

Semino, E., Demjén, Z., Hardie, A., Payne, S., & Rayson, P. (2017). *Metaphor, cancer and the end of life: A corpus-based study.* Routledge.

Simon, G., Árvay, K., Bajzát, T. B., K. Molnár, E., Prótár, N., & Szlávich, E. (2022). Metaforikus kreativitás és érzelemszabályozás – Metaforamintázatok a közösségi médiában a járvány idején [Metaphorical creativity and emotion regulation – Metaphor patterns on social media at the time of the pandemic]. In G. Szabó (Ed.), *Érzelmek és járványpolitizálás: Politikai érzelemmenedzserek és érzelemszabályozási ajánlataik Magyarországon a COVID-19 pandémia idején* (pp. 82–111). ELTE Eötvös Kiadó.

Sontag, S. (1978). *Illness as metaphor.* Farrar Straus Giroux.

Szabó, L. P. (2020). Háború járvány idején–Hogyan beszél Orbán Viktor a koronavírusról [War during the pandemic – How Viktor Orbán talks about the coronavirus]. In B. Böcskei, A. Körösényi, & A. Szabó (Eds.), *Vírusba oltott politika: Világjárvány és politikatudomány* (pp. 123–134). TK Politikatudományi Intézet–Napvilág.

Szabó, L. P., & Béni, A. (2021). Vírusháború: A Covid19 járvány metaforikus ábrázolása a magyar hírportálokon [Viruswars: The metaphoric depiction of the Covid-19 pandemic on Hungarian news portals]. *Médiakutató*, 22(3/4), 59–68.

Szabó, L. P., & Farkas, X. (2022). „Küzdelem a vírus ellen" – Orbán Viktor érzelemszabályozási ajánlatai a koronavírus-járvány első és második hullámában [The fight against the virus – Viktor Orbán's emotion regulation offers during the first and second waves of the coronavirus pandemic]. In G. Szabó (Ed.), *Érzelmek és járványpolitizálás: Politikai érzelemmenedzserek és érzelemszabályozási ajánlataik Magyarországon a COVID-19 pandémia idején* (pp. 23–39). ELTE Eötvös Kiadó.

Szabó, L. P., & Szabó, G. (2022). Attack of the critics: Metaphorical delegitimisation in Viktor Orbán's discourse during the Covid-19 pandemic. *Journal of Language and Politics*, 21(2), 255–276. https://doi.org/10.1075/jlp.21068.sza

Venables, W. N., & Ripley, B. D. (2002). *Modern applied statistics with S* (4th ed.). Springer.

Wickham, H. (2016). *ggplot2: Elegant graphics for data analysis*. Springer.

World Health Organization. (n.d.). *Hungary: WHO coronavirus disease (COVID-19) dashboard*. World Health Organization. https://covid19.who.int/region/euro/country/hu

Metaphors as markers for suicidal intent: Patterns in metaphorical language used in online forum posts about suicidal thoughts

Gábor Simon[1] – Tímea Borbála Bajzát[1] – Kata Árvay[1] – Júlia Ballagó[2,4] – Kitti Hauber[1] – Zsuzsanna Havasi[1] – Ágnes Kuna[1] – Emese K. Molnár[1] – Noémi Prótár[1] – Eszter Szlávich[1] – Zsuzsa Kaló[3]

ABSTRACT

Increasing attention is being given to the linguistic analysis of metaphors in mental health research. Previous studies have highlighted the importance of figurative language in monitoring the presuicidal syndrome. However, only limited scholarly attention has been paid to the systematic exploration of the relationship between suicidal tendencies and metaphorical language use. Our research project aims to detect reoccurring patterns of metaphorization that may contribute to the diagnosis of presuicidal syndrome. To achieve this goal, we explore the patterns of metaphorical expressions used in online support-seeking discourse on suicidal thoughts. The present paper reports on the preliminary results of the research: it outlines the corpus design and the methodological framework, and provides an exploratory analysis of the conceptual domains frequently involved in metaphorization. The analysis is based on publicly available forum posts about suicide (PsyMet Corpus). In addition to automatically annotated morphosyntactic phenomena, the analysis also includes the manual annotation of metaphorical linguistic constructions based on the MetaID protocol, supplemented by identifying metaphorical source domains. The paper first discusses the potential role of metaphor in identifying (or at least aiding understanding of) suicidal tendencies, then presents the methodological framework of the research, before summarizing the conclusions drawn from the pilot analysis of a sample of 46 posts. The significance of the study rests on the hypothesis that the identification of the patterns of metaphorization can improve both diagnosis and psychological intervention.

Keywords: metaphor, suicidal thoughts, corpus, annotation

---

[1] ELTE Eötvös Loránd University Budapest, Institute of Hungarian Linguistics and Finno-Ugric Studies
[2] University of Debrecen, Institute of Hungarian Linguistics
[3] ELTE Eötvös Loránd University Budapest, Institute of Psychology
[4] HUN-REN Research Centre for Linguistics, Budapest

1. Introduction

Based on currently available statistical data,[5] the number of deaths caused by suicide in Hungary has increased in the last three years. Between 2000 and 2020 the frequency of deaths caused by suicide dropped continuously before rising again following the COVID-19 pandemic. Moreover, while the figures for 2018 show a decrease in successful suicides during that period, Hungary was clearly ranked as the third country in the EU for per capita suicide deaths. These data motivate our research on the language of suicidal thoughts and behavior, with the aim of exploring the metaphorical expressions used in pre-suicidal syndrome. Following the literature on discursive suicidology (Erdős, 2006),[6] we assume that reoccurring patterns of metaphorical language use observable in online discourse can be considered a special type of "cry for help" phenomenon:[7] a(n) (un)conscious expression of mental health issues and/or suicidal intention with the aim of seeking support from society. Thus, a systematic analysis of metaphorical patterns in online posts about suicidal thoughts and intention may result in (i) a set of particular types of metaphorical expressions that strongly mark suicidal intention, and (ii) a database in which the density of metaphorical language use in online discourse about suicidal thoughts can be measured. We also assume that the distribution of metaphorical expressions in the analyzed texts correlates with the intensity of suicidal thoughts; i.e., a greater number of associated metaphors used in the text indicates stronger suicidal intention. Consequently, the findings of the research may contribute to preventive intervention by aiding the evaluation of the seriousness of the subject's intention.

Previous research listed the following general symptoms of presuicidal syndrome (Ringel, 1976; Erdős, 2006, pp. 48, 50, 94; Yaseen et al., 2018): narrowing of the situation, change in experiencing time, lack of anticipation

---

[5] The data are presented on the homepage of the Central Bureau for Statistics (https://www.ksh.hu/ffi/1-16.html, last access: 19 January 2024).

[6] "Discursive suicidology examines thematizations and directly relates these social constructions to areas of human action. The examined texts are, on the one hand, produced by people preparing for and committing suicide, and on the other hand, everyday knowledge and language about suicide, as well as forms that are the subject of public discourse and considered worthy of recording: media texts, literary works, proverbs, etc." (Erdős, 2006, p. 67).

[7] About the "cry for help" phenomenon and its recent investigation see Young (2019, pp. 225–237) and Sikveland (2023).

or expectations for the future, narrow-mindedness, and high frequency of negation. A recent overview of papers published on the language of suicide between 2000 and 2021 (75 studies in total, carried out in various countries including, but not limited to the USA, the UK, China, Australia, Chile, France, the Netherlands, Germany, Japan, and Mexico) identified potential predictors of suicidal thoughts and behavior as mainly prosodic, lexical, and morphosyntactic features, with methodology based on counting words and part-of-speech categories (i.e., measuring the frequency of using verbs, nouns, first and second person pronouns, function words, prepositions, modifiers and adjectives), and analyzing the usage of intensifiers and superlatives (Homan et al., 2022).

In the last decade specifically, the realm of social media has been given special attention. A recent study (combining textual analysis with neural networks and machine learning to automatically detect suicidal ideation) shows that suicidal posts on Reddit can be characterized by a lexical profile using the categories of authenticity, anxiety, mentality, depression, negativity, and sentimental despondency (Aldhyani et al., 2020). Nevertheless, we can agree with Homan and her colleagues in their general assessment that the majority of the literature to date "merely reveals what at-risk individuals talk about", while the question of "how individuals express themselves" has yet to be fully answered (Homan et al., 2022, p. 15). Metaphor has already entered the scope of scholarly attention; Erdős B. (2006, pp. 58–59, 63, 87, 103), for example, mentions some of the most frequently used metaphors in emergency telephone calls about suicide intentions (*falling out of the world, pit, sleeping, having a rest, journey* or *boundaries*). However, reoccurring metaphorical markers of presuicidal syndrome have not been explored systematically.

In the wider realm, metaphors have proved to be an essential feature not only of thinking but also talking about mental health problems. Metaphorical expressions (linguistic structures motivated by and used for expressing metaphorical meaning in the discourse) may help patients in describing their sensations and experiences (Tay, 2017, p. 371); thus, they serve therapeutic purposes, and beyond representational function, they contribute to building a relationship between doctor and patient, and researcher and participant (Knapton & Rundblad, 2018). To mention only a few recent studies, linguistic metaphors are used to better understand the experiences of the users of synthetic cannabinoids (Kaló et al., 2020), to handle PTSD in therapy with veterans (Foley, 2015), and to explain the person-like character of voices in voice-hearing (Collins et al., 2023). In addition, the use of metaphors to discuss mental health problems is not confined to the realm of professional healthcare discourse: Hazel Price demonstrated that mania is described in contemporary English newspapers as a "journey on a rollercoaster" (see Price 2022, pp. 64–65). To summarize, exploring metaphorical expressions sheds new light on the sharing of individual experiences of mental health problems, construing a personal identity with a particular mental state, and creating a supportive interpersonal context for handling these states. Consequently, identifying and analyzing metaphorical language in available resources tops the agenda in contemporary medical linguistic research. However, as Price (2022, pp. 64–65) points out, this kind of metaphor analysis is "only possible through a close reading of the corpus", since metaphors do not have specific linguistic markers (that can be automatically extracted from large corpora), and they are not limited to the level of individual words.

The present paper proposes a methodological framework for identifying the use of metaphors in communicating suicidal intentions. The brief literature overview outlined above highlights the following unanswered questions: (i) How dominant is metaphorical language in the online posts about suicidal thoughts? (ii) What are the reoccurring patterns of metaphorical language use in Hungarian online posts on suicidal thoughts? (iii) What are the most salient conceptual domains in the metaphorical language related to presuicidal syndrome? With a systematic corpus annotation and data analysis, the study findings aim to provide answers to these questions and shed light on a new aspect of discursive suicidology; namely, the metaphorical markers of suicidal intentions. To these ends, a specific research corpus and a protocol for metaphor identification are required. In what follows, the infrastructure of the analysis and its methodological framework is briefly discussed, before the preliminary results of the processing of a pilot sample of the corpus are presented.

2. Material and methods

To provide answers to the questions outlined above, a small-scale research corpus (the PsyMet corpus) was created, within which all metaphorical expressions were identified and annotated. Online posts were sampled from a voluntary community support site for people with mental disorders and difficulties (bura.hu), from three topics dedicated to suicide: *Öngyilkosság* 'Suicide', *Szuicid gondolatok* 'Suicidal thoughts' and *Krízis, öngyilkossági szándék* 'Crisis, suicidal intention'. The selected texts were posted between 2010 and 2021,[8] while the sampling process was carried out in the spring of 2023. All the posts reporting on actual or past suicidal thoughts and/or attempts from a first-person perspective were sampled, resulting in a total of 406 texts. Of this material, approximately 10% (46 posts, 3786 tokens altogether) was selected for a pilot corpus, which was then used to conduct a small-scale annotation study with 9 annotators, each of whom worked independently on their designated portion of the pilot dataset.[9] The present paper discusses the results of this pilot analysis.

The annotation was based on the MetaID protocol (Simon et al., 2023), a hybrid, morpheme-based language-specific adaptation of the Metaphor Identification Process Vrije Universiteit (MIPVU, Steen et al., 2010). This procedure is a dictionary-based word-sense-disambiguation task, in which the basic meaning and the contextual meaning of the unit of analysis are compared on the basis of the dictionary entry, and when a cross-domain mapping can be identified between the two, the given unit receives a metaphoric label. In the method employed by the present study, the unit of analysis is the morpheme, since Hungarian is an agglutinative language, in which also inflectional case markers can initiate metaphorical meaning. Put simply, the protocol employed identifies metaphorical usage below the word-level. Moreover, the MetaID method also allows identifying metaphorization above the word level, since the annotator explores the argument structure constructions organized around verbs, and allocates labels of semantic relations between the components of metaphorical multi-word expression (based on Cognitive Grammar, see Langacker, 2013). Finally, the collocational behavior

---

[8] This was the period when the users actively used at least one of the topics chosen for sampling.
[9] The annotators are members of the MetaID Research Group (within the ELTE DiAGram Research Centre for Functional Linguistics organization, https://diagram.elte.hu/en/). After a joint annotation of one text (discussing all the emerging issues of metaphor identification), all members annotated 5 posts individually. Then, a pairwise curation was carried out, ensuring the reliability if the annotation process. About the overall reliability of the MetaId protocol see Simon et al., 2023.

of the lemmas of the text was measured in a large-scale reference corpus, and if the metaphorical expression (a multi-word unit of Hungarian in this case) proved to be a strong collocation in the reference corpus, its components received idiomatic metaphor labels. To summarize, metaphor annotation comprised two layers in the analysis: the components of metaphor-related[10] expressions (mtags set) and the semantic relations between them (mrel set). Table 1 summarizes the tags provided by the protocol (for a more detailed explanation of the annotation procedure see Simon et al., 2023).

Table 1. *The set of labels used in MetaID protocol*

Set	Tag	Function	Example
mtags	MKK, Metaforához kapcsolódó kifejezés	Metaphor-related Expression	*rom* 'ruin' in (1)
	MKI, Metaforához kapcsolódó inflexió	Metaphor-related Inflection	*ban* 'in' in (1)
	MKA, Metaforához kapcsolódó argumentum	Metaphor-related Argument	*életem* 'my life' in (1)
	MKKomp, Metaforához kapcsolódó komponens	Metaphor-related Component	*rom* 'ruin' in (1)[11]
	MKKid, Metaforához kapcsolódó idiomatikus kifejezés	Metaphor-related Idiomatic Expression	in the expression *hosszú ideje* 'for a long time' the attribute *hosszú* 'long' (it is strongly collocated with the noun *idő* 'time' in Hungarian)
	MKAid, Metaforához kapcsolódó idiomatikus argumentum	Metaphor-related Idiomatic Argument	*késsel* 'with knife' in (2)

---

[10] Note that – in accordance with the original method – the MetaID protocol can mark only the potentiality of metaphorical meaning generation in the corpus. Whether there is an actual metaphorization in the process of understanding the texts is a question that can be answered via experimental methods.

[11] Note that one lemma can receive more than one label in the protocol: the noun rom 'ruin' is a metaphor in its own right (labelled as MKK) and also a nominal component of an inflectional metaphor (labelled as MKKomp).

Set	Tag	Function	Example
	MKKompid, Metaforához kapcsolódó idiomatikus komponens	Metaphor-related Idiomatic Component	in the expression *hosszú ideje* 'for a long time' the nominal lemma *idő* 'time' (it is strongly collocated with the adjective *hosszú* 'long' in Hungarian)
	dMKK, direkt Metaforához kapcsolódó idiomatikus kifejezés	Direct Metaphor-related Idiomatic Expression	in the expression *mintha égnének az idegeim* 'as if my nerves were on fire' the lemma *ég* 'burn/be on fire' (it is directly used as metaphor in the context)
	dMKKid, direkt Metaforához kapcsolódó kifejezés	Direct Metaphor-related Expression	*szurkál* 'stab' in (2)
	MZ, Metaforazászló	Metaphor Flag	*mintha* 'as if' in (2)
	MKKimp, Metaforához kapcsolódó implicit kifejezés	Implicit Metaphor-Related Expression	any pronoun that refers back to a tagged metaphorical lemma via coreference
mrel	tr	trajector (the primary figure[12] of the meaning of a verb)	*életem* 'my life' as the subject of being in ruins in (1)
	lm	landmark (the secondary figure of the meaning of a verb)	*késsel* 'with knife' as the direct object of the verb *szurkál* 'stab' in (2)
	ela	semantic elaboration of an aspect of the meaning of an expression	the elaboration of *rom* 'ruin' as a physical container in (1)

(Continued)

---

[12] In Cognitive Grammar, relational meanings (expressed by verbs, adjectives, participles, inflections, preverbs and postpositions in Hungarian) include participants, one of which is more prominent (the primary focal participant), while the other is in the background of our attention. The participants are called figures in this framework.

Table 1. (Continued)

Set	Tag	Function	Example
	poss	possessive relation	in the expression *a szörnyűségnek vége legyen* 'let the horror have its end' there is a possessive relation between the noun *szörnyűség* 'horror' and the noun *vég* 'end'
	expm	explicating metaphorical meaning (via metaphor flag)	the conjunction *mintha* 'as if' highlights that being stabbed with knives is a metaphorical description of being in crisis
	r	technical label for handling flexible word order in Hungarian	in the expression *nem adtam fel* 'I didn't give up' the preverb *fel* 'up' is connected to the main verb *ad* 'give' with the r relation

Examples (1) and (2) from the pilot corpus illustrate two types of metaphorical expressions.

(1) *Romokban az életem.* 'My life is in ruins.' (Krízis, öngyilkossági szándék_2587)

(2) [...] *minden másodperc olyan, mintha 1000 késsel szurkálnának* [...] 'every second is like being stabbed with 1000 knives' (Krízis, öngyilkossági szándék_2587)[13]

In (1) there are two metaphors: the noun *rom* 'ruin' refers here to the state of being destroyed in or after a crisis (where LIFE is conceptualized as a

---

The primary figure attracts more attention and prominence, while the secondary figure remains in the background. (See Langacker, 2013, pp. 70–73.)

[13] The examples were translated by the first author of the present study.

BUILDING). Thus, both the nominal predicate (*romokban* '[be] in ruins') and its argument (*életem* 'my life') can be labeled as metaphorical: the latter is the argument of the predicate, and it expresses the primary figure of the relational meaning 'being in ruins', thus, a trajector relational label can be allocated between the predicate and the argument. On the other hand, the inessive case marker *-ban* 'in' construes here the whole scenario (BEING IN LIFE-CRISIS) as BEING IN A PHYSICAL CONTAINER, therefore a metaphorical inflection and a metaphorical component can be marked within the word form *Romokban* 'in ruins', allocating an elaborative relation between the two. In (2) there is a direct idiomatic metaphor with a metaphor flag: the conjunction *mintha* 'as if' explicitly marks that the scenario of being stubbed with knives needs to be interpreted figuratively. Consequently, the verb *szurkál* 'stab' is a direct (i.e., explicated) metaphor connected to the conjunction as a metaphor flag with an "expm" relation. Moreover, the expression *késsel szurkál* 'stab with a knife' is a stable collocation in Hungarian (with a logDice score of 7.466); hence, the components can be labeled as idiomatic (dMKKid and MKAid) with a landmark relation between them. Figure 1. demonstrates how these expressions were annotated in the corpus.

The infrastructure of the analysis consists of further language resources supporting the process of annotation. To store the sampled texts, their metadata, and the results of the annotation, a git-based system was used on the GitHub platform. All the annotations were carried out in the INCEpTION semantic annotation platform (Klie et al., 2018). For the task of word-sense-disambiguation, The Concise Dictionary of Hungarian (Pusztai, 2003) was used, while the Hungarian Gigaword Corpus (v.2.0.5, Oravecz et al., 2014)[14] served as a reference corpus for measuring idiomaticity, using the threshold of 6 in logDice score (Rychlý, 2008).

---

[14] The Hungarian Gigaword Corpus is available here: https://clara.nytud.hu/mnsz2-dev/en/

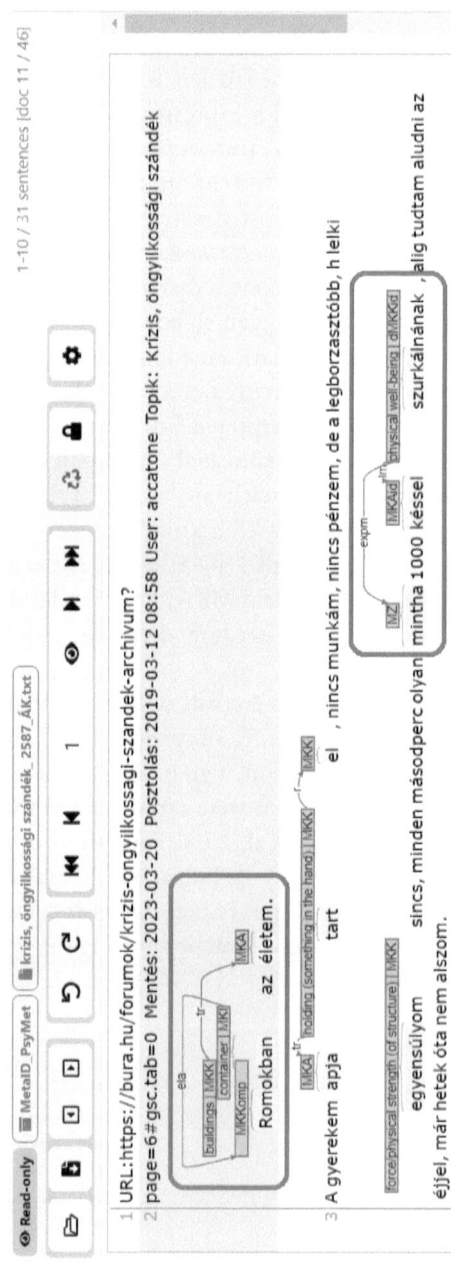

Figure 1. *The annotation of examples (1) and (2) in the INCEpTION platform*

3. Results and discussion
3.1. Quantitative analysis

Altogether in the pilot corpus, 754 labels were allocated. The relative frequency of metaphorical tokens was 19.92%; i.e., on average, every fifth token in the sample received a metaphorical label. Since one token may be labeled with more than one category (like *rom* 'ruin' in (1), which is both a metaphor in itself and a component of an inflectional metaphor), and because some labels mark that a token or morph only contributes to a metaphor (e.g., arguments, components, or metaphor flags), it is worth counting only those labels that initiate metaphorical meaning generation (MKK, MKKid, MKI, dMKK, dMKKid, MKKimp) to obtain the number of individual metaphors in the pilot corpus. In this way, 417 metaphors were identified, thus indicating that in more than 10% of the sample (11.02%), metaphorical language use plays a central role. In addition, 88.50% of the metaphor-related expressions had at least one argument or component; therefore, it can be asserted that the majority of metaphors are realized in multi-word expressions. Finally, the percentage of all allocated metaphors proved to be idiomatic was 6.71%, which is a relatively low proportion. Therefore, it can be asserted that although metaphorization is frequent in the sample, it is not dominated by metaphorical expressions as prefabricated units of Hungarian.

Concerning the annotated semantic relations, the data show that elaboration (31.04%) and the specification of the secondary figure of the process designated by the verb (i.e., the landmark, 37.91%) dominate the sample (335 annotated relations altogether). Elaborative relations are very common in attributive (adjective + noun) constructions (as in *hosszú ideje* 'for a long time') and in inflectional metaphors (as in *Romokban* 'in ruins'). The landmark participant of a process or relation belongs to the background of the scenario in terms of attention direction; i.e., it is the participant with which an action happens. As an example, knives are the tools with which the act of stabbing is accomplished in (2). Consequently, two kinds of patterns seem to be typical among the metaphors in the pilot corpus. The first focuses on the secondary participant (mainly the patient, the recipient, the beneficiary, the instrument or the circumstance of the process) instead of the primary participant (i.e., the agent), while the second focuses on the specification of a component in inflectional or in metaphorical attributive constructions. Especially the former deserves more attention from the perspective of the analysis because it demonstrates that the subjective reports on suicidal thoughts highlight the scenario and its details rather than the actor and their role in it, backgrounding the activity of the person in crisis and/or foregrounding them as a passive participant in the situation. This finding may shed light on the linguistic realization of constriction, one of the main components of presuicidal syndrome (see Ringel, 1976).

3.2. Exploratory qualitative analysis

Another important methodological innovation in the pilot study was the identification of typical source domains for metaphorical structures. These are the conceptual structures in terms of which another, more abstract concept is understood. In other words, metaphors unfold as mappings from the source domain (e.g., RUINS OF A BUILDING) to the target domains (e.g., PERSONAL LIFE DEMOLISHED BY CRISES, see (1)). At the present stage of the research, the default meaning identified by the dictionary has been employed in source domain labeling. In the context of a small-scale corpus annotation, the results presented here are relevant only from an exploratory point of view, and the development of an appropriate methodology is ongoing.

The source domains identified in this study are categorized as follows: FORCE, BATTLE, OBJECT, SPACE, MOVING, PERSON/ANTHROPOMORPHIC and STATE.[15] In addition to sorting the instances with metaphorical potentiality into the semantic groups presented above, an attempt was made to order them in terms of linguistic polarization, i.e., highlighting positive and negative domains.[16] As an example, the FORCE frame can motivate both ends of the polarity scale: it is characterized by a prevalence of expressions that linguistically convey a 'loss of control' (and hence vulnerability) and those that conceptualize the desire of the speaker to 'regain control'. The lemma *ural* 'to control' often appeared in these cases, as did the lemma *bír* 'endure'. Furthermore, a

---

[15] We aimed to maintain a higher level of abstraction, but we plan to use more detailed ontologies for categorization in the future, for example, the semantic tag set of the USAS analyzer.

[16] The polarity of metaphorical expressions (i.e., whether or not they describe scenarios as positive or negative events or actions) can show that the post's author focuses on overcoming suicidal intention or the bad feelings related to it. Therefore, investigating polarity may play an important role in prevention. Two members of the research group evaluated the positive or negative meaning through discussion.

linguistically more elaborated metaphorization of this category was detected: *visszaráncigáltak a hajamnál fogva* 'dragged me back by my hair'. The BATTLE source domain could not be separated strictly from the FORCE domain. One of the most typical was the verb *küzd* 'to fight'; however, for example, the lemma *túlél* 'to survive' and *roham* 'attack' (in the following context: *nem bírom ki mostanában sírásrohamok nélkül* 'I can't go without a crying fit these days', lit. 'I can't go without the attacks of crying these days') also occurred. *Küzd* and *túlél* focus on the speaker's actions, but *roham* refers to the occurrence of presuicidal thoughts. Moreover, presuicidal thoughts are frequently anthropomorphized as an active and destructive entity. For instance, *az jár a fejemben* 'that's on my mind' (lit. 'that goes in my head'), and *késsel szurkál* 'stabs with a knife'. The conceptualized result of coping with presuicidal thoughts appeared as states on the positive side of polarization; e.g., *szabadság* 'freedom', *egyensúly* 'balance' and *egzisztencia* 'existence'. Finally, SPATIALITY is related exclusively to hopelessness and presuicidal thoughts, with examples from the corpus including *pokol* 'hell', *kör* 'circle', and *rom* 'ruins'.

Summarizing the findings of the exploratory qualitative analysis, having suicidal thoughts is depicted metaphorically in the sample as being and moving in (general or specific) SPACE, encountering PERSONIFIED ENTITIES, and using or lacking FORCE. The linguistic elaborators of coping with presuicidal thoughts typically activated the domain of FORCE, BATTLE and STATE. However, these preliminary results must be considered in the context of our pilot sample.

4. Conclusion

The present study summarized the motivation, the theoretical and methodological background, and the preliminary results of a larger project focusing on the identification and analysis of metaphorical expressions in online discourse about suicidal thoughts. The small-scale exploration of a subset of our total sample showed that (i) metaphors are relatively frequent in subjective confessions of suicidal intention (in the form of online posts); (ii) the dominant linguistic pattern of these expressions highlights the secondary (i.e., inactive) figure of the construed scenario, and (iii) negative polarity with the domains FORCE, BATTLE, SPACE and PERSON are more frequent. The limitation of this pilot study lies in the small amount of processed data; however, it is anticipated that both the size and depth of corpus annotation will be systematically expanded, using a more detailed semantic ontology (and a more elaborated procedure) for source domain labeling. One long-term objective is that the project may support the automatic detection of suicide risk in online conversations. Using the annotated corpus as input material, large language models can be trained to identify metaphorical expressions in texts. Based on the detected structures, an algorithm can assess whether or not the pattern of metaphorical language use in online communication about suicidal intention (e.g., counseling via emails or posting support-seeking comments in forums) requires professional intervention from the therapists. For this, both metaphor detection and the evaluation of the posts need to be standardized in terms of the level of suicide risk. Exploring metaphor patterns on the one hand, and identifying a correlation between these patterns and suicide risk on the other, may lead to the long-term goal of successful suicide prevention.

References

Aldhyani, T. H. H., Alsubari, S. N., Alshebami, A. S., Alkahtani, H., & Ahmed, Z. A. T. (2022). Detecting and analyzing suicidal ideation on social media using deep learning and machine learning models. *International Journal of Environmental Research and Public Health*, *19*(19), 12635. https://doi.org/10.3390/ijerph191912635

Collins, L., Brezina, V., Demjén, Z., Semino, E., & Woods, A. (2022). Corpus linguistics and clinical psychology. *International Journal of Corpus Linguistics*, *28*(1), 28–59. https://doi.org/10.1075/ijcl.21019.col

Erdős, M. B. (2006). *A nyelvben élő kapcsolat. Egy öngyilkosság-megelőző sürgősségi telefonszolgálat beszélgetéseinek vizsgálata.* = A relationship that lives in language. An investigation of conversations in a suicide prevention emergency telephone service. Typotex.

Foley, P. S. (2015). The metaphors they carry: Exploring how veterans use metaphor to describe experiences of PTSD. *Journal of Poetry Therapy*, *28*(2), 129–146. https://doi.org/10.1080/08893675.2015.1011375

Homan, S., Gabi, M., Klee, N., Bachmann, S., Moser, A.-M., Duri', M., Michel, S., Bertram, A.-M., Maatz, A., Seiler, G., Stark, E., & Kleim, B. (2022). Linguistic features of suicidal thoughts and behaviors: A systematic review. *Clinical Psychology Review, 95*, 102161. https://doi.org/10.1016/j.cpr.2022.102161

Kaló, Z., Kassai, S., Rácz, J., & Van Hout, M. C. (2020). Synthetic cannabinoids (SCs) in metaphors: A metaphorical analysis of user experiences of synthetic cannabinoids in two countries. *International Journal of Mental Health and Addiction, 18*, 160–176. https://doi.org/10.1007/s11469-018-9970-0

Klie, J.-C., Bugert, M., Beto Boullosa, Eckart, R., & Gurevych, I. (2018). The INCEpTION Platform: Machine-assisted and knowledge-oriented interactive annotation. *Proceedings of System Demonstrations of the 27th International Conference on Computational Linguistics (COLING 2018)*, 5–9.

Knapton, O., & Rundblad, G. (2018). Metaphor, discourse dynamics and register: applications to written descriptions of mental health problems. *Text & Talk, 38*(3), 389–410. https://doi.org/10.1515/text-2018-0005

Langacker, R. W. (2013). *Essentials of cognitive grammar*. Oxford University Press.

Lao, C., Lane, J., & Suominen, H. (2022). Analyzing suicide risk from linguistic features in social media: Evaluation study. *JMIR Formative Research, 6*(8), e35563. https://doi.org/10.2196/35563

Nacey, S., Dorst, A. G., Krennmayr, T. & Reijnierse, W. G. (2019). *Metaphor identification in multiple languages: MIPVU around the world*. John Benjamins Publishing Company.

Oravecz, C., Váradi, T., & Sass, B. (2014). The Hungarian Gigaword Corpus. *Proceedings of LREC 2014*, 1719–1723.

Price, H. (2022). *The language of mental illness*. Cambridge University Press.

Pusztai, F. (2003). *Akadémiai magyar értelmező kéziszótár = Dictionary of the Hungarian language*. Akadémiai Kiadó.

Ringel, E. (1976). The Presuicidal Syndrome. *Suicide and Life-Threatening Behavior, 6*(3), 131–149. https://doi.org/10.1111/j.1943-278x.1976.tb00328.x

Rychlý, P. (2008). A lexicographer-friendly association score. *Proceedings of Recent Advances in Slavonic Natural Language Processing RASLAN*, 6–9.

Sikveland, R. O., & Stokoe, E. (2023). A cry for "help"? How crisis negotiators overcome suicidal people's resistance to offers of assistance. *Journal of Language and Social Psychology*, 42(5-6), 565–588. https://doi.org/10.1177/0261927x231185734

Simon, G., Bajzát, T. B., Ballagó, J., Havasi, Z., Molnár, E. K., & Szlávich, E. (2023). When MIPVU goes to no man's land: a new language resource for hybrid, morpheme-based metaphor identification in Hungarian. *Language Resources and Evaluation*. https://doi.org/10.1007/s10579-023-09705-9

Steen, G. J., Dorst, A. G., J. Berenike Herrmann, Kaal, A., Krennmayr, T., & Pasma, T. (2010). *A Method for Linguistic Metaphor Identification*. John Benjamins Publishing.

Tay, D. (2017). Using Metaphor in Healthcare. Mental health. *The Routledge Handbook of Metaphor and Language*, 317–384. Routledge. https://doi.org/10.4324/9781315672953-39

Yaseen, Z. S., Hawes, M., Barzilay, S., & Galynker, I. (2018). Predictive validity of proposed diagnostic criteria for the Suicide Crisis Syndrome: An acute presuicidal state. *Suicide and Life-Threatening Behavior*, 49(4), 1124–1135. https://doi.org/10.1111/sltb.12495

Young, G. (2019). The Cry for help in psychological injury and law: Concepts and review. *Psychological Injury and Law*, 12(3-4), 225–237. https://doi.org/10.1007/s12207-019-09360-y

Semmelweis Medical Linguistics Investigations

Edited by Katalin Fogarasi and Dániel Mány /
Semmelweis University, Institute of Languages for Specific Purposes

The Semmelweis Medical Linguistics Investigations series explores how language fundamentally shapes healthcare communication, practice, education, and policy. It provides a dedicated platform for interdisciplinary research at the intersection of medicine and linguistics, offering insights into how language practices impact patient safety, clinical efficiency, and equitable care. The diversity of methodological approaches supports both theoretical innovation and practical application. The series builds on a growing recognition that language is not merely a medium of transmission in healthcare. Effective communication is integral to accurate diagnosis, informed consent, continuity of care, and trust between patients and providers. With its roots at Semmelweis University in Budapest – an institution with a longstanding tradition in medical excellence – the series is positioned to become a cornerstone of international medical linguistics research.

Vol. 1 Katalin Fogarasi and Dániel Mány (eds.): Impact of Sociocultural Factors on Health Communication. In collaboration with Sarah Bigi, Zsófia Demjén, Jan Engberg, Pascaline Faure and Rita Temmerman. 2025.

www.peterlang.com

www.ingramcontent.com/pod-product-compliance
Ingram Content Group UK Ltd.
Pitfield, Milton Keynes, MK11 3LW, UK
UKHW041923210426
5322IPUK00002B/26